T0136416

Merged Evolution

WORLD FUTURES GENERAL EVOLUTION STUDIES
A series edited by Ervin Laszlo
The General Evolution Research Group
The Club of Budapest

VOLUME 1
**NATURE AND HISTORY: THE EVOLUTIONARY APPROACH
FOR SOCIAL SCIENTISTS**
Ignazio Masulli

VOLUME 2 – KEYNOTE VOLUME
THE NEW EVOLUTIONARY PARADIGM
Edited by Ervin Laszlo

VOLUME 3
THE AGE OF BIFURCATION: UNDERSTANDING THE CHANGING WORLD
Ervin Laszlo

VOLUME 4
COOPERATION: BEYOND THE AGE OF COMPETITION
Edited by Allan Combs

VOLUME 5
**THE EVOLUTION OF COGNITIVE MAPS: NEW PARADIGMS
FOR THE TWENTY-FIRST CENTURY**
Edited by Ervin Laszlo and Ignazio Masulli with Robert Artigiani and Vilmos Csányi

VOLUME 6
THE EVOLVING MIND
Ben Goertzel

VOLUME 7
CHAOS AND THE EVOLVING ECOLOGICAL UNIVERSE
Sally J. Goerner

VOLUME 8
**CONSTRAINTS AND POSSIBILITIES: THE EVOLUTION OF KNOWLEDGE
AND THE KNOWLEDGE OF EVOLUTION**
Mauro Ceruti

VOLUME 9
**EVOLUTIONARY CHANGE: TOWARD A SYSTEMIC THEORY OF DEVELOPMENT
AND MALDEVELOPMENT**
Aron Katsenelinboigen

VOLUME 10
**INSTINCT AND REVELATION: REFLECTIONS ON THE ORIGINS
OF NUMINOUS PERCEPTION**
Alondra Yvette Oubré

VOLUME 11
**THE EVOLUTIONARY TRAJECTORY: THE GROWTH OF INFORMATION
IN THE HISTORY AND FUTURE OF EARTH**
Richard L. Coren

VOLUME 12
**THE MIND OF SOCIETY: FROM A FRUITFUL ANALOGY OF MINSKY TO A
PRODIGIOUS IDEA OF TEILHARD DE CHARDIN**
Yvon Provençal

See the back of this book for other titles in World Futures General Evolution Studies.

Merged Evolution

Long-Term Implications
of Biotechnology
and Information Technology

Susantha Goonatilake

Center for Studies of Social Change
New School for Social Research
New York, New York, USA

Gordon and Breach Publishers

Australia • Canada • China • France • Germany • India •
Japan • Luxembourg • Malaysia • The Netherlands •
Russia • Singapore • Switzerland

Amsteldijk 166
1st Floor
1079 LH Amsterdam
The Netherlands

British Library Cataloguing in Publication Data

Goonatilake, Susantha
    Merged evolution : long-term implications of
    biotechnology and information technology. – (World
    futures general evolution studies ; v. 14 –
    ISSN 1043-9331)
    1. Information technology 2. Biotechnology 3. Evolution
    I. Title
    303.4'833

    ISBN   90-5700-521-2

Contents

List of Figures   vii

Introduction to the Series   ix

Preface   xi

Introduction   1

I   THREE LINEAGES AND TWO TECHNOLOGIES   11

    1   Biological Evolution: The Genetic Lineage   13

    2   The Cultural Stream of Science   23

    3   The Computer Information Flowline   35

    4   The Exosomatic Lineage Develops Its Autonomy   47

    5   Biotechnology   71

II THE THREE LINEAGES MERGE   85

    6   The Merging of Culture and Artificial Information   87

    7   The Merging of Culture and Genes   117

    8   The Merging of Biology and Computing   147

III CONSEQUENCES   165

    9   The Macro Properties of Merged Evolution   167

    10 An Extended Sociology: The Structure
        of New "Communities"   197

Bibliography   221

Index   255

Figures

1. Flow of information down human history
   passing through key transformations   25

2. Forces buffeting stream of scientific knowledge   32

3. Formation of concepts   33

4. Range of human skills, partially or fully being informatized   44

5. Culture and artefactual information merges   113

6. Merging of culture into genes   144

7. Merging of genes into culture   145

8. Merging of biological information
   and artefactual information   164

9. Some stages in the evolution of information envelopes   183

10. Cross-envelope information flows   186

11. Isolated lineage "tunnels" through time giving rise to
    changing world views, which gradually become richer   192

12. Three lineages merge giving rise to changed world views.
    Views suddenly become richer. Histories accelerate   193

13. Merged Evolution   194

Introduction to the Series

The *World Futures General Evolution Studies* series is associated with the journal *World Futures: The Journal of General Evolution*. It provides a venue for monographs and multiauthored book-length works that fall within the scope of the journal. The common focus is the emerging field of general evolutionary theory. Such works, either empirical or practical, deal with the evolutionary perspective innate in the change from the contemporary world to its foreseeable future.

The examination of contemporary world issues benefits from the systematic exploration of the evolutionary perspective. This happens especially when empirical and practical approaches are combined in the effort.

The *World Futures General Evolution Studies* series and journal are the only internationally published forums dedicated to the general evolution paradigms. The series is also the first to publish book-length treatments in this area.

The editor hopes that the readership will expand across disciplines where scholars from new fields will contribute books that propose general evolution theory in novel contexts.

Preface

This book is written on the premise that long-term implications of biotechnology and information technology have strong evolutionary implications . . . so far not adequately addressed. These evolutionary implications result from the merger, through new technologies, of three streams of information: genetic (biological), cultural, and "artefactual" information in computers.

The volume is divided into three sections. The first section describes the three streams and their characteristics. The part of this section dealing with biology and culture has aspects familiar to biologists and sociologists, respectively — but perhaps not to each other. The portion on the stream of computer information is not that well known. Some of these ideas of evolution of the three streams were dealt with by the author in an earlier work: *Evolution of Information: Lineages in Genes, Culture and Artefact*, Pinter, London/New York, 1992. The first section also has two chapters covering the basic elements and characteristics of biotechnology and information technology, especially as they would affect aspects of evolution described in later chapters.

The second part of this volume discusses merging of the three streams arising from biotechnology and information technology. The results are three merged streams of, respectively, genetic-cultural, cultural-artefactual, and genetic-artefactual information. Different modes of merging, both indirect and direct, are covered in detail.

Section three addresses implications of the merging. It describes implications for evolutionary processes on earth as well as dynamics of the new merged 'communities,' including their subjective and ethical aspects.

The ideas in this book have been developed over the years by the author. Portions have been presented as papers at various conferences as well as in technical organs and books.

Conferences include: "The International Colloquium on the Social Mastery of Technology," Lyon, France, 1991; "The Third Artificial Life Conference," Santa Fe, New Mexico, 1992; "*INTERFACE '92*," Atlanta, Georgia; "The UNESCO Science and Culture Forum — Toward Eco-Ethics: Alternative Visions of Culture, Science, Technology and Nature," Belem, Brazil,

1992; "XIIIth World Conference of World Futures," Turku, Finland; "The Symposium on New Epistemologies" at the World Congress of Sociology, Bielefeld, Germany, 1994; "The World Academy of Arts and Sciences Biannual Conference," Minneapolis, Minnesota, 1994; "The International Seminar on Evolutionary Systems," the Konrad Lorenz Institute, Vienna, Austria, 1995; "Washington Evolutionary Systems Society: 4th Interdisciplinary Conference on General Evolutionary Systems," Washington, DC, 1996; and "The Conference on the Quest for a Unified Theory of Information," Vienna University of Technology, Austria, 1996.

Among the technical organs are: *Futures Research Quarterly; Journal of Social and Evolutionary Systems; Futures, Leonardo* and *Ecodecision*. Some of the ideas have appeared in books such as *The Decolonization of Imagination: Culture, Knowledge and Power*, Jan Nederveen Pieterse and Bhikhu Parekh (eds.), Zed Press, 1993; *The Future of Cultures*, UNESCO, Paris, 1994; *The Future of Asian Cultures*, UNESCO, Bangkok, 1994; *The Knowledge Base of Future Studies*, Richard E. Slaughter (ed.), Routledge, Kegan and Paul, 1997; and *Mining Civilizational Knowledge*, Susantha Goonatilake, Indiana University Press, 1998. Some of the subject matter on biotechnology and information technology was gathered in 1994, while I was writing a chapter on new technologies for the United Nations *Report on the World Social Situation* — issued every four years.

I thank various participants in these conferences and editors of journals and books for their valuable comments, criticisms and suggestions. The manuscript in a preliminary form was read by Profs. Stanley Salthe, Georgis Kampis and Erwin Laszlo. Some chapters were read by the late Prof. Jonas Salk. I am grateful to them for valuable suggestions. The shortcomings that remain are of course mine.

INTRODUCTION

A major transformation is occurring today because of two new key technologies: information technology and biotechnology. This book is about the larger, long-range consequences of their impact.

These two technologies come as a major culmination of a series of previous technologies that have shaped human institutions. They are today poised to have a dramatic effect on virtually the entire humankind, much more so than all these earlier technologies. Their long-range effects have not been examined adequately in the existing literature. This book intends to fill this gap.

In the conventional scheme of historical evolution, it is usual to classify a sequence of technology and societal stages. These stages vary from hunter gatherers and pastoralists, using for example, stone tools, through metal-using agricultural societies with attendant city cultures, to industrial societies.

Almost all contemporary societies have at least partially gone through these stages, with even the least industrialized societies having pockets of industrial technology. The technological societal shift underway currently has been characterized as a movement toward an "Information Society" where the majority of the population (as in the contemporary developed "OECD" countries) are engaged in activities that directly or indirectly deal with information. Other countries, it is expected would sooner or later follow in the footsteps of the OECD countries.

If animal power and iron tools characterized agriculture societies, and steam power and engines characterized the early period of the Industrial Revolution, then Information Technology provides the new all-pervasive set of artefacts for information societies. Information technology is, however, not the only technology that is very rapidly transforming the contemporary production process. The second, often ignored by conventional evolutionary scenarios of societies, is biotechnology.

These two new "third wave" technologies are more "generic" than all the earlier technologies since the Industrial Revolution (OECD, 1989, pp. 52–55). The two technologies will also have a major impact on many of our current problems, whether they deal with ecology, biodiversity, cultural diversity, or the sustainability of the earth.

1

During the immediate and medium future, the processes and products of these technologies will penetrate all economies intensively. Freeman (1987) gave the range of application and pervasive impact of the two technologies in products and processes. He indicated that information technology would have a more pervasive impact than all the earlier technologies. Information artefacts would become rapidly incorporated in an increasing number of products and processes. The fate of biotechnology was not yet clear to Freeman and he gave four scenarios on the degree of impact. However, the development in biotechnology in the last five years or so tends to favor his scenarios for the more pervasive impact.

In the case of information technology, the technology enhances or substitutes for human information. It is in this sense a substitute for human culture, those items of information which humans learn either at home (through primary socialization), or at school and university (through secondary and tertiary socialization). But the effects go much beyond that. In its role of substituting for human mental work, information technology in fact substitutes for a variety of human roles, resulting in, as it were, a parallel occupational or role structure beside the human one.

The impact of biotechnology is on the other hand different; it acts not on culture but on biology. The biological impact affects plant, animal and human life. Biotechnology rearranges the genetic heritage of nature.

How do these technologies that intrude so intimately on culture and biology appear in contrast to earlier technologies; and how do their accelerating impacts on society and nature, differ from technology's effects in earlier historical epochs?

Life emerged 3–4 billion years ago and in the course of its evolution, produced myriad combinations of the four chemical bases (A, C, T, H) of the DNA molecule, giving rise to the biological essence of life on earth, its genetic basis. The new biotechnology allows the possibility of a deep and pervasive shuffling of this entire heritage, of potentially all biological information. The applications of the new biotechnology would therefore have major repercussions on existing agriculture and husbandry, medicine and industrial processes. But this shuffling of genetic information is not the random one that occurs under nature. It is now a human driven one, governed by human vicissitudes, by the market place, by the current dynamics of international relations, class structures and cultural perceptions. It is also a shuffling of the genetic heritage under very unequal social relations. The existing world social order is, in effect, influencing the shuffling of genes to produce a new genetic order that partly mirrors it. This shuffling has moved away from the random shuffling of nature to a very selective, restrictive one controlled by a few humans.

This restrictive shuffling erodes existing genetic information stores, changes existing plants and animals and potentially makes for major environmental problems. The natural environment, the oxygen we breath, the present climate and its flora and fauna are all the results of a long biological evolution and processes of adaptation. These are now questioned by the current interventions. The present multitude of life forms is being endangered by the homogenizing tendencies of the new biotechnology. Biotechnology will also question existing agricultural and industrial production systems, trade patterns, ecologies and ethics.

Although there are some animals that possess learned, acquired behavior as opposed to a genetically determined one, it is humankind that is defined by the ability for culture. Only humans have this most malleable of information systems, their culture. And it is culture that enabled humans to bootstrap out of animal existence to civilization. It is this cultural information that is now been increasingly cloned by the new information technology.

Information technology extracts selective essences of human culture and embodies them in diverse products. These products are now spreading out to virtually every possible human cultural and mental activity. As prices drop dramatically these artefacts of encapsulated culture will penetrate the humblest of product and soon, the humblest of home. This encapsulated culture is a mirroring of living human culture, and this reflection increasingly interacts with and at least partially controls its original.

The two new technologies dealing with biological information and information in artefacts are extremely malleable to social factors, that is, to cultural information, much more malleable than any other technology. Their very pliability allows for both highly skewed social structures and their opposite, the widest democracy.

As the two technologies in the coming decades sweep through many human activities, they will rearrange biology and culture. They cut a swath through the biological and cultural landscape as no other technology has hitherto done. They supplant the effects of the various other technologies since the Industrial Revolution — steam, electricity, and oil-based ones. Their rearranging power goes beyond the neolithic revolution, a 'mere' five to ten thousand or so years ago, which gave us agriculture; and in changing biology, the rearranging goes to a much longer time frame, to thousands of millions of years.

Both the two technologies require in relative terms much less energy and materials than the earlier industrial technologies. They, therefore, could change the demand spectrum of the world into one that is less energy- and material-consuming. As energy and material guzzling smoke stack industries are partially bypassed, it could lead to a less environmentally stressed earth. If, on the other hand, the erosion of biodiversity that presently concurrently occurs with the introduction of biotechnology in agriculture is unchecked, the stress on the earth's environment could increase.

The industrial revolution was built on 19th-century technology and the particular raw material and industrial product exchanges that this entailed gave in to the present North-South agenda. The new technology will dramatically change the composition of North-South trade as hitherto agricultural and industrial commodities are changed by the new technologies. It will, therefore, question existing international relations and stress the many international regulatory agencies that exist today.

The interaction of the two new technologies on human society, culture, economics and ethics have been hitherto studied in the same way conventional studies on the impact of other technologies have been done. That is, commentators have looked at short time spans and seen the impact, for example, on various institutions. But the new technologies have a much more pervasive character. They impinge on and substitute for biology — including human biology — and culture. In this, they influence human as well as biological destiny in a much more pervasive manner than all earlier technologies. This demands a much deeper look at the long-range implications of the technology. The long-range perspective requires examining the implications of the technology on evolutionary processes in biology and culture.

Information as a Variable

The deep transformations being wrought by the two new technologies pose a set of key and crucial questions. To describe these and suggest answers, several disciplinary approaches have been conventionally used. These include such subjects as biology, ecology, economics, anthropology, sociology, and the underlying physics and chemistry of the global system, including entropic phenomena. Yet, these approach the problems from their individual disciplinary backgrounds and there is no common denominator that unifies the different approaches.

In this book, the variable of "information" is taken to be a common denominator in all the changes wrought by the new technologies — especially the long-range evolutionary ones — and is used to describe them(OECD, 1989, pp. 52–55).

As a concept, "information" has been used in a variety of meanings. The first widespread attempt to use information as an overarching concept was in the 1940s and 1950s in the early years of cybernetics. The concept of information implicit in these approaches was the mathematical one developed by Shannon and Weaver (1949) and derived from the concept of information used in communication. This was a very narrow concept, rightfully rejected by several biologists as not able to encompass the richness of biological phenomena (Maruyama, 1976, Waddington, 1976, Brooks and Wiley, 1986). It has also been rejected by those involved in the subbranch of computing, Artificial Intelligence (AI) (Boden, 1980). Such a narrow concept would also be clearly inadequate for the more complex social phenomena.

There has been a loss of confidence in the early hegemony acquired by this view of information (Marijuan, 1996, p. 86). The "sciences of the artificial" as epitomized by this approach are now in retreat (Marijuan, 1996, p. 93). Yet, there is emerging now a new interest in information as a variable to be used in many disciplines (Marijuan, 1996, p. 87).

With the collapse of the relevance of the old information theory, new ones are being proposed. Theories have also been suggested where information is even considered a basic property of the universe, in much the same way as energy and matter is. Information in this fundamental sense is being defined as the capacity to organize a system (Stonier, 1996, pp. 135–140). A role for information at the quantum level, the most foundational level of physics is also being proposed in some other theoretical approaches. Here, how a quantum system obtains information about its 'outside' — the environment — is addressed, transcending the view from both the 'outside' and 'inside' (Grossing,1988, pp. 225–238).

The physicist Matsuno has noted that the physical changes that deal with historical changes, namely evolution, give a diachronic view of information as historical flow of information. Synchronic information is only a limiting case — a snap shot — of these diachronic processes. The view from such a historically derived process as it unfolds, it has also been surmised, gives an 'internalist' view of the world (Matsuno, 1996, pp. 111–118). Such perspectives from 'within' have also been suggested to describe some proesses in physics, leading to an 'endophysics' (Rossler, 1987, pp. 25–46, Rossler, 1996, pp. 211–219). A form of 'subjectivity,' particular viewpoints, has thus crept into some discussions on long-term changes in physics.

Some of these new approaches take into account the philosophy of evolutionary systems that deal with environments and change. These new attempts are in keeping with the trend of the times where overarching theoretical schemes are suggested, through, for example, various theories of complex, nonlinear, self-organizing systems (Fleissner Hofkirchner, 1996, pp. 243–248).

Biologists, working at a less theoretical and a more pragmatic level, have suggested the use of the information concept as being a set of instructions on how to deal with the environment (Waddington, 1976. See also Boulding, 1978). It is this pragmatic notion of information that is implied in the discussion in this book. We also bring in other overarching perspectives such as the 'views from within' that come with the new general theories of evolution.

Information in this sense of a set of instructions to deal with the environment is coded in the biological realm in genes. Such information also exists in human culture as a set of proclivities and instructions on how to interact with the environment. Similar information also exists in the new computer-based information artefacts.

Some new perspectives take the position that in a variety of realms, there are information activities across individual entities — not just within them. These interacting entities, it has been suggested, constitute 'societies'. Thus a cell is a 'society of enzymes'; the organism, 'a society of cells'; the nervous system, 'a sociey of neurons' and there is of course the society of human individuals (Marijuan, 1996, pp. 87–96).

The three information realms — in biological, cultural and machine systems — constitute lineages of information which transmit information diachronically from generation to generation. In biological systems, genes act as carriers of this information, resulting in a chain that connects existing living beings (some, as in the case of humans with, for example, three billion base pairs of DNA and a hundred thousand genes) with the earliest ancestors four billion years or so ago (say with only a few genes and a short string of DNA). The result of biological evolution is a branching-out tree whose constituent genetic information, bifurcates and changes corresponding to environmental pressures. This gives a constantly changing set of instructions on how to deal with the environment. With the passage of time, in some of the later species, these sets of instructions have grown increasingly more elaborate, a phylogenetic tendency being common to all such evolving systems.

The next information lineage system is that of culture. Several animals exhibit the ability to transmit learned information to their offspring, resulting in a chain of information that stretches backwards in time from the present. It is, however, in primates and most importantly in humans, that culture becomes an important intermediary with nature as a means of fitting into an ecological niche.

Cultural information held by humans has increased many, many fold from that of the earliest humans to that of today's world. Even the hunter gatherer groups of earliest times would have possessed large amounts of cultural information as studies on contemporary hunter gatherers reveal (Pfeiffer, 1969). The agricultural revolution, growth of cities and the arrival of specialized personnel like craftsmen, priests and medical practitioners increased this stock of knowledge. During the last three centuries, the effects of the Scientific Revolution and the Industrial Revolution increased dramatically the stock of cultural information. Since then new branches have grown on the tree of cultural information. And like the genetic one, it is continuously growing and bifurcating.

Of cultural knowledge, scientific knowledge is the most formalized. According to some estimates, its exponential rate of growth is such that it doubles every eleven years or so, a rate greater than the doubling rate of population in the developed countries (Price, 1963, Open University, 1971). Increasingly, this information is being stored not so much in the heads of humans but in artefacts, especially computing devices. And at least part of the processing of this information is being done by similar artefacts.

Cultural information seems now thus to be "spilling over" into artefacts. This process is similar to an earlier spilling over of genetic systems to culture. When genetic systems were not sufficiently flexible and elaborate enough to deal with the more rapid changes in the environment, cultural systems emerged in humans to help cope with the environment. The result in the case of the present "cultural spillover" to artefacts that store and process cultural information is an emerging lineage of information artefacts.

Such artefacts precede today's computers and can be traced through a long genealogy, stretching from the knots on a string and notches on barks in early prehistoric times, through the abacus, Napier's Rods of the 17th century, through the office machinery of the late 19th century, to present day computers. During the last forty years, computers as a new information system on earth, have grown explosively.

Computers have been going through a generation of changes every few years, increasing their power by a magnitude while cutting their costs by half. The result is that computer devices have been getting smaller, faster, cheaper, more sophisticated and more widespread. Newer technologies such as opto electronics, molecular switches and nano electronics promise in the foreseeable future enormous capacities rivalling biological information systems including that of the human brain.

The continuing drop in prices of these artefacts means that they are being ubiquitously embedded in a range of products. Already the simplest of such devices in the developed world probably exceed their human population. By the end of this decade, there would thus be more computing devices than the human population. (See Chapter 4 for details).

Not only are these devices increasingly populating the world, they are increasing the skills they perform. The very earliest computer applications replaced rudimentary mental skills, such as those of arithmetic. Since then, skills in the workplace that are being replaced fully or partially by these devices have increased, extending now to skills of professionals.

The present computing artefacts are still relatively crude and not autonomous, but a branch of computing based on biological models is rapidly emerging that has relatively autonomous characteristics and does not require detailed programming by humans. Such technologies as genetic algorithms, neural networks and Artificial Intelligence programs promise a whole new set of relatively autonomous information artefacts in the immediate future.

In the same way that humans exchange information culturally through conversation, and organisms swap chromosomes, computers pass information synchronically — that is, horizontally. In addition, as in the other two information realms, there is also in computers an information transmission forward, through time, diachronic transmission. That is, instead of information being exchanged between computers only at a particular time, there is also information transmitted down through time from one computer to another, constituting a lineage of computer information, a diachronic, historical flow.

Since computers have existed only for 40 years or so, this diachronic lineage is short. Further, this information that is transmitted down is still of a relatively unchanging kind, limited to a tight domain. It is unlike the more indeterminate, loosely coupled information flows associated with biology and culture. However, there are indications that similar loose information flows with evolutionary characteristics are also appearing in the computer diachronic flow, especially with the newer autonomous techniques.

But each of the three information lineages associated with biology, culture and computing artefacts, are encroaching upon and are being encroached upon by the other two lineages. The information lineage of biology is encroached upon by computer information and culture. And the lineage of computer information is encroached upon by culture and biology. And, both computer information and biology in turn affect cultural information. Dynamic interactions therefore occur as a result between all three information lineages.

It is these dynamics of the three lineages as they are affected by biotechnology and information technology that this book describes. The special focus would be the evolutionary implications of the two new technologies on both biological nature and human society and culture.

The new technologies deal with influences across several domains — for example across biology, computing, and human society and culture. To give an adequate description, it is necessary to gather together large amounts of data from different fields. In the following pages, therefore, information from biology, computer sciences and the social sciences are gathered together to describe different processes. This exercise by necessity must cross unidisciplinary boundaries and approaches. And, although sometimes technical details from within a narrow discipline will be presented, these will be attempted within the common general framework of this book.

In the following chapters we will sketch the information characteristics of the three lineages; describe the pervasive growth of information technology and biotechnology and show how a resultant mixing of the information in the three lineages has profound implications for both biological and cultural life on earth.

SECTION 1

THREE LINEAGES AND TWO TECHNOLOGIES

1 : BIOLOGICAL EVOLUTION: THE GENETIC LINEAGE

The first lineage of information is that of living beings. Its characteristics have become increasingly clear since Linnaeus laid out a taxonomy of living matter in the 18th century and Darwin and Wallace described biological evolution in the 19th century. In this chapter we will sketch the essential features of evolution in biology. Although much of what we recall here could be received wisdom for many, these essential features are described for the purpose of a complete narrative. Further, the case of biological evolution provides the most rigorously studied case of evolution. The essential general properties of evolutionary lineages which biology yields will be echoed in the other two lineages.

The solar system was formed about six billion years ago, nearly nine billion years after the coming into being of the Universe. In a relatively short time after the solar system was formed, life emerged on earth. Geological considerations give a figure as early as 4.6 billion years for the first life forms on earth (Dickerson, 1978, pp. 16, 70–86). There are no fossils from that early period, but one can conjure and reconstruct the emergence of life based on chemical experiments and existing fossil and genetic remnants. The formation of life was the result of a self organization of complex chemicals from the simpler ones that emerged as the earth cooled (Kuppers, 1990, p. 163). The original hypothesis of Oparin and Haldane in the 1920s and 1930s was that the radiation from the sun helped set in chemical processes that aided the synthesis of a large number of complex organic molecules from the prevailing soup of water, carbon dioxide and ammonia. Aspects of this theory were demonstrated in the 1950s by Urey and Miller through laboratory experiments that tried to emulate the early conditions of life on earth. Subjecting a mixture of simple chemicals that would have been found in the pre-biotic earth to an energy source in the form of electrical sparks that presumably substituted for the lightning in the original earth, they were able to synthesize many organic compounds, the precursors of proteins. Since the 1950s, these experiments of creating the precursors of life have been replicated in different laboratories, producing different building blocks of life.

Yet, evidence is accumulating challenging Miller and his colleagues' original hypothesis. This includes recent information on planetary formation which has cast doubt on whether the early earth had clouds of ammonia and methane. Consequently, current work suggest different routes to the formation of life.

Living organisms have also been found at many spots on the ocean-bed hot springs giving rise to a view that it was in these hot pressurized places that life first arose. In the seemingly hostile environment of hydrothermal vents in the ocean floor, strange life forms like blind fish and giant tube worms have been discovered (Durand et al., 1993, pp. 39–44). The RNA of microbes living in these vents, it has been found, are the nearest to those of the first organisms on earth. These similarities between the life material of early organisms and present ones have also suggested that life arose in such hydrothermal vents of the earth's crust in its early history. It has been speculated that at such spots of high temperature, emerging organisms could absorb more energy from nutrients, and so gave rise to life (Holm, 1992, p. 1).

Fossils have been found of a well established community of microbes with eleven different types of living organisms in rocks in Western Australia that are 3.5 billion years old. It appears that a 'mere' one billion years after the emergence of life on earth it had become well established. During this time the earth was still being bombarded by asteroids, which implies that if life had not taken a firm hold it would have been quickly eliminated. This suggests that the emergence of life, once the chemicals and conditions were in place, would have taken place rapidly through a relatively simple process.

Contemporary life forms consists of the macromolecule DNA with an intermediary RNA that helps form proteins. But proteins are required for the manufacture of both DNA and RNA, leading to a circular chicken or egg question of which came first? Recent research has shown that RNA can be both a blueprint as well as a catalyst helping in its own replication. RNA in this light becomes the ancestor of DNA, probably RNA emerging before proteins.

Illustrative of RNA's role of precursor to DNA as a life molecule, a section of RNA made in the lab has been able to reproduce itself. It was able to make use of the organic material in a test tube and make copies of itself. These copies soon entered into an evolutionary process that yielded new molecules, a vital step in the formation of complex chemical compounds.(Joyce, 1993, pp. 1205–1212). Other researchers have randomly generated literally trillions of different RNA strands to emulate the possibilities in the early earth. Out of this collection, at least sixty molecules emerged that could connect with each other and so develop the complex ladder of life (Lauhon & Szostak, 1993, pp. A1087–A1087).

The arrival of photosynthesis, a biochemical means of releasing oxygen, was an important landmark in the history of life on earth. All life forms after that had to take into account the existence of oxygen in the atmosphere. Another important step was the arrival of the cell, by which the genetic material was contained in a central area. The cell also allowed for higher levels of organization by life forms through different arrangements of collections of cells. Later, sexual reproduction allowed the speeding up of the evolutionary process by the possibility of a greater shuffling of genetic material.

The earliest life forms were in the sea. About 500 million years ago, the first jawed fish appeared, leading respectively to bony fish and those with cartilage, like sharks. During the Devonian Age 350–400 million years ago the first life forms begin the colonization of the earth. Initially these were plants, to be followed by worms, mollusks and anthrapods. These lacked much mobility because unlike the sea, gravity dragged them down. When bony fish with bony structures emerged from the sea to the land they could be more mobile and larger because of their skeletons.

Fish rapidly readjusted to the land, the gills that served them under water metamorphasized on land to lungs. This age of amphibians gave way to the age of reptiles. The latter dominated the Mesozoic era, whose last period the Triassic, saw the arrival of the largest land animals, the dinosaurs. The Jurassic which followed, saw reptiles evolving into the earliest mammals as well as to birds. Many more mammals with very diverse life forms, existed in the Cenozoic than today. Mammals acquired a placenta, giving rise to shy nocturnal insect eating, small animals. These mammals branched out to numerous niches leading ultimately to primates. Primates, some of whom emerged when dinosaurs still existed, were initially small and squirrel like. They had the distinction of having an overlapping binocular vision, forepaws that could grasp and above all, an increased brain size.

These initial primates living in trees led ultimately to humans. Primates that lived on the outskirts of the forests with access to open land led to an adaptation to a more erect posture. A feedback loop between tool use and the neocortex probably led to the expansion of the brain. With the growth of speech centers, humans could communicate with each other much more intensely. Modulated speech replaced crude gesture and the stage was set for learning from each other. Learning exists in some of the most primitive of organisms, but learning and transmission of the learned information down a line is restricted to only those with culture. Cultural animals exist in several species but the acquisition of speech gave humans the largest capacity for culture. This was as it were, a final culmination of a biological evolutionary process.

The Evolutionary Process

How did these myriad of life forms come into being, what were the processes involved? The descriptions are in the details of the evolutionary process as described by a series of writers. They range from the original formulation by Darwin and Wallace, through the descriptions of the inheritance mechanism by Mendel, through the New Synthesis to the more recent work on molecular genetics.

The evolutionary process in biology has a few key tenets. First, is that the world of the living is in a constant state of flux and change, new species emerge while others become extinct. This process is largely gradual. All later species are derived from earlier ones, the origin of all life can be traced to one common origin. The genetic code is today thus universal, although there is no reason for this to have been so.

The code in its inception could have been arbitrary and could have been constituted of other chemical characteristics. Thus, although the amino acid glycine is specified in all species by the triplet GGC, there is nothing in glycine that requires that it be specified by this particular triplet and not by any other (Ridley, 1985, p. 10). Probably the carriers of early variants of the code got shouldered out by carriers of the present one.

The engine of the evolutionary process according to the Darwinian-derived view is natural selection. Any trait that favors an organism or its offspring is favored through natural selection. Natural selection occurs through broad processes — the generation of variety and selection to fit the environment. The variety of possible biological elements generated in a set of individual organisms is vast. This variety is created largely through random processes (Brandon, 1990, pp. 3–39).

But those that survive to pass their genetic characteristics to their offspring are those who have the most adaptive mechanisms to deal with their environment. The environment includes for example, the general climate, predators and competitors. The micro environment into which adaptation takes place is the niche. These niches vary as to a host of physical factors that include temperature, pressure, moisture, availability of food and predators (Brandon, 1990, pp. 47–49).

Those organisms that are not eliminated by the environment live on to pass their characteristics to their progeny. This does not necessarily mean a brutal struggle for existence, those organisms that are neutral to the environment, as the work of Kimura shows, also do not get eliminated and hence survive (Kimura, 1985). A current view of adaptation is that the environment presents "problems" which are then subject to a "solution" by the organism. Thus, the problems presented by flight are solved by a variety of processes. Reptiles gradually alter bones, muscles and skin, bringing forth a wing, bones become lighter and feathers develop aerodynamic characteristics. If these winged birds are now given another problem, say adaptation to a watery home, they gradually change their wings to become flippers as happened in the evolution of penguins (Lewontin, 1978, pp. 212–30).

Living things are classified — among other categories — into species. Members of the same species can interbreed, exchange their genes and so pass on their traits to offspring. Because of natural selection, there are structural similarities in related species. A particular makeup of their bodies that gives a survival advantage is transferred down.

Genetic Transmission

Darwin did not specify the exact mechanisms of the transfer of inherited characteristics (Ridley, 1985, p. 23). It was Mendel, nearly one hundred years ago who gave an exact mathematical description of the inheritance mechanism through his experiments on peas in his monastic garden. In later years from 1920 to 1950 through the Modern Synthesis, Mendelian genetics were combined with population dynamics to give a more comprehensive explanation. Since the 1950s, the deep changes wrought by discoveries of the molecular basis of life have brought the evolutionary changes down to the level of chemistry.

The fundamental discoveries of molecular biology describe the exact mechanisms of the transmission process. From the molecular view, the unit of hereditary transmission, the gene, is but a section of the macro molecule DNA. This molecule is composed of a sequence of four nucleotides. These are Adenine(A), Cytosine(C), Guanine(G) and Thymine(T). These are strung along each strand of the double helix structure of the DNA. A single DNA can have as many as 200,000 bases in it or in the case of humans, nearly 3 billion with approximately one hundred thousand genes. There is also much unused DNA material, so called junk DNA, the human genome having approximately 95% 'junk'.

In higher organisms, the DNA resides in the nucleus in chromosomes. The chromosomes divide the genetic matter among themselves. At reproduction, the different segments of chromosomes are exchanged resulting in the reorganization of the hereditary material. A massive variety of new genetic combinations becomes possible because of this process.

Genes in a reproductive community are spread over the community, constituting a large pool. Any individual organism at a given time holds only a small part of this genetic pool. Evolution takes place through selection from this pool and not by selection through the individual. It is the population dynamics of such choices through the genetic pool that are described in the mathematical explanations of the New Synthesis.

Species evolve in interaction with their environments. But part of that environment constitutes other species which also respond by changing their evolutionary development corresponding to changes in their environments. The result is the coevolution of species with their environment.

The genetic information is in various sections of the DNA which correspond to different genes. They give instructions for the manufacture of proteins. The particular set of proteins which comes into being as a result gives rise to a particular organism (Kuppers, 1990, p. xviii).

The actual process of the use of the genetic material is through an intermediary molecule RNA, from which it is copied into proteins. This mode of transmitting genetic information in DNA transcribing it into messenger RNA, which then translates them to proteins gives the various building blocks of organisms. The different characteristics of organisms, their form, sex and behavior are the result of the particular sequence of amino acids which constitute the different proteins.

The diversity and the variations in the evolutionary process are created by mutations in the genetic information caused by a variety of factors. Mutations can result in an error in replication of the DNA or, for example, by radiation knocking off one of the bases.

Researchers are discovering some exceptions in the classical Mendelian molecular genetic world. The junk sections of the genome, it appears according to one formulation are not junk at all, but have the function of correcting the errors in the active portions of DNA that code for proteins (Coghlan, 1992, p. 4). The DNA itself now appears to be a very dynamic entity with a high degree of flexibility (Ho, Saunders and Fox, 1986, pp. 23–24).

DNA on occasion does also pass from species to species by hitching a ride on a parasite. Genes also jump from chromosome to chromosome. They also do not always inhabit one fixed location; in transferring from parent to progeny, they may also leap from one spot to another. DNA also responds to its environment in the cell, sometimes this environment directing the mutation (Rennie, 1993).

These newly found dynamic properties of the genome are modifying some of the central arguments accepted earlier. They, however, enrich the received wisdom, not overthrow the basic arguments.

The result of the evolutionary process is that past genetic information is passed down the lineage of species. Particular portions of information that have been useful in dealing with the environment in the past are passed onto the future, by and large, unchanged. Life is not continuously reinvented, but readapted with minor modifications. Information, therefore, tends to conserve itself.

Thus, today's life forms contain a memory of the earliest prebiotic experience. These include particular reaction pathways, the sequence of nucleotides or amino acids. In modern DNA, memories of ancient struggles and the resulting adaptations reside. Genes constitute a library of these past successful strategies (Eigen et al., 1982, p. 10, Ayala, 1978, p. 26). As a consequence of this conservativeness, humans share 99% of their genes with chimpanzees, and 40% with plants (Washburn, 1960, p. 11).

In the evolutionary process, while conservation of past memory is retained, novelty is also constantly created. The general thrust of evolution is however not predictable in an exact manner. A strong element of indeterminateness and lack of exact prediction exist in biological processes. The future in biological systems is, therefore, partially open. Evolution is a process of becoming, not of being.

As evolutionary time lapses, there is more time for nature to experiment with the environment, for life to have more "conversations" and encounters with it. The result is that more complex organisms with a larger battery of responses to the environment appear later in evolutionary history. Early organisms could not have more than a few genes in them, there would be insufficient time for a battery of responses that code for the environment to have been tested out and incorporated in an organism early on. Thus, primates or, for that matter, humans with 100,000 genes and three billion base pairs in their genetic code, could not have appeared until late in evolutionary history. There simply would not have been adequate time for enough of nature's experiments.

There is thus a phylogenetic tendency in evolution, the more complex organisms appearing later. It is, as it were, a form of progressivism built into evolutionary processes. But this progressivism in the biological system taken as a whole does not exclude newer versions of smaller organisms like bacteria and viruses, constantly appearing on the scene later on in evolutionary history.

The phylogenetic ascendancy in evolution can be demonstrated by counting the number of genes in the different organisms, or, in a more formal sense by the information content that they encode for. Information theory was a mathematical theory of communication developed in the late 1940s and 1950s which used a measure of information based on statistical criteria, the bit. This measure, however, has limited uses in the biological field as has been pointed out by several workers in the field. It, for example, does not allow for the semantics of information, its context and meaning.

Yet, even with these limitations, bit counts on the content of genetic information are possible and provide for some crude indication of the growth of complexity through evolution. Such measures have been made by several workers in the last two decades and thus illustrate the growth in complexity of the information. Such measures show that "evolution leads to the formation of organisms with the greatest of experience, with the highest rate of gaining this and to the storage of further information" (Holzmuller, 1984, p. 130).

The encoded information is also a window to the external world and has been seen by some theorists as ecological perspectives or 'theories' that change with the environment. Such a Gestalt encoded in a genome is seen as a means of structuring the world outside, having its own 'subjectivity' on the world, its own 'world view' to the environment outside (Marjorie Greene, 1985, Jerison, 1985, Nagel, 1974). As the lineages course through time these 'subjectivities', and world views — termed "egocentricities" by Morin (1981) — change. The need to take into account such particular internalist views is consonant with current discussions on the need to have internalist views' in physics, especially in processes where history and evolution are important (Matsuno, Koichiro, 1996, pp. 111–118, Rossler, 1987, pp. 25–46, Rossler, 1996, 211–219).

The path of evolution is generally gradual with micro changes leading, for example, to new species. But there have been in geological-time terms, sudden bursts of rapid evolutionary change. There have been suggestions that evolution makes major changes precisely because of these sudden jumps — through a process of punctuated equilibrium (Eldredge & Gould, 1972, pp. 82–115). It has also been shown that the micro evolutionary processes described in the literature are in fact also compatible with these sudden bursts as they are with the more gradualist ones (Ayala, 1985).

Salthe has described nesting of compartments within a hierarchy as a common characteristic of biological organization. Thus ecosystems can be considered as collections of cells which in turn can be considered collections of molecules (Salthe, 1985). Information, it has been noted does not percolate only within the horizontal layers of this hierarchy, it also percolates vertically. Information percolates upwards and downwards in the hierarchical chain (Conrad, 1996, pp. 97–109).

The DNA molecule is a physical entity and as such it obeys general physical laws including those of thermodynamics. The Second Law of Thermodynamics states that the entropy of a closed system increases. Entropy can be described in various ways, one such measure being that of disorder and randomness. So, what the Second Law states is that in a closed system, there is a tendency for increased disorder. This is usually implied as the physical law that gives the arrow of time, a direction to the future of the universe which is towards increased randomness in its physical structures leading ultimately to its heat death.

But, in the case of biological systems, the tendency through evolution is for decreases in randomness, a greater organization and a greater complexity with the phylogenetic process. This phenomenon implies that in evolution, there is a reduction in entropy, a fact first pointed out by Schroedinger (1945) as characterizing all life. But since the total entropy of the world has to increase, this means that living matter reduces entropy only by either importing energy or matter while at the same time exporting entropy outside its boundaries. In fact recently, Brooks and Wiley (1986) have attempted to deduce all the laws of biological evolution from the viewpoint of entropy.

Thermodynamically, living matter thus acts as an open system, open to import and export of matter and energy. The thermodynamics of open systems have been described in detail in the work of Prigogine

(1980) who has shown that open systems have also the ability to self organize, to create order out of chaos. The evolutionary process thus proceeds by a process of self organization of disparate elements. The beginning of life itself is a process of self organization of stereo-chemical properties of molecules (Ho et al. 1986). Biological systems are thus self organizing systems in which novelty is introduced to prior information (Mayr, 1985).

The self organizing aspects and novelty creation have been termed auotopoiesis by the Chilean biologists Varela and Maturana (Varela et al., 1974, pp. 187–96). This is the process through which living systems continuously renew themselves in such a fashion that their regulatory mechanisms and the integrity of their structures are maintained. A self organizing system develops internal hierarchies of organization and also has the property of agency. It plays a part in developing its own individuation (Salthe, 1989, pp. 201).

Biological evolutionary processes, then, have the properties of interacting with an environment, adaptation, speciation, memory retention, creation of novelty, phylogenesis, evolving world views, self organization, growth of internal hierarchies and auotopoiesis, properties we shall now see are echoed in cultural systems as well.

2: THE CULTURAL STREAM OF SCIENCE

There is a wide variety in human societies and social groups across the world. These differences arise, generally speaking, according to different modes of intervening with the physical and social environments. The social structures and cultures of societies are consequently deeply conditioned by these interventions. A wide variation results within given broad technological limits in actual societies. (For examples of these variations in hunter gatherer and pastoral societies, see Leakey and Lewin, 1977; Bonte, 1981; for pre-capitalist societies in general, see Kahn & Llobera, 1981; "feudal" type of societies are discussed in Bloch, 1961, Coulborn, 1956; capitalist and socialist industrial societies in Bendix, 1963, Davis & Scase, 1985, Birnbaum, 1980, Noble, 1981).

The intellectual means through which humans deal with these environments is culture. These environments, however, are both the social worlds of fellow human beings, as well as the physical environments in which they live. So culture becomes, in essence, a means of how to deal with both the physical world as well as the social world.

All societies have structural cleavages and hierarchies that divide them into classes and strata. The learning of culture, the acculturization process occurs essentially within these strata, within classes and other groups in society. Subcultures particular only to some of these strata also arise and exist. It is along a framework set by these social cleavages that these subcultures are learned, internalized and transmitted down generations, down, for example, a class, ethnic group or profession.

The social structure is then the skeletal framework through which culture flows down generations. A particular 'flow line of culture' associated with a particular social division, whether it be a class, ethnic group, or profession or a narrower stratum, thus extends backwards across time to past generations. And this cultural lineage presumably will extend also into future generations, if the social strata survive into the future. Thus "a given culture trait can be fully understood only if seen as the end point of specific sequences of events reaching back into the remote past" (Kluckhohn, 1959).

From this perspective, the long flow of human history can be viewed as a sequence of changes in the social structure, accompanied by a set of changing cultural flow systems cascading through time. These cultural flow lines stream down the outlines made by the social structure as it interacts with the environment.

The different "stages of human history" correspond to the different socio-technological systems as they interact with different socio-physical environments. With different means of interacting with the environment ("forces of production"), the flow lines of culture shift when the socio-physical environment changes. Any such ensuing cultural system can be seen as a historical unfolding of cultural information lineages, where information is transmitted diachronically down generations.

A formulation of social change in the above manner takes into account more meaningfully the mechanics of actual social transformations and the interactions with culture than the simpler unilinear schemes evolved in the 19th and early 20th centuries, to describe what was then but a set of unique transformations in Europe. The social world as seen today is much more varied than the simpler descriptions of an earlier era.

We are today aware of different complexities and nuances and wide variations in societies. These are, among others, differing initial conditions, differing actors, differing key influences. Hence we do not have to recourse to simple single factor causes as in the 19th century. The complexities of the current world are such that different technologies, forms of ownership, traditions and social stratification arrangements jostle with each other in a continuously unfolding historical process. Corresponding to these jostling social structures are their associated cultures, sets of information that flow down and jostle with each other. This scheme of multiple cultural flow lines jostling with each other allows for representing a variety of interactions, among others, between technology, social structure and culture, so that the richness of actual historical transformations is captured. (Some of the dynamics of long-term social change given above have been argued more fully in Susantha Goonatilake, 1991.) Evoking sets of lineages as a central organizing principle for viewing culture takes into account the many cultural variations in today's world. The model of societal evolution and cultural flow that ensues is essentially multilinear.

In actual societies these jostling multiple modes of production are accompanied by different subcultures that correspond to various social divisions. These divisions include those of class, creed, ethnicity, profession and craft which have their own lineages of culture. These lineages 'cut' synchronously reveal little islands of subcultures on top of greater continents of culture, little universes of specialized information and meanings atop broader more general ones. An example would be the subculture of the profession of modern surgery which sits atop the more general West European culture.

The cultural lineage changes with changes in the interactions between society and its environment. When new environmental factors emerge, the existing socio-technological order does not match the given world outside. Innovations, new information in the cultural flow lines of how to deal with the changed environment, now occur. These innovations in the mode of interacting with the environment lead at crucial times to major socio-technological shifts. Here, a disjuncture occurs and if the innovations either in technology or in the social sphere or both are sufficiently deep, a new societal configuration results. A fresh rearrangement of cultural flow lines, with new additional flow lines now emerges (see Figure 1).

There are changes of skill and occupational patterns, of transmission belts of culture, corresponding to such rearrangements. Consequently new social lines are added to the earlier ones. The cultural flow lines now transmit new accretions of culture, while other newly added cultural elements help maintain the system. This equilibrium continues till new innovations arise at a new point of instability.

These disjunctures, are "revolutions," necessary steps in socio-cultural evolution paralleling speciation in biological evolution. From this

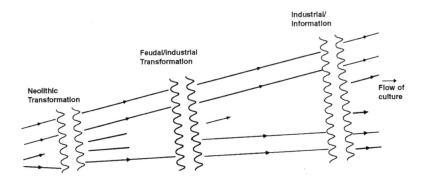

Figure 1   Flow of information down human history passing through key transformations

viewpoint, a revolution occurs "when a society is driven, either by internal perturbations or altered environmental inputs, through a 'catastrophe' to a bifurcation point, where it makes a nonlinear leap to a new level of stability" (Artigiani, 1987, p. 252). At the new level, society is more complex, and more interconnected (Artigiani, 1986).

Cultural information speciates and bifurcates in a parallel manner to the genetic lineage, as it changes its internal information stores in response to changes in the environment. A tree-like structure as in the traditional evolutionary tree of biology results; in this case, it is the tree of knowledge. The stock of cultural knowledge that constitutes the tree is vast and has been continuously growing.

The stock of culture held by the very earliest humans corresponds to those of today's hunter gatherer groups. It has been estimated that the latter's knowledge would, if formally collected, fill a library of thousands of volumes (Pfeiffer, 1969). Since these earliest groups, cultural information on earth has grown enormously. Population growth increased the number of culture creators and culture "processors," as did the growth of cities. The latter provided a central meeting place for the collection of cultural knowledge, its rapid exchange and its differentiation into different subcarriers.

The most formalized system of cultural information is scientific knowledge. With the Scientific and Industrial Revolutions, modes of interacting with nature changed dramatically from the times associated with agriculture. In addition, the formal acquisition and processing of cultural information intensified.

Consequently, the cultural tree of information now stands besides the genetic tree as a constantly increasing and continuously bifurcating system, a set of parallel instructions on how to deal with the environment. It is science and technology that today stands as a major reservoir of information for interactions with the environment. It is the cultural information associated with it that is the most crucial. And it is the cultural information that is most relevant to the main theme of this book, namely the impact of information technology and biotechnology.

The Culture of Science

Recent work on the social bases of science has described how these cultural trees of science are constructed in interactions with their environments. And, for any meaningful discussion today on human culture's interaction with the environment, it is necessary to recall these discussions.

These social influences on scientific knowledge can be identified at three broad levels. The first, at the level of the immediate peer group of scientists, is the one that has been studied most intensively by the school of the social construction of science (Collins, 1975; Pinch, 1976; Brown, 1984; Knorr-Certinca, 1981; Pickering, 1984, pp. 85–117). The second exists at the level of the influence of national level socio-economic factors such as funding on science and national formal and informal policies of science (Sklair, 1972; Ezrahi, 1971; Farley, 1977; Mackenzie, 1978; Barnes, 1982). At the third level are the macro long-range historical changes in society such as those that occurred at the time of the Renaissance, in the mercantilist period or the Weimar Republic (Hessen, 1930; Needham, 1956; Forman, 1971).

The Scientific Revolution took place shortly after the Renaissance and so the emergence of science has been linked to the Renaissance's and mercantile capitalism's social effects (Needham, 1972). The crowning moment of the Scientific Revolution was the work of Newton. The latter's results lay in the fields of motion and optics which were essential for the navigation and ballistics of the mercantilist period. Hence Newton's efforts have been linked to these social requirements of mercantile capitalism (Hessen, 1930). Centuries later, in 20th-century physics, quantum mechanics created a profound philosophical revolution by introducing aspects of uncertainty at the level of the very small. Quantum mechanics arose in the Weimar Republic, a time of great social uncertainty and doubt in Germany. The arrival and ready acceptance of the strange epistemology of quantum mechanics has been related to this prevailing Zeitgeist of uncertainty in Germany at the time (Forman, 1971).

The impact on science of these macro level changes is difficult to prove and must remain speculative. But at a less global level are contemporary results of how science is affected by social, political and economic factors at the national level. These national effects result in variations in science and technology practices for example between the United States, Japan, Britain, France, Germany and Sweden. A study indicates that the differences in these countries are due to several factors such as the history of the country, funding sources for science, allocations for R&D and coordinating mechanisms (Lederman, 1987, pp. 1125–1133). The general thrust of this study has been replicated in several other country examples.

Thus, Ireland which occupied a peripheral position in Europe had British colonial influences. These led to a particular development of science and of scientific institutions that paralleled the growth of science in other small, peripheral countries. These trends continued to shape science until recent times (Yearly, 1987, pp. 191–210).

Science grew significantly in France in the early decades of this century because there was strong support by the government, a strong lobby and resulting improvements in scientific institutions. In the early 20th century, 'supply push' forces from science were influential in France in contrast to other European countries which were influenced by a 'demand pull' of economic and political factors. Yet other countries eventually overtook France due to a combination of factors that included institutional conflicts, ideological factors and epistemological differences (Shinn, 1989, pp. 659–683).

The effects of differences in national approaches to science are seen in the field of high temperature superconductivity in the United States and Japan. To deal with the area, Japan developed a strategy at a national level using national level institutions. In contrast, the United States did not have a national level strategy. With the United States emphasis on individuality, hundreds of strategies existed, each having its own response, thus preventing the United States from making a concerted effort (Crow, 1989, pp. 322–344).

Science's results reach their public through publications. National differences show up also in publications behavior. Thus, a study of publication behavior in the field of cardiovascular research in Nordic countries revealed a strong correlation between the regional location of the research and citing behavior, including those who are cited. An article in a U.S. journal was cited more by other U.S. journals. Because the United States is a much larger entity, this gave rise to a problem of cognitive access for research done and published in the Nordic countries (Luukkonen, 1990, pp. 167–184). Such problems of peripherality increase in the case of Third World countries, specially the smaller ones. This is reflected in publication behavior of developing countries, where strong differences exist among those who write respectively for local journals and for Western journals. Thus, a study on publication practices in Korea and Philippines shows that those who publish locally tend to cite local sources more than those who publish internationally, while the latter tend to cite international sources (Lancaster et al., 1990, pp. 239–244).

Apart from this difference in cognitive access there are other differences between developed and developing countries. One is a strong dependency link between the two. Detailed studies of developing countries show these dependency links. Whether it be training, building of local institutions or funding, many developing countries are strongly dependent on the developed countries. These include the choice of research topics which are generally based on cues from colleagues in developed countries. Developing country researchers tend to use the same equipment and the same international scientific literature as their developed country counterparts (Goonatilake, 1984).

These national level influences on the movement and growth of science have been shown in a variety of other studies. These studies covered national level influences on the biometry/Mendelism controversy (Mackenzie and Barnes, 1978), on the spontaneous generation/biology controversy (Farley, 1977), on the growth of statistics (Mackenzie, 1978), and on 19th century cerebral anatomy (Rose, and Rose, 1976).

Scientists at their work do not operate at a "national level." In their day-to-day work they are huddled in small groups and teams. Even if they are working in different laboratories or institutions, only a small group is at the forefront of research — the invisible college — and it is to this group that the scientist basically addresses his work. A spate of studies have indicated that at the production of science, this most intimate small group level is suffused with strong social influences that affect the scientific output.

Thus, studies such as those on lasers and gravitational waves indicate that interpretations of scientific results are mediated by social factors (Collins, 1975). This social mediation has been confirmed in several other studies such as those on quantum mechanics (Collins, 1975), the weak neutral current (Pickering, 1989, pp. 217–232) and radar motor research (Gilbert, 1976). Latour (1979) has explored the construction of scientific fact in the social setting of the laboratory. It appears from these and other studies that formal scientific rationality is constructed from social commitments (Wynne, 1976). Following the same trend, Pinch (1976) has suggested that scientific theories are themselves multi dimensional and that a theory means different things to different practitioners.

This social conditioning is also seen in scientific journals. Each scientific journal develops a particular style and imprint because of social factors. The journal's own unique history helps in this growth, as do other factors, including the role of professional associations, frequency of the journal, its market size, and aesthetic beliefs of the editors as well as the scholarly community itself (Horowitz, 1987, pp. 125–130).

The social influence of science has been recently explored in a different direction by feminists, some of whom have rhetorically asked "Whose Science" (Harding, 1991, Harding, 1986, Haraway, 1988, pp. 575–599)? Feminists have shown that science has developed through largely a male trajectory, leaving out female inputs. This has inevitably brought masculine metaphors as a dominant feature of science (Hallberg, 1990, pp. 27–34). Science it appears has a strong patriarchal imprint. The trajectory science has taken through particular sets of key figures such as Plato and Francis Bacon has implied an unconscious and often conscious exploitation of nature and a stigmatization of motherhood (Jansen, 1990, pp. 235–246). It also has led to a particular world view that for example, searches for "master molecules" and is guided by a hierarchical view of nature rather than an interactionist one (Witt et al., 1989, pp. 253–259). This patriarchal science, according to some feminist research, rests heavily on linear thinking, quantification and reductionism at the expense of many other means of organizing knowledge (Witt et al., 1989, pp. 253–259). The result is a phantom objectivity that ignores alternative constructions of reality (Jansen, 1988).

Because of these studies on the social underpinnings of science, it appears that several social factors shape science — major social transformations, national level social and political forces, forces at the level of the laboratory and journal, and patriarchy. Science then becomes a social field in which various interpersonal and other relationships jostle with each other and designate and determine the correct problem to be studied, the correct methodology, the correct result and its significance (Bourdieu, 1991, pp. 3–26).

Science progresses by yielding theoretical constructs through which particular problems can be understood. Especially at important junctures in science, at paradigmatic breaks, new theories are born to fit new empirical results. Like a child playing with a construction set, at such a juncture a scientist builds a new conceptual framework to fit into the available results (Barnes, 1982, p. 90). The building blocks of such a framework are different conceptual elements. These cultural elements for theory have historically come from a variety of sources. Some have come from the past, as when the atomic perspective abandoned after the Greeks was revived in the 18th and 19th centuries (Pagel, 1973, p. 104) or when Laplace's explanation for the formation of the planets as due to a collapse of a cloud of dust was revived in the mid-20th century. Other examples of such revivals from the past include Boltzmann's atomistic-kinetic theory (Wiener, 1973, p. 89) the indeterminacy principle of Grimaldi through Heisenberg (Schroedinger, 1957, p. 92), and Newton's particle view of light through Einstein (Wiener ibid.)

Such conceptual elements come also from the general culture. Thus, evolutionary theory was influenced by a variety of cultural elements in the society at large in early- and mid-19th century. These cultural elements came from comparative anatomy, paleontology and ontogeny (Gould, 1983). Other influences were from philosophical, literal, social, economic and political ideas and debates of the time (Young, 1973, p. 348). These influences included those of Adam Smith, Malthus and the theologian William Paley (Young 1973, 373–6).

Some of these cultural elements that go to build science could be in fact somewhat arbitrary, like the *a priori* elements held by different theoreticians. Feuer has detailed such *a priorii* elements that were brought into science. One such example is the transport of Mendelief's mystical ideas into his successful theory of the periodic table (Feuer, 1978). Holton has discussed how a limited set of 'themes' and 'anti themes' — such as for example, "continuity and discontinuity," reductionism and holism" etc. — have helped build the major theoretical edifices of science (Holton, 1973).

Some of these extra-disciplinary cultural building blocks of science emanate from the transfer of metaphors. These metaphors could come from the same discipline, from another related discipline or from completely unrelated ones, even from the poetic imagination of the scientist. Metaphor in this light is 'the pregnant mother' of scientific thought (Turner, 1987, pp. 44–61). It transports insights, gives nudges to the imagination and transports theories from one domain to another (Rothbart, 1984, pp. 595–615).

The extra disciplinary inputs into the construction of the cultural stream called science are many. Now, seen from this perspective of the social construction of science, what broad sense can we make of the cultural stream of science? Let us stand aside from the snapshots of the practice of science that these studies on the social construction of science reveal. Let us instead take these studies and try to "run the snapshots together as a movie." This gives a time dimension to these studies and a changing picture emerges.

This picture is of a cultural stream that moves forward and breaks into new disciplines or subdisciplines as fresh new subjects of enquiry are invented. Physics breaks into many subdisciplines; Biology into yet others. The stream bifurcates and grows branches. The driving mechanisms for this movement onward of the branches, that is of new knowledge, are the social forces we already sketched (see Figure 2). These social forces operate at the level of macro social changes, at the level of the nation and at the micro level of the small groups within which scientists practice their craft and influence science. In practicing their craft scientists build new meanings for the phenomena at hand and form new conceptual structures from cultural elements (see Figure 3). This conceptual structuring draws upon past cultural elements, elements from other disciplines or metaphors from the culture in the general environment. The resulting cultural stream that emerges as science is developed within a particular social context, which is the environment against which the cultural and conceptual elements are tested for fit. These environmental factors include both formal and group-specific informal criteria for what is "correct science" (Susantha Goonatilake, 1982, Susantha Goonatilake, 1984). Science thus grows like a tree buffeted by social forces. It is like the tree of biology, another tree of information.

If one were to view physical reality as some sort of blackboard, then these socially driven efforts of science are like scrawls on the blackboard that illuminate particular areas. But this is not the only scrawl

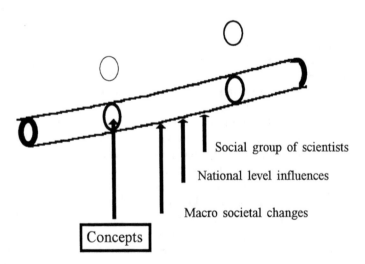

Figure 2 Forces buffeting stream of scientific knowledge

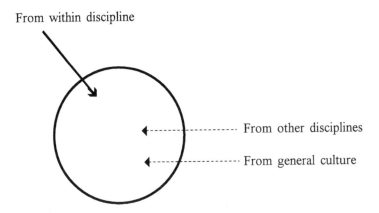

Figure 3 Formation of concepts

that is conceivably possible. Given different starting points for the science — that is, given different key questions at the beginning of science — one could have a different trajectory for science. If then the budding science system had different sets of practitioners with different sets of problems, different epistemological givens, differing national priorities etc, one would get an entirely different scrawl on the blackboard of reality, an entirely different tree of knowledge. It is like life beginning on another planet having different physical conditions. If life were to form on another planet, one would have different sets of biological forms and an entirely different tree of evolution.

Scientific practitioners in a particular discipline view the world through the latter's disciplinary lenses. When a physicist or a chemist or a biologist, thinks of an atom, they approach it through the current problems they have at hand. Apart from such common entities as atoms, there are a wide variety of concepts that are specific to a discipline. Thus a bacterium and its behavior is specific to a biologist and not usually to a physicist. A discipline therefore brings a particular perspective from which to view the world outside, a particular social subjectivity. When scientists are socialized through their professions these subjectivities are particularly honed so that essentially they yield what amounts to a worm's eye view of the world. In their training they are given the collective memory of the discipline as it has advanced through the centuries and decades. And as the discipline advances further, one can picture the scientist crawling through these particular windows to reality afforded by the subject. As the discipline moves forward, it is bounded by the discipline's epistemological boundaries and handed down social perspectives which are jealously guarded by its practitioners (Barnes, 1982, p. 90).

However, when new experimental or other results appear that confound the received wisdom and the existing apparatus through which the world is viewed, there is a change in the ruling window through which the discipline views the world. The existing worm's eye view of the discipline has a major change now, a paradigmatic change occurs. At times of such disjunctures, the old cultural order changes and there are now different lenses through which the scientist views the world.

Of all the cultural elements, it is science that affects most intimately today's interventions with nature. Especially the two technologies in which we are interested in this book are driven by science. So, although science is only but a part of the field of culture, it is for the purpose of this book the most central.

One can now summarize the properties of this cultural lineage of science that have been described. These properties have parallels with the biological one — and include speciation (to, in this case, disciplines and subdisciplines), the persistence of past memory, self construction (social construction by interactions between members), subjectivities associated with a lineage (in the manner of a particular discipline's 'views' on how to deal with the data on the world that is given to it, a phenomenon parallel to other social subjectivities in larger social lineages and equivalent to, say class or group consciousness), and sudden changes in cognition as in paradigmatic changes (Kuhn, 1962).

3: THE COMPUTER INFORMATION FLOWLINE

In the previous chapters, two well known evolutionary lineages have been discussed. They are in the genetic and cultural domain. In addition to these two an incipient evolutionary lineage of artificial (exosomatic) information devices is being rapidly formed. We discuss this lineage in this chapter and the next.

The rise of this lineage is fueled by both technological developments as well as particular social factors. As a result of the rise of this lineage many social roles are being fully or partly replaced by the technology.

Such extra-cultural and extra-biological, "exosomatic information systems", in fact predate humans. Thus, a bird that uses a twig it had placed earlier as a marker for remembering where it was building its nest uses an exosomatic information device of the simplest kind. So does a chimpanzee who uses plastic markers to communicate with humans, as in a celebrated set of experiments in chimpanzee communications (Premack, 1971, pp. 808–822).

Human mechanical manipulation of symbols — artefactual information processing — begins with the use of those objects closest to humans, their own fingers or toes. Different counting systems based on fives or tens are living remnants of such prehistoric information processing. Twigs and pebbles or markings on a cave wall were also manipulated for similar ends, as exosomatic means of recording and processing information. Writing, the development of letters and numbers and their manipulations on an external medium, were further steps in this same mode of externalization. With the introduction of the abacus a few thousand years ago mechanical operations took another step. The abacus, based on a system of "twos and fives," was an extrapolation of the system based on two hands and five fingers. However, it is during the last few centuries that a very rapid acceleration in externalization of information storage and manipulation has occurred.

In 17th-century Europe John Napier, a Scotsman, invented a means by which through a set of rods, multiplication was made possible by simply adding sets of numbers. Napier's other invention, logarithms, gave rise to the other calculating device — slide rules. In 1623, a machine was developed by Wilhelm Schickard that could add, subtract, multiply and divide. Soon after, in 1642, Blaise Pascal made a machine that could do additions and subtractions. Leibniz, using toothed wheels, improved Pascal's machine so that it could both multiply and divide (Pask and Curran, 1982, p. 7).

The major leap in artefactual information handling was made by the 19th-century polymath Charles Babbage. He used the ideas of Wilhelm Schickard who had developed punched cards to control the patterns woven in an automatic loom, to feed data and instructions to a calculating machine (Bromley, 1983). However, neither of Babbage's two inventions, the Difference Engine or the Analytical Engine, were completed. His Analytical Engine, which used punched cards to supply data and instructions and had an arithmetic logic device and a control unit, had the basic outlines for the mid-20th-century computer. His scheme had a system for input of data and instructions, storage for information, a control unit that allowed instructions to be carried out in a given sequence, an arithmetic logic unit to manipulate data and an output for the machine (Pask and Curran, 1982, p. 11). Babbage's associate Lady Lovelace also identified two other aspects of contemporary computer programming, namely the loop and the branch. In repetitive calculations, the loop allowed the same instructions to be automatically carried out over and over again. The branch allowed a set of operations to be carried out separately and to be later fed into the mainstream of calculations (Pask and Curren, 12).

In 1890, Herman Hollerith of the U.S. combined mechanical devices with the newly developing electrical technology to yield a machine that had punched cards to represent data and electromagnetically driven wheels and rods that did arithmetic (Pask and Curran, 16). Nearly half a century later, in the 1940s, the German, Konrad Zuse and IBM separately built machines that reduced Babbage's original vision to working hardware (Pask and Curran, p. 16). The IBM machine Mark I had 78 adding machines and desk calculators controlled by instructions channeled through punched holes.

In subsequent machines, electronic devices quickly replaced the slow operating electromechanical devices. The first electronic (valve) based machine was the Colossus I of Britain in 1943 (Pask and Curran, p. 11) while the first American machine the ENIAC (Electronic Numerical Integrator and Calculator) was commissioned in 1946 (Sherman, 1985, pp. 65–75). The latter operated 1,500 times faster than the Mark I and had 20,000 electronic valves.

With the development of the transistor, valves were in turn replaced; the fully transistorized computer appeared in 1956 (Ibid). A key landmark and turning point in the sequence of subsequent events was the development in 1971 of the computer on a chip; where a complete set of components and circuits was etched on a very small space. This first chip of 1971 possessed the computational power of the first ENIAC, cost far less and occupied a fraction of the space of the ENIAC which had 18,000 valves, consumed 180 kilowatts, covered 300 cubic feet and weighed 30 tons (Pask & Curran, 1982, p. 18).

Subsequent progress in electronics, especially through developments in integrated circuits, have produced a veritable revolution every few years in the size and power of computers. The level of integration since then has increased. Large Scale Integration (LSI) followed, leading to an increase in the number of components, followed by Very Large Scale Integration (VLSI) and Ultra Large Scale Integration (ULSI). Millions of components are today found on a chip the size of a thumbnail and the tendency towards microminiaturization is continuing to accelerate. It is the chip that forms the core of information technology.

Information Society and Information Technology

A central driving force in the increased use of information technology is the recent emergence of an "information society" in the developed countries. This growth is centered around the primacy of the service sector and its use of information. The growth of an exosomatic lineage tied to the new information technology is directly related to the growth of this information society. It is useful to briefly overview the growth of information society and its relationship to information technology.

The new societal profiles that have emerged in developed countries have been designated by different authors under various labels. Once, the information society was designated the "service society" (Marien, 1983). Roughly the same connotation was given to the "post industrial society" (Bell, 1973) or the "technocratic age" (Brzezinski, 1970). The word "electronic age," and the "age of information," were labels given by Marshall McLuhan (McLuhan, 1964) and "knowledge society" was the label given by Peter Drucker (Drucker, 1969).

The term "information society" itself was first used in the late 1960s in Japan (Kohyama, 1968), to be later repeated in a Japanese Government Plan, *The Plan for an Information Society* (Masuda, 1981). Other variants to describe the new social profiles included (Marien, 1983) "telematic society" (Martin, 1981), as well as the "Infoglut age". Although there is often an overlap and a lack of conceptual clarity in these formulations, one can discern a common thread of a clear and dominant shift towards information-related activities.

These tendencies towards information activities are influenced by a complex mixture of political, economic and intellectual factors (Noble, 1986). "Information" activities in many of these definitions include technical, clerical and service activities which are now being rapidly encroached upon by the new information technology.

The shift to dominance of the "information sector" has occurred gradually over the last hundred years. Marc Porat (1978) determined that between 1860 and 1906, the single largest labor group in the United States was agriculture. Between 1906 and 1964, the industrial work force became predominant, reaching a peak of 40 percent in 1946. By the 1950s, the proportion of the industrial work force had begun to decline and by the 1970s, it was only 25 percent. From 1954 on, what Porat (1978) has described as information workers, had become the largest group, rising from 5 percent of the labor force in 1860 to nearly 50 percent by the mid-1970s.

Based on a study in the mid-1970s, Porat claimed that the United States was by then essentially an information-based economy and that already by 1967 over one-fourth of the GNP was in the production, processing and distribution of information goods and services. By the beginning of the 1970s, nearly half the U.S. workers held jobs involved in the production, processing and distribution of symbols and hence were, "information workers."(Porat 1978).

Porat's methodology was applied by the OECD (1981) to a number of developed capitalist countries. And, it was clear that the economy had indeed shifted towards information goods and services. A more disaggregated analysis of these trends indicates that almost three-fourth of this growth was due to information-handling services (OECD 1981). A study of nine OECD member countries also showed that there had been a substantial growth of the information labor force and that the information sector had become a major sector for employment in all the countries surveyed.

Although the former Soviet Union and the hitherto planned economies had different societal characteristics from developed market economies, a shift to information-type societies was already being recorded in these countries by the 1970s as in the prognosis from Dobrov (Dobrov, 1979). The latter assumed technology as a total system and noted that software and what he called "Orgware" (Organizational ware — "the specialized organizational component of technology") would be dominant in the future. It is noted that what he meant by both software and orgware were information-based systems. In such a system, the major economic activity would be the creation and exchange of information.

Clearly, a fundamental shift in the social structure was underway in all developed countries, whatever their social systems. The information and communication economy that has thus emerged in developed countries is being rapidly fueled by developments in both communication and computer technology. Many of the activities in Porat's information sectors are being mechanized. The shift to an information society is thus being accompanied also by a shift to electronic means of information processing.

We can get some indication of the pervasive impact of the shift to information technology by considering the number of social roles that are being replaced fully or partially by the new technology. These give a very vivid perspective on the importance and impact of the technology and the creation of a set of information lineages parallel to the human cultural ones.

Replacement of Social Roles by Information Technology

The new technology encroaches upon a whole range of social roles and their attendant cultural systems. These roles vary from those at the commanding heights of the society and economy, through the levels of professional work, to white collar work, to skilled craftsman-type manual work, to unskilled work. This increasing encroachment by information technology on the occupational structures of developed economies can be indicated by examining a sample of occupational slots — from top to bottom.

Here the encroachment of the new technology continues across almost the entire job spectrum. In market economies, control of the economy at the higher level is by a profit-seeking private sector guided by fiscal and other means, while in the hitherto planned economies it had been by top level planners and the political elite. To both these control functions of the economy, at the level of private profit-seeking and macro planning, the new information technology had brought great changes.

In long-range forecasting of developed market economies conventional computer technology, as for example in input-output tables had been used for decades. Now more intelligent and skilled Artificial Intelligence systems are increasingly beginning to be used. These include for example, neural systems used for long-range business and economic forecasting, many of which have outperformed human systems (Ormerod, 1990).

At the level of the market, investment decisions of when to invest, and under what conditions, have been formalized and incorporated in computer programs in many professional activities of the financial system. Stock market offerings, their performance in the market as well as analyses and suggestions for the best buy are done on computer systems. And, buying and selling at major stock exchanges, or at foreign exchange centers has been at least partly done for several years by automated computer programs. The potential effect of these programs is suggested by the fact that the sudden collapse of the market in October 1987 as well as its subsequent recovery was due to automatic computer programs that had been used for trading (Knight, 1987). These programs, it should be noted were relatively 'dumb' ones, very different from the expert systems, neural networks and genetic algorithms that have since moved in (Geister, 1986).

With development of intelligent systems, skill replacement in finance by the technology is moving up. Many of the more challenging programs today are increasingly neural networks (Culbertson, 1990). Neural computers have been used for forecasting the Standard & Poor's Index, currency trading and equities trading (Chithelen, 1989). In addition, a whole array of new AI techniques based on genetic algorithms, chaos theory, fuzzy logic, neural networks and hybrids thereof are entering the field (Suran Goonatilake and Khebbal, 1995, Suran Goonatilake and Treleaven, 1995, The ghost, 1993).

The new information technology has also come to play an increasing role at different levels of micro economic decision making and management. Computerized decision making is encroaching on several levels with varied impacts on different social and occupational strata, as the following illustrative examples suggest.

Systems that automatically retrieve, find and act on information have already affected a wide variety of office jobs. And when increasingly in the future, this computer intervention is through AI based intelligent systems, the skills encroached upon would be quite significant. For example, a broad range of narrow management skills can be replaced by expert systems (Clay, 1989). Currently, the management functions that could be handled include scheduling and forecasting, personell management and procurement. Some AI based systems have also replaced management functions in discovering basic principles in business, forecasting and making profitable decisions (Coats, 1986).

There has been a strong impact of the new technology not only in the micro economic sphere of finance but also in other office work. These devices today encroach on several existing social roles in the office. The partial roles of higher management are thus being informatised through Management Support Systems. These include financial and market analysis systems, some having expert systems and neural networks (Di Giammarino and Kuckuk, 1991). For non-routine, higher level banking functions, loan application software, such as those with neural networks have replaced some managerial human skills (Culbertson, 1990, Smith, 1991). In the middle management clerical and other office jobs, many of the existing functions and roles have, or are being, fully or partially usurped by the machine (Marti and Zeillenger, 1982).

With the increased mechanization of the office, there has been a considerable degree of change in a wide variety of more routine office work that has replaced several clerical functions. Already the widespread use of desktop computer terminals and such devices as word processors has brought deep changes. More recently, grammar and style correction programs that partially replace the editing function has been a move, one step higher in the writing skill ladder. Widely expected within the next few years are developed versions of the rudimentary voice-driven word processing systems that are already on the market. These examples of encroachments of information technology cover almost the entire office work spectrum, from the higher executive through middle management to the clerical level (Giuliano, 1982; Wessells, 1990).

As in office management, in manufacturing too, almost the whole chain of skills and human roles are being fully or partially replaced by informatics. Thus Computer Assisted Design (CAD) and Computer Assisted Manufacture (CAM) have transferred some of the work of engineers to computer programs. In Computer Assisted Design, — CAD — computer graphics at the terminal are used to design, draft and analyze a product to be manufactured. Among the many applications of CAD have been the design of printed circuit boards, aircraft and automobiles. The use of CAD has yielded dramatic gains in the productivity of engineers and architects. Thus, Boeing estimated that the use of CAD had doubled the productivity of its engineers (Wessels, 1990, p. 32).

Lower down the manufacturing hierarchy are those who actually do the manufacture. Information technology is encroaching on the activities of both skilled and unskilled workers. Machinists for example, were some of the most highly skilled workers in industry who required years of experience to learn their craft. They were responsible for the use of drills, machine tools, and other equipment used in industry to produce different products. These activities have now been computerized through Computer Numerical Control (CNC). Here, a computer controls and guides milling machines, lathes and drills (Wessells, 1990, p. 33).

At lower levels of skill, robotic devices have successfully replaced, fully or partially, many unskilled worker functions and helped cut costs, as for example, in the automobile industries. Thus, welding on the assembly line, a semiskilled job, has been replaced by welding robots at lower cost.

In the chain of manufacturing jobs, thus virtually the complete array of human roles from those of highly skilled professionals through technicians and skilled workers to the unskilled have been encroached upon, in part or fully, by the new technology. Very deep changes in the respective roles of humans and machines have thus been occurring (Ayres and Miller, 1982; Hudson, 1982; Bylinsky and Moore, 1983). These changes affect almost the totality of social roles in the classical industrial job spectrum.

The combined encroachments into both white collar and manufacturing activities of the new technology in one industry can be seen by taking the air transport system. Here, CAD/CAM and other techniques common to advanced manufacturing are regularly used in aircraft manufacturing activities. The mechanical maintenance of the aircraft also depends on computer assistance, including use of expert systems that help diagnose faults. Running an airline utilizes the whole spectrum of information technology in office management, a highly visible computerized activity being booking systems. Flight simulators have for decades taken the partial role of trainer. These simulations, with newer computer technology have now become far more realistic, as have computer assisted air control systems which have augmented the activities of human controllers. The actual flying activity of a pilot has been heavily encroached upon in the newer generation of airplanes that 'fly by wire', while fully automating the flying of civilian aircraft is not a major technical difficulty, as has already been demonstrated in the case of some military aircraft (Sterling, 1991, p. 6).

Taking one other professional field — health care — as an illustration of the spread of technology, one can see the full or partial replacement of human functions across the entire occupational spectrum in the field. This spectrum covers human skills connected with drugs, from the discovery of new drugs by tailor-making chemicals on the basis of computer graphics, to the manufacturing process carried out on the basis of CAD/CAM, FMS (Flexible Manufacturing System) or CIM (Computer Integrated Manufacture), to testing the drug and following its efficiency through computerized data collection and analysis.

On the medical practicing side, some doctors have used for some time now expert systems for narrow diagnostic purposes. In fact one of the first expert systems to be made was MYCIN, an effective medical diagnosis system (Yu, 1979, p. 242, 1279–1282).

Imaging devices such as CAT, PET and similar systems and life support systems in the medical field that are heavily computer intensive are becoming increasingly pervasive. More recently, 'electronic' dissections and operations have been used on computer generated images of an organ to help surgeons. And, in the foreseeable future, robotic scalpels and knives would do precision surgery with finer tolerances than would humans, pin pointing with accuracy surgical interventions especially in delicate operations such as on the brain (Holusha, 1993).

The evidence we have presented from the different occupation structures suggests that a large number of hitherto human social functions are being fully or partly informatized across the entire job spectrum. The computer is thus encroaching on the functions of macro economic planners, key corporate decision makers, various professionally and technically qualified workers, and various skilled and unskilled clerical and manual workers.

These tendencies illustrate the rapid and pervasive encroachment by technology on social roles. What was a human and social function, has now become increasingly a machine function. The social roles in the occupational structure have been increasingly taken by machine roles (see Figure 4). A new "occupational structure," a new set of roles based on machines seems to be thus hiving off from the human one.

Globalization

The social roles that are being cloned by information artefacts are the result of differentiation of work into more and more specialized functions, into an increasing array of narrower and narrower social slots.

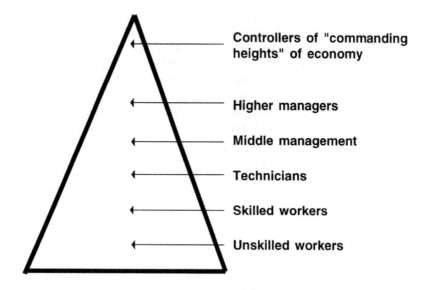

Figure 4   Range of human skills, partially or fully being informatized

An opposite trend is seen in the integrating and globalizing tendencies that are engulfing the world. These tendencies are political, economic, cultural, religious and above all technological.

If the information society described national tendencies, then this process of globalization describes an associated emerging web of information rings around the world.

Global communication had become one of the world's fastest growing industries. And the rapidly developing pervasive communication network (Pelet, 1987) was giving rise to a vast network of data girdling the world (Miles et al., 1988) growing at an exponential rate (Kobayashi, 1983). The ensuing transborder data flows were ignoring and bypassing local and national decision making (Schiller, 1981, p. 112) and raising questions of privacy, sovereignty, cultural identity and vulnerability of countries which have no control over their data flows (UNCTC, 1983).

What has been called the "global electronic machine" today consists of several components. These include hundreds of millions of tons of coaxial cable buried under the seas or underground, electronic devices and chips and orbiting satellites. These connect billions of radios, televisions, telephones, computers, fax machines and telex machines. As new technical developments like fiber optics and high capacity satellites come increasingly into the system, the interconnectedness increases dramatically (Pelton, 1989, p. 9).

The act of translating electronic signals to optical ones and vice versa as in current wired systems is not very efficient. As electrons are replaced by light waves in communication networks for processing, the full potential of fiber optics will be realized. In such a situation bandwidth would become 'as cheap as water'. It allows the possibility to transmit to every home or school on line selected contents of entire libraries such as that of the Library of Congress (Chan, 1995, pp. 72–76).

Electronic communities such as those on the Internet exchange information very rapidly across borders and have a sense of immediacy as they communicate with, support or compete electronically with foreign-based compatriots. Much of the data being exchanged and processed globally, are being cycled through computing artefacts.

Symptomatic of the pervasiveness of electronic links to the present global order is the fact that on a single day currency trading globally across the electronic system at the end of 1992 stood at one trillion U.S. dollars, equivalent to the funds held by all the central banks in the world (*New York Times*, September 25, 1992). This financial globalizing tendency is intimately linked to the new information and communications technologies, which are rapidly being integrated with each other.

Telecommunication links in developing countries are far less pervasive than in developed countries. Yet, as the world's decisions become increasingly integrated, those few that have the telecommunication links in developing countries are those who have influence on decisions in their countries and who in turn are affected by global trends. It is through these influential links that global financial transactions and telecommuting signals pass and key decisions take place.

The growth of the information society and information artefacts in the developed world has now spilled over to the global arena. Information artefacts now increasingly interconnect the globe. The growth of these transnational links results in, and is accompanied by, the growth of an explosion of information artefacts. It is the new ocean in which humans are being increasingly immersed.

This chapter has documented the rapid growth of computerized systems fuelled by a set of unique historical circumstances. These include developments in technology, the growth of the information society; the extensive replacement of human skills by computer programs and the knitting of both human and artefactual systems into a globalizing whole. These tendencies are intensifying rapidly at present. These and other deep dynamics are pushing information handling associated with computers to an increased autonomy, a tendency that is explored in the next chapter.

4: THE EXOSOMATIC LINEAGE DEVELOPS ITS AUTONOMY

The growth of information artefacts and their encroachment of social roles that were documented in the previous chapter is not just a development of yet another technology. It also leads to an increasingly autonomous lineage of information.

This development is fueled by deep changes in technology and society. This could be illustrated by taking up for discussion a few of the changes that are driving informatization inexorably forward. Some of these trends are partly extrapolations of ones sketched in the previous chapter and some are additional, deeper ones. Some are quantitative extensions of trends of the last chapter, others are qualitative ones. Because this lineage of artefacts is still nascent, and unlike those of the biological and cultural lineages, not yet part of common knowledge, it is necessary to highlight here some of these trends that influence its rapid growth.

These trends include the exponential growth of information, the accelerated growth of extremely high capacity and cheap computing artefacts, and the growth of autonomous characteristics in these artefacts. These result in an artefactual information lineage which is growing explosively. It has, as will be illustrated, many of the evolutionary characteristics common to the biological and cultural lineages. To describe some of these processes require digressing into some technical detail.

The Exponential Growth of Information

Information is growing today at an exponential rate much higher than the handling capacity of unaided human effort. This necessarily demands a high degree of mechanization.

Thus, it has been observed, more information of a general non-scientific kind has been produced during the last 30 years than in the previous 5,000 years (Large, 1984). A weekday issue of *the New York Times* carries more information than the average person in 17th century England was exposed to in his entire life (Wurman, 1989, p. 28). Further, the number of books in the leading libraries of the West doubles every 14 years, and even this fast growth is lagging behind the absolute growth of raw information (Wurman, 32).

As another indirect indicator of the growth, one could note that the English language today contains roughly 500,000 words, five times greater than in the time of Shakespeare (Wurman, 28). Pool noted that from 1960 to 1977 the number of words made available to Americans through the various media grew at a rate of 8.9% per year or more than double the 3.7% per year growth rate for the gross domestic product. And taking into account population growth, the words actually consumed per capita grew at a rate of 1.2% per year. The supply of information exceeds its consumption (Wurman, 28).

To take another example, from 1940 to 1970, the number of checks written in the United States increased tenfold and by 1980 over 40 billion checks were being written every year. This volume was far greater than could be processed by manual means alone. This rapid growth necessitated (and was accompanied by) the entry, a few decades ago, of computers into the banking sector. Electronic processing of funds has today become widespread in the major financial centers of the world and is growing rapidly. Checks, for example, are today handled through automated means using optical scanners that can read over ten thousand characters per second, processing in a minute more checks than a human worker of the precomputer age could do in a full day (Wessells, 1990, p. 29).

Indicative of this overencompassing encroachment of information technology in routine financial transactions is the fact that in only the week "the economy melted" in October, 1987, namely the largest financial crash since the Great Crash of 1929, there were 2.3 billion financial transactions in the U.S., more than occurred in the entire year of 1967 — twenty years previously (Sculley, 1989, p. 218). By the early 1980s, in one day a large commercial bank would electronically transfer roughly 30 billion U.S. dollars a day by computer (Parker, 1983). And towards the end of the decade, close to 100 trillion dollars, of fund transfers occurred electronically every year through cable and satellite (Pelton, 1989, p. 10). The volume of financial transactions had grown so enormous that it had become mandatory for computer mediation to be used for several functions and transactions. Electronic financial and currency links had now girdled the globe and were growing rapidly. The international *daily* traffic of currency trading was estimated at the end of 1992 at one trillion U.S. dollars, having increased by 50% over the three-years period up to 1992 (Greenhouse, 1992). Today's computer technology has therefore created a huge new electronic economy, what has been called the new "electronic commons." In this "network of money," cash is no longer something tangible like gold or paper but is transmitted by electronic signals in computers (Kurtzman, 1993).

The rapid growth of financial information and the necessity of computer mediation is being paralleled in other information spheres. Here again exponential growth necessitates computer mediation.

The above trends are for general nonscientific knowledge. But most of the new data is being generated by science. A few decades ago De Solla Price showed that the number of scientific books and journals had grown at an exponential rate since the mid-17th century. This rate was higher than the rate of growth of the population (Open University, 1971). More recent estimates indicate that the quantum of scientific information is now doubling every five years, and in the near future is expected to double every four years (Wurman, 1989, 32).

But in some scientific observation and experimental systems, such as in the Human Genome Project or in the satellite-based Hubble and other telescopes, the outpouring of information is far greater. Thus in astronomy, computers and automatic sensors are gathering such huge quantities of data that it has been referred to as 'trawling the heavens' for data. During the next few years, because of this massive outpouring, certain fields of astronomy would collect tens and hundreds of the times of data that had been collected in the entire history of humankind (Trawling the Heavens, 1995, pp. 107–108).

In addition, immediate access to databases all over the world, which is fast becoming a reality, would result in scientific personnel wallowing in a trillion bytes a day, in what has been described as attempting to drink from a fire hose (Waldrop, 1990). This high volume of information being generated today in certain sectors is thus simply beyond the physical capacity of humans alone to keep in track (Denning, 1990, pp. 402–406). To give another related example, when a communication system exchanges information at 100 (one hundred) gigabits per second, this is much higher than can be tackled by human mediated systems such as telexes and telephones alone (Pelton, 1982). It has to be hived off from humans to the machine lineage as humans alone would not be able to cope.

The emergence of large international information systems would facilitate a large-scale shift from human processing to machine processing of information. The shift of cultural information to a machine mode will increasingly result in a global information network that handles machine data (Pelton, 1982). Machine to machine data flows are consequently growing more rapidly than those from human to human, or human to machine traffic (Pelton, 1982).

Machine handling will not only be limited to a routine collection of data, or to preliminary analysis, but because of the pressures from the exponential growth of data, increasing use will be made of automated means of comprehending this information. Already, the problem of searching in large data bases is being facilitated by data mining programs. These scour massive data bases, even navigating a large network like the Internet, and then seek out, identify and retrieve relevant data. In such functions, these electronic agents take the role of a human research assistant.

There is a very rapid growth of information that cannot be handled by humans alone and which require exosomatic devices. Some of this growth is due to information generated by exosomatic devices themselves. Consequently, the exosomatic, artefactual information system is growing rapidly, faster than the human one and now increasingly requires its own devices to make sense of it.

Growth of Density of Chips

The rapid growth of new information is not the sole factor fueling the exosomatic line. The rapid growth of the artefactual system is also being fueled by technical developments that are increasing enormously the capacities of key elements in computers.

Thus, the number of components that could be placed on a silicon chip has been increasing quickly. The most commonly used type of chip is the dynamic-random access memory chip, DRAM. It is here that new manufacturing techniques are perfected before being used on the more complex logic chips.

Over twenty years ago, in 1975 at the beginning of the chip era, there was available either commercially or in demonstration models one kilobyte (1,000 bytes, IK) of memory per chip. In 1977 this had risen to 4K; in 1979 to 16K; in 1981 to 64; in 1983 to 256K; in 1984 to 4 megabytes (4 million bytes, 4,000K); in 1988 to 16 megabytes and by 1990 64 megabytes (Hannah & Soreff, 1983) were available in demonstration models. In 1991, the highest capacity commercially available chip was a 4 million transistor chip capable of holding 4 megabytes, which was equivalent to one and a half times the words in a large novel such as the "Great Gatsby" (*New York Times*, Dec 29, 1991, p. 5). In early 1993, Toshiba was showing demonstration models of DRAM chips with a 256 megabyte capacity, each such chip having the capacity to hold 11,000 pages of text. These chips were expected to be commercially available by 1998 (Marbach, 1993, p. 93) Between 1972 and 1992, the amount of data that a commercially available DRAM chip could hold thus increased over 4,000 times, from 1,000 bytes to 4 million bytes in 1992.

The amount of information that could be held on a thumb nail size chip was increasing by leaps and bounds. The increase in capacity of memory chips is directly paralleled by the increase in logic processing chips, with broadly similar manufacturing processes underlying both.

As a consequence of the progress illustrated by these examples, the memory and processing speed of computers double and the prices halve every two years or so. This exponential growth in memory capacity of chips is referred to as Moore's "Law" which "asserts" that the number of components on a chip doubles every two years. (Hanna & Soreff, 1983, p. 22). In the mid-1970s Moore's Law was amended as the pace of doubling was accelerating; so that today the number of chips doubles every 18 months (*The New York Times*, December 29, 1991, p. 5). This geometric development it appears is not slowing down and is probably still accelerating. Today's microprocessors are nearly 100,000 times as powerful as their ancestors in the 1950s. If these trends continue, in twenty-five years (say in 2020) a single desktop computer will be as powerful as all the computers in Silicon Valley today (Patterson, 1995, pp. 62–67).

The resulting reduction of prices of components by the operation of Moore's Law is illustrated by the fact that in 1985, costs had dropped to a 10,000th of the figure in 1950 (Ayres, 1987). As newer chips are introduced every two years or so, similar cost relationships would result between the old and the newest chips.

Secondary Storage

Unlike the human brain, present computer design stores data not only in the primary storage of DRAMs but also in secondary, more permanent storage such as discs and tapes. Here too, transformations are taking place in a manner parallel to those of DRAMs and processing chips.

In the last few years large amounts of data has been made available on CD-ROM (Read Only Memory) discs. Encyclopedias, data bases, and collections of books are now appearing by the hundreds and offering not just cheap storage but also multimedia capabilities, where sight, sound, text and numbers interact. The basic costs of memory storage in the existing technology in CD-ROM has become almost absurdly small relative to other storage formats.

Today on a CD approximately 300,000 pages of text can be stored. Such a disc when in volume production can be stamped for just US $1 (*Time* Oct. 21, 1990, 80). The rest of the costs for today's CD-ROMs that sell anywhere between a few dollars to hundreds of dollars, are for the preparation of the material to be stored, copyright, profit margins and so on. This means that the cost per book of 300 pages stamped on a CD-ROM can go down to US $ .001, (that is US cts. 0.1). If the computer to read the CD-ROM exists, this is truly affordable storage even in the poorest Third World context. The technology of CD-ROMs is basically derived from that of CD audio records. A technology, DVD — Digital Video Disc, is now on the market that gives a video the size of a CD, thus doing for the video market what was done to the audio market by CD. This format is now about to encroach the computer market as DVD-ROMs with very much higher capacity than CD-ROMs. These DVD-ROMs are expected to rapidly displace CD-ROMs in a matter of years. This development will further enhance secondary storage and make its costs become still smaller.

New research using the innovative technique called near-field scanning optical microscopy has also yielded secondary storage densities one hundred times as great as in compact discs and three hundred times more than in existing magnetic storage systems (Markoff, 1993). This technique could potentially store 45 (forty five) billion (10^9) bits of information per inch or, alternatively would be able to store a novel the length of "War and Peace" on a pin head (Markoff, 1992).

Computer Densities Rivaling Brain Capacities

The continued miniaturization driven by technology now faces certain physical limits associated with the current silicon technology used for transistors. Limits to etching of circuits and heat disposal of the current technology are being reached. Some of the limits now being approached in existing silicon technologies have forced the search for other techniques in micro miniaturization. These newer techniques include the stacking of components three dimensionally, the use of molecular switches, nano technology and opto-electronics. To illustrate the potential for massive growth in these technologies and the implications for the associated information technology, it is useful to overview some of these developments now being pursued (Markoff, 1992).

The capacity of chips could be increased by stacking components one above the other in a volume, instead of printing the circuits on the surface of a silicon wafer. There would thus be layers of components with connections between them. With this technology, "in principle, we could build a solid cube of transistors that would rival the human brain in circuit complexity but perform at speeds hundreds of thousands of times faster than neurons" (Hanna & Soreff, 1983, p. 24). Such a cube of components would have problems of heat disposal to be probably solved by intense cooling or by the new developments in super conductors which operate without resistance and so eliminate the problem of heat generation (Sutton, 1987).

In an emerging molecular approach to microminiaturization, the switching on and off of an electric current — the standard method of binary operation in electronic devices — is through a molecule. Such molecular computers are expected to perform a central role in the coming decades.

One technique of molecular level chips using 'spectral hole burning' could technically store 10^{12} bits (one trillion bits) per square centimeter. This density is based on having the storage devices laid out on a flat surface. If, however, they were stacked on top of each other the density that could be conceived of, would be 10^{18} bits per cubic cm. The human brain holds 10^9 bits per square centimeter; so that in about 750 cubic centimeters, it stores the equivalent of about a thousand billion (10^{12}) bits of data. So, the storage density achievable through spectral hole burning is a thousand times that of the human brain. These molecular devices would also be very fast, well beyond the THZ (one THZ equals 1 million MHZ) range (in comparison, the fastest Intel 486 chip in 1994 operates at 66 MHZ and a fast Pentium, its successor, at 100 MHZ.) With this type of technology, the information in every book ever written can be fitted into an area of 20 cm^2 or, if stacked three dimensionally, into a volume the size of a cube of sugar and accessed virtually instantly (Suran Goonatilake, 1991a, p. 26)

Another approach to infinitesimally small cheap devices is through the rapidly developing technology of the very small — nano technology. Nanotechnology aims at the manufacture of very tiny artefacts and machines. Machine parts would be at the size level of an atom, often built using the same photo lithographic techniques that ensure cheap production of silicon chips. Today's transistors in chips are more than five hundred times as thick as individual silicon atoms. Yet, atomic level switches have already been demonstrated using the scanning tunneling microscope which has the ability to pick up, move and deposit individual atoms of silicon. A development using this technique and storing a bit in a cluster of 1,000 atoms, could give the entire contents of the U.S. Library of Congress in a 12" wide silicon disc, current technologies requiring 250,000 such disks (Yam, 1991, p. 20). As a consequence, "a shirt-pocket supercomputer may be in the cards, as well as memory chips that hold a library"(Port, 1991, pp. 54–55).

Further down the road of infinitesimal miniaturization, is at the level of using an electron to represent one bit. This technique has been demonstrated at the laboratory level in devices called Coulomb Blockade devices. Today's chips use 500,000 electrons to represent one bit. Using these Coulomb Blockade techniques, a one electron level chip could hold a million (10^{12}) bits of information on a British fifty pence coin (Clery, 1993).

The use of optical devices for computer components would also accelerate the process of micro miniaturization very much further. There are several parallel approaches being pursued in optical computing. The Swiss are working on a technique that can store holograms on top of one another on a single polymer, which offers massive storage possibilities of the order of 100 million (10^8) bits per square centimeter (Bains, 1990). Another approach using very tiny lasers can potentially store 6.5 trillion (6.5×10^{12} bits - equivalent to 1 million novels) in a cubic centimeter volume (*New York Times*, Sept 1, 1991, p. 43).

Use of optical devices based on holography in optical neural computers has enormous information processing and storage possibilities. Using this technique, a volume hologram the size of one cubic centimeter could specify more than a trillion (10^{18}) connections (Abu-Mostafa et al., 1987). In contrast, the human brain consists of roughly 1,000 billion (10^{12}) neurons. And as each neuron is connected with as many as 10,000 (10^4) others, this gives roughly 10 million billion (10^{16}) interconnections for the brain (*Cabling of the brain Economist*, 15 June 1985, p. 84). These yield packing densities for the optical device of an order much higher than in brains.

The limits of silicon are being reached in three to four computer generations' time, that is in say, ten years. The technologies under development after that, at the molecular, atomic, electron or photonic level will expand capacities enormously, to the level of the infinitesimally small. These emerging technologies would also allow for extremely high capacity permanent secondary storage.

Many of these technologies are today at the developmental or experimental stage. Some will develop faster than others, others for a variety of reasons will drop out on the wayside. Only some will reach commercial viability. Yet, each of these emerging technologies have the capacity to develop cheap computing artefacts exceeding the storage capacity of biological neural material, including the human brain. At least, a few would do so in the foreseeable future.

"Artificial Intelligences" and Machine "Creativity"

In most current applications, computers have been used to process information so that relatively routine mental applications could be done faster. A qualitative change in the use of computers is through "Artificial Intelligence" (AI) and intelligent techniques, by which computers enter less routine fields, where more creative processing is required. The mass entry of at least some AI applications would deeply change the contours of the artefactual information system, tending to make a lineage with increasingly autonomous characteristics.

Artificial Intelligence (AI) developments in both software and hardware allow computers to enter the realm of manipulation of symbols, words, ideas and knowledge — areas normally limited to humans (Gregorio, 1987; Doi et al., 1987). The AI field covers the ability to understand normal speech, read documents, process images and do deductive and inductive thinking. In operational terms, AI includes the ability to learn and do induction, speech and pattern recognition, natural language use, robotics, neural networks, genetic algorithms, fuzzy logic and expert systems.

In the 1980s, an over-hyped and over-ambitious scheme by the Japanese, the Fifth Generation Computer program, saw major efforts in AI, but could not reach its stated goals (Feigenbaum and McCorduck, 1983). Parallel programs were also launched in America and Western Europe (Torrero, 1985). Although this program's ambitious goals were not reached, the field was taken sufficiently seriously that by the mid 1980s in the United States, over half of the leading 500 companies — the "Fortune 500" — had projects in Artificial Intelligence research (UNIDO, 1986).

The 1990s have seen some major trends not foreseen at the time the Fifth Generation program was launched, and which are today penetrating significant areas of computer applications. But before discussing these, it would be useful to briefly recall some significant AI successes of the past to give a flavor of its goals and potential.

These past successes include Winograd's program called SHRDLU which attempted modeling natural language capacities and which could hold a dialogue in words, with some representation of the real world. Through this natural language dialogue, the program could manipulate its "world" of a few simple solid geometric objects. A similar attempt was the "kitchen world" of the LUIGI program (Scraggs, 1975). This program could "converse" with understanding on its conceptual world, which consisted of utensils and food items. In both these programs, an integral model of the external real world was manipulated. Another rather rudimentary natural language system was INTELLECT (Kaplan and Ferris, 1982) which was used to interrogate data bases (Alexander, 1982, p. 140).

Based on current work, computers with some practical facility for natural language abilities are expected to be widespread within the next decade (Unenohara and Linuma, 1989). The Japanese have been using rudimentary computerized translation systems for quite some time. But they are developing a context-sensitive electronic dictionary that will give much more effective and understandable translations (Pollack, 1992). Although the time when one could ring up anybody in the world and chat freely in one's language of choice through automatic translation is yet in the future, there have been major developments recently. Already by the mid-1990s voice recognition devices with some contextual understanding are beginning to be widely used by telephone companies. In the near future, interpreter telephones would be used in limited applications such as making travel reservations (Pollack, 1993).

An area where the computer has encroached relatively successfully upon the human arena is mathematical theorem proving. Indicative of the potential in the field, the American Mathematical Society has for example devoted special issues of its journal to the subject (Bledsoe & Loveland, 1984; Wang, 1984). Successful examples of theorem proving have included the classical Newell and Simon "Logic Theorist" used for propositional logic and Gelernts's program for elementary geometry which produced proofs hitherto unknown to humans. Wang developed a program for Propositional Logic, and Robinson produced a system for first order predicate calculus. The Boyer-Moore Theorem Prover (BMTP) stated theorems and proved them automatically. These latter theorems have been considered to be in a class difficult if done by humans (Boyer and Moore, 1979).

Computer systems that learn and improve on their performance have been seen in widely different areas. One of the earliest successful examples was Samuel's Program for playing checkers (draughts) (Samuel, 1959, pp. 210–229). This had a learning system which helped it increasingly better its performance based on its past successes. The program improved by playing against human opponents as well as by following already published games played between masters. This program eventually beat its creator and later, also some champion players (Michie, 1974). A similar successful program was Mostow's "FOO" for playing cards. Mostow's program took general advice on how to play the game such as play "this way" or play "such a card, during such an occasion" (Mostow & Hayes, 1979), Mostow, 1981).

There have been many AI systems that learn by induction, that is by making generalizations from specific knowledge elements (Cohen & Feigenbaum, 1982, p. 373). Some have been able to discover new concepts. A well documented case is Meta DENDRAL which learnt sets of rules that are used in chemical analysis (Buchanan and Mitchell, 1978, pp. 297–312), and the AM (Automatic Mathematician) which discovered new concepts in mathematics (Lenat, 1883). Another system HACKER had by a process of learning by doing, aided computer programmers acquire programming skills (Sussman, 1975). BACON, a very successful program in science developed by Simon "rediscovered" several well known scientific laws (Langley, 1977, pp. 6, 505–507). BACON, given raw data, examined them and made generalizations. The "rediscoveries" included were Ohm's Law in electricity, Newton's law of gravitation, Kepler's Law of planetary motion, Boyle's Law of gases, Snell's Law in optics and Black's Law governing specific heat (Langley ibid). In a similar vein GLAUBER, another program by Simon discovers qualitative laws, not quantitative ones like BACON (Boden, 1990, pp. 197–200). More recent developments in AI fall into a few significant classes: neural networks, genetic algorithms and fuzzy logic. It is in these categories that major advances have recently been made in moving computers towards more human-like abilities.

Whereas conventional programs deal with facts and raw information, expert systems deal with knowledge and professional "lore." This expert's lore is not formally recorded in textbooks and often the expert is also unaware of how the solution is arrived at. The lore consists of hunches and "heuristics" (rules of thumb), acquired over a lifetime's experiences, which are combined with the more formal knowledge in the expert area. An expert system combines this knowledge with an inference system (Michie and Johnston, 1985, p. 34).

With the arrival of expert systems, professional skills, such as those of lawyers, doctors, engineers and accountants were now being encroached upon by computers (Michie and Johnston, 1985, p. 34). Expert systems can in narrow demarcated areas be equal to, or perform better than human professionals. Some of these areas have included medical diagnosis, mineral exploration, analysis of organic compounds and classifying crop diseases (Michi and Johnston, 1985, p. 34, Forsyth and Naylor,1986, p. 186, Rennels and Shortcliffe, 1987).

An expert system that has been quite successful is *DENDRAL* which analyzes data from instruments to give the constituent elements and the molecular structure of a chemical compound (Michie and Johnston, 1985, p. 44). Another widely known system, *MYCIN*, helped diagnose infectious diseases more accurately than their human counterparts (Yu, 1979, pp. 1279–82). An expanded, more generalized version, called "essential *MYCIN*" or *EMYCIN* was very successful. Doctors using this had signed 85% of the reports generated by the system unchanged (Osborn, 1979). Other expert systems have helped "prospect" for buried treasure using geological and other data (Duda et al., 1981), while another *MOLGEN* has helped in genetic engineering (Michie & Johnston, 1985, pp. 44–46).

Expert systems are in what has been termed the symbolic realm of AI, that is in manipulation of symbols. There are other AI developments that are making rapid progress, that do not require overt manipulation of symbols. And, these are transcending some of the limitations of expert systems. One of these — neural networks — have within the last few years shown considerable promise. Neural computers are based on the assumption that systems can be developed which, when connected together and having sufficient complexity, automatically process information. This approach was initially based on how the brain itself organizes information (Ferry, 1986, p. 37).

Self-organization systems of computing were attempted in the decades after World War II but were given up because of the limited number of neuron-like elements then available for experimentation. Contemporary specialists believe that if a computer is wired up as in a brain, the system would start to learn and intelligent behavior would emerge by the machine organizing itself (Clark, 1987). The computer's elements would be like neurons — and their interconnections like the nervous system's synapses. In a Neural Network, no single element by itself determines the output of a computing system; the *collective* output of all the units in the system determines this.

Neural networks have been very successful in certain areas especially where previous symbolic AI approaches had failed or had given meager results (Rumelhart and McLelland, 1986). Neural networks have exhibited associative memories as in the way humans remember a particular person's face, or evoke a cluster of associated memories such as those of age, height, job, name, family and shared experiences (Tank and Hopfield, 1987).

Neural networks unlike other AI systems do not require detailed programming of the reasoning strategies. Instead, the network is trained by presenting repeated examples of an object or processes. A neural network used for recognizing a face would not require detailed formal descriptions through a program as done in traditional, symbolic AI. What is done in a neural network is to show the network repeated examples of different faces, allowing natural interconnections to occur. The network then automatically builds up a representation of a typical face so that when a face is held up to the network, it would now recognize it as such.(Abu-Mostafa and Psaltis, 1987). Thus, a neural system will build up generalizations of knowledge from examples presented to it. The representation of any item so recognized is not located in any one particular memory location, but instead it is spread out over the whole network. Further, the same network can hold representations of many other objects by a process of "superposition" (Clark, 1987).

This superpositional storage allows neural networks to be robust. This means that even if the network does not have the complete information about a particular object or concept, it can still come to conclusions based on the available partial knowledge.

Neural systems have shown promise in other applications, especially where conventional means were not very successful. One such success was in the "traveling salesman" problem — where the optimal route to be taken by a traveling salesman going to several cities was to be identified — and which had defied conventional AI (Abu Mostafa & Psaltis, 1987). Neural networks have also successfully read handwriting directly into a computer. Similarly, neural network-based speech recognition systems have moved up from the laboratory stage. NETtalk, a neural system which converted text automatically into speech has been successful, outperforming another system which used symbolic AI methods and which had taken many man years to build

(Sejnowski and Rosenberg, 1986). Neural networks have functioned very well and outperformed human experts in credit evaluation. Credit evaluation is done by banks and credit companies before granting loans. Factors such as age, income and performance of past loans are important in correct evaluations. Neural networks, when trained with past performance data, have automatically identified worthy credit risks, while rejecting unworthy ones (Leigh, 1995).

Other areas where neural networks have achieved very high performance is in sonar detection (Churchland, 1995) in detecting chemicals in the environment, and in computer vision to recognize objects (Boden, 1988) . Neural networks have also been developed to drive a computer-simulated tractor trailer truck and to sift out explosive chemicals at airports (Brody, 1990). Neural networks have also been used for diagnosis and treatment in medicine. Given an unfamiliar diagnosis, the system prompts suggestions for treatment based on diagnoses similar to the one at hand (Smith, 1986).

Neural networks offer a natural way for computing systems to learn from their environment. The natural analogy is how the child learns from the environment in which he or she lives. Here, the programs themselves do not need detailed expertise in a problem area. They require only a means of testing trial solutions to see how well they meet established criteria. Once these criteria are established the computer itself gropes around testing for possible solutions for a fit. A large number of applications of neural networks are now being made world wide.

There is another potentially very powerful means of computing also based on biological principles that is developing very fast. This is genetic algorithms, which uses an evolutionary approach to problem solving. In genetic algorithms, pioneered nearly twenty-five years ago by John Holland, solutions are evolved in a manner mimicking Darwinian evolution. Programmers set up a test to check whether trial solutions meet certain established criteria. Once the criteria are set, the program itself gropes around for solutions that fit the criteria in a trial-and-error manner. Parts of a program — strings — are exchanged randomly so that the solutions can be tested for fit to an established criterion (Walbridge, 1989, pp. 47–53.).

The genetic algorithm process broadly fits the manner through which biological evolution proceeds, where chromosomes exchange genes during the evolutionary process. This system of arriving at solutions without detailed programming has been successful in a variety of uses such as design of civil engineering trusses, scheduling jobs in a factory and recognitions of a face or a language in the presence of background "noise" (Walbridge, 1989).

A new form of software, 'agents', is emerging rapidly that will scour the data terrain and identify predesignated items of data. It will not only identify, but also partly process the data. These agents are still in their infancy but are bound to grow. The increasing deluge of information demands it, as well as newer programming techniques allowing for it. Already by the mid-1990s, there were a handful in commercial operation. Some existing ones could do routine secretarial tasks like scheduling meetings and automatically responding to incoming electronic mail. In some of the future artefacts in the emerging genre, learning aspects will be built in so that the agent studies the user's habits and later gives what he regularly asks for. Some will venture into broad cyberspace and interact with other people's agents, exchanging information and responding to each other (Schwartz, 1994).

Another newer AI approach, fuzzy logic, is a method of getting computers to deal with grey, "common sense pictures of an uncertain world" (Kosko and Isaka, 1993, pp. 76–81). This approach to logical thinking has proved very useful, especially in control systems. Fuzzy logic had become wide spread by the mid 1990s in many control devices such as in household appliances and lifts (McNeil and Freiberger, 1993, 319).

These newer computing approaches are also being combined to yield 'hybrid' systems that bring together the advantages of each. There are now developments where rules of fuzzy systems are generated through neural networks (Kosko and Isaka, 1993, pp. 76–81). Other hybrid approaches that have features of neural networks, genetic algorithms or fuzzy logic in different combinations to give synergistic effects are being explored (Suran Goonatilake, and Khebbal, 1995).

If the search for artificial intelligence can be crudely categorized by the dominant themes of the different decades, it would probably read as follows. The 1950s was the decade of neural nets, the 1960s of heuristic search, the 1970s of expert systems and 1980s of machine learning (Forsyth and Naylor, 1986, p. 1), and the 1990s probably of connectionist devices, genetic algorithms, fuzzy logic and hybrid systems thereof with human interventions.

Artificial intelligence aims at a higher form of machine processing of information. And so, the question can be posed: are any of AI-based computers creative? Can they create new ideas or novel systems that were unknown before? Even a simple calculating device often gives an answer that was not known before, so that in that very restricted, rather trivial sense such a device produces a new result every time it operates. But when one normally discusses creativity something higher is meant.

New developments in expert system-based devices for example tend to make the computer become a research assistant in scientific work, more than a mere number crunching slave. A computer, and say an astrophysicist, could after such developments carry on a "conversation" at a higher level of conceptualization. Here, alternative models and descriptions in astronomy would be "discussed" and "debated" between the human and machine, and a "consensus" arrived at (Hut and Sussman, 1987).

There have been several classical examples of creativity in AI. The AM (Automatic Mathematician) (Lenat, 1983) program discovered concepts in two fields of mathematics, namely set theory and elementary mathematics. Starting with a knowledge base of over 100 concepts, obtained from the mathematical field of finite set theory, AM was fed with knowledge of mathematical aesthetics. As it operated, it developed new concepts as well as hypotheses. With its initial set of concepts, AM independently discovered many well known results in set theory. After further activity, AM discovered many of the simple arithmetic operations. It discovered multiplication through four different means. The ability to raise numbers to the fourth power, as well as taking fourth roots were also discovered. Although at an elementary level, AM could go very much beyond its initial set of concepts and rediscover some key mathematical results.

A recent example of a computer-generated proof in mathematics has raised effusive praise from human mathematicians. The program had solved a conjecture that had baffled the best mathematicians for 60 years. The program was a general one, designed to reason, not to solve a particular problem like a chess program does. This has been hailed as the crowning achievement in over 30 years of computer-based theorem proving and was considered "clearly a form of computer thinking" (Kolata, 1996 b: p. C1).

In the EURISKO program, heuristics worked on themselves, and their performance was constantly monitored by the program. Heuristics helped to generate other better heuristics (Lenat, 1983). EURISKO when applied to VLSI (Very Large Scale Integration) circuit design came up with a three dimensional AND/OR gate which was very novel and had not been thought of before (Forsyth and Naylor, 1986, p. 216).

A connectionist device generates internally generalized models that it did not have before. So, in this sense, it is 'creative' vis-à-vis its previous state. But these models and solutions may not be novel to humans. Yet it is not difficult to foresee neural networks delivering solutions that would surprise their creators, because the detailed workings of the problem are unknown to the user, implying that the solutions are creative. Connectionist devices are still new, and in the future we could expect significantly creative responses. In a similar way, the solutions of genetic algorithms are novel because the solutions the programs evolve towards could not have been known before.

There seems to be no formal unbreakable barrier between human and ultimate machine creativity. Already a VLSI design by the EURISKO program has been given a patent (Forsyth and Naylor, 1986, p. 216). And one expert system in an area of biochemistry has been listed as a coauthor of a paper published in a scientific journal (Boden, 1990, p. 134).

The trends in AI that have been charted here are only a beginning (Rothfeder, 1986). With the creation of machines that have more intelligence and creativity, they will in turn help design and develop successor systems that will be still more intelligent. Because of this process, artificial intelligence becomes an intelligence amplifier.

By the early 1990s computers had sufficiently advanced to be tested in a contest based on the so called Turing Test. This test, named after the British computer scientist Alan Turing, states that if a person after interacting with a device through a telecommunication system cannot state whether the entity he is communicating with is human or not, and if he is in fact communicating with a machine, then that machine passes the "Turing Test" for an adequate intelligence capacity (Markoff, 1991). The computers that competed in a recently held Turing test did not have some of the most recent technologies. Yet there were few programs, which led some of the judges to believe they were interacting with humans. But the successes of these winning programs, it should be noted, had as much to do with their ability to analyze language structures and present them, than with real human-like understanding.

The structural information processing that has been dealt with in the examples given above are not the most difficult aspects of human intelligence to emulate. It is the more commonsensical aspects that have proved the most difficult for computers to process. Douglas Lenat has been working on the codification of commonsensical knowledge for almost 10 years. These are the information handling so easy to do by humans but that has failed computers. His project has collected hundreds of thousands of such commonsensical views of the world that humans take for granted. The database is not yet complete.

But by mid-1995, the system was fast reaching a level at which it could serve as the base for future accretions. Together with a natural language processing program it will be able to gradually expand its base by automatically adding on uses that it is unfamiliar with. Once that threshold is reached, the system will be able to operate on its own, learning its way, and adding on further information. Such a program for example, once added to a future word processing program will not only check grammar and spelling but also content (Lenat, 1995, pp. 80–82).

Still, AI systems, although they may outperform humans in narrow fields are not about to replace general human thought. Yet, the directions that have been highlighted here and the examples that have been given, show the deep potential that AI has in the future.

Computing Devices Spread Pervasively

Fueled by the underlying technology trends given earlier, the growth of the information industry in recent decades has been very rapid.

Already by 1985, there were more computers than people in the United States including tiny microprocessors embedded in a variety of household devices and consumer goods. Further, in the same year, microprocessors were being manufactured at a rate of more than a million a day. Yet only 4 million computers were produced in that year, so that only 1% of microprocessors end up in computers and only 20% in pure electronic systems. The remainder were being used in other artefacts like cars (Kairamo, 1987, p. 41) . Already by 1985, electronics constituted a larger portion of costs of automobiles than sheet metal (Kairamo, 1987, p. 41). Consumer appliances in homes today contain many hidden computers which have complex control functions in such equipment as washing machines, sewing machines, microwave ovens, VCRs and a variety of other consumer goods (Birnbaum, 1985). Further, the use of computing power in American society has progressed to the point where some citizens will soon own more computing power than the amount projected 30 years ago as the *total* national requirement for the United States (Anderson, 1986, p. 79).

In the late 1970s, Osborne compared the degree of improvements associated with the microelectronic technology with an imagined similar progress in aeronautics. In this case, the airplane would by the late

1970s, he calculated, be carrying half a million (500,000) passengers, at a speed of 20 million (20,000,000) miles per hour at an air ticket cost of less then one penny (Osborne, 1979). In 1986, the cost of a chip with the capacity of the ENIAC the first American computer (which then cost $5 million) was $5, a million times cheaper at the nominal rate of the dollar (Anderson, 1986, p. 17). In the early 1990s, Jerry Sauders, chairman of the Advanced Micro Devices Corporation put the nature of these advances in different words: " If cars evolved at the rate of semi-conductors, we would all be driving Rolls-Royces that go a million miles an hour and cost 25 [US]cents" (*Denser, Faster, Cheaper The New York Times*, 1991, p. 5).

If one sees down the time horizon of the next 10 years, (and more so of the next 20 years), one would see 'completely inexpensive computing power' (Markoff, 1992, p. D1). And, ubiquitousness of computing will soon be such that it could be a wearable product. Prototypes at MIT suggest that there will be chips in one's shoes powered by the mechanical act of walking and there will be chips embedded in the clothes that one wears (Markoff, 1995, pp. 14–15). Computing devices have become the cheapest and most ubiquitous technology ever.

The Third Lineage Comes into its Own

Most information transmission in the computer, artefactual realm is synchronous, that is exchanges of information are between computing artefacts for purposes of solving current problems. This would correspond to synchronous information exchanges between humans in the form of conversation to solve current problems or of 'idle' chatter. But just as humans transmit information diachronically down through time, there is also the diachronous transmission in artefacts. Through this process a lineage that extends backwards and forwards through time is created.

Computers have existed for only a few decades, so the lineage of information that is handed down from one set of information artefacts to another is still short, perhaps not more than 40 years. But it is growing rapidly in importance as computer use grows exponentially.

The growth of the technology is also fueled by socioeconomic factors that are driving some societies to have a preponderant information sector. Most of that information is being increasingly cycled through computers. The explosive growth of computer-processed information is also helped by the exponential growth of information and formal knowledge which by the early decades of the 21st century, will be so large that humans alone would not be able to cope with this growth, requiring an increased hiving off to machine processing.

These tendencies are combined with rapidly falling price per unit of computation in the technology. It is reasonable to expect that consequently, there would soon be more computing devices in the world than there would be people, although they would be unevenly distributed.

Thus, embedded microcontrollers are single purpose computers that do a variety of little jobs in many artefacts including microwave ovens and video games and many, many other devices. One of their first uses were in the hand-held calculators of the 1970s. A typical car today uses about 15 such separate chips, the number expecting to double before the end of the decade (Calem, 1994). Already the electronics in an automobile, essentially carried through these devices cost twice as much as the steel in a car (Zuckerman, 1995). In the average U.S. home, Motorola estimates that from virtually zero microcontrollers in 1980, use would zoom to about three hundred by the end of the century. Indicative of the massive proliferation of cheap computing, it was estimated in 1993 that there were a total of 1.7 billion such microcontroller chips sold world wide (Calem, 1994).

Computer devices are also increasingly being interconnected through a rapidly developing pervasive communication network, as the world telecommunication system is today being integrated with that of computer devices (Pelet, 1987). The emerging vast network of data girdling the world is growing at an exponential rate. As machine to machine information is increasing rapidly, this information girdle will be one that increasingly handles machine data.

This machine-to-machine traffic in the future will be mediated through devices that include AI characteristics (Feigenbaum & McCorduck, 1983). Such a system would become an active, intelligent one. It would be able to summarize information, follow particular relationships, be a "consultant" on narrow areas giving advice and suggesting solutions. The consumer for this type of actively processed information would not necessarily be a human but could also likely be another machine (Feigenbaum & Macorduch ibid).

The information that is handed down from machine to machine is rigid in that a computer is still not very flexible as to the set of responses it has with its environment. The responses are mostly tight and foreordained by one element from its environment, namely human programmers, just as insects are tightly controlled by their genetic programming. But new developments in autonomous techniques including those that use learning systems, genetic algorithms, and neural networks and hybrids thereof provide for the lineage to become more adaptive to the environment and so change its internal stores accordingly.

Under the latter circumstances, it is no longer possible for a human programmer to know in detail the artefact's responses to the environment. When there are densely interconnected devices with AI characteristics, the autonomous nature of these evolutionary processes in the artefactual system would increase very significantly. The lineages now become true lineages in the biological sense in that they change in a nontrivial sense their internal characteristics after interacting with the environment. The internal information system in these devices is also constructed through these interactions with the environment; that is, they are self constructed. The detailed properties of these densely interconnected devices cannot be predicted beforehand; they are emergent. The artefactual line now develops by constructing itself through a process of becoming.

The artefactual realm is also tending to exhibit another characteristic of evolutionary lineages, namely that of sudden change, a disjuncture, as in punctuated equilibrium in biological phenomena and sudden changes in social cognition in culture as in paradigmatic shifts. Work done on computational ecologies of even relatively simple computer systems connected together like airline booking systems has been shown to exhibit such sudden disjunctures (Huberman and Hogg, 1988).

The artefactual lineage also interacts with its external world, its environment, through its input and output devices. The information in computer artefacts has a particular window to the environment, given say by its program and input-output devices. It samples and interacts only with one aspect of the environment, sampling as it were a particular niche. In this sense, the artefactual lineage also has particular "subjectivities," different sublineages having different ones that change when their internal states change.

The rapid replacement of human computational functions by artificial devices means that even in a notional sense, it will no longer be possible for humans to keep in track the detailed workings in these devices. Even 30 years ago, when most computers were mostly functioning as fast-running sophisticated addition and subtraction machines, it was not physically possible for a human to check independently all the calculations being done in detail, simply because of the huge manpower and time constraints.

These constraints have increased geometrically in recent years. With thousands of million microprocessors at the turn of the century, even if the total human population was harnessed in a tight organizational framework, it would not be possible to keep track of all the computation being done currently through these machines to give the same output at the same time. Even today a human using a rudimentary device like a calculator cannot follow or check its detailed workings. He assumes implicitly that it is correct.

When mass produced computing devices have AI features, it would lead to a "xeroxing" of machine intelligence (Smith and Debenham, 1983). Ultimately in one scenario this artificial intelligence revolution could "upgrade and mass produce the finest intellectual decision making of society's scholars for public consumption" (Smith and Debenham 1983).

In tightly demarcated areas of cultural information, artefacts such as expert systems can replace professional expertise. When a learning system is added to the system, or is "hybridized" with genetic algorithms or neural networks, it develops its knowledge system on its own, outside of the knowledge that had been acquired by the professional expert. This new knowledge, the generalizations and the laws that such a system acquires is made outside detailed human instruction, and so is partly acquired outside the existing human-generated cultural flow.

When those AI machines are interconnected, the output of one such machine would feed another as an input, without going through human intermediaries. In such cases, humans will not be able even in principle, to follow the information processing, that is the reasoning, the logic, the sequence of steps etc. that was involved. Such a flow of information would be "opaque to human attempts to follow" the operation of the machines (Michie and Johnston, 1985).

The interconnected system of information machines are in clusters and networks. They constitute also islands of information. When the artefactual information in these islands within such nets gets both some autonomy as well as an opaqueness to the human actors, they tend to develop increasingly as separate entities. These islands also develop as tree-like structures. These islands would tend to bifurcate as the total information within the system grows, like disciplines in scientific cultural information bifurcating into further islands with the growth of knowledge. These bifurcations would be not due to human interactions alone but increasingly also to machine interventions.

Initially, the artefactual flow lines will follow the outlines of existing disciplines. Yet, increasingly there will be a continuous exchange of information between different artificial information flow lines. For meaningful exchanges of information to occur, it has to be structured. With the intelligent information processing filtering this exchange through AI systems, new fault lines in existing classifications, new flow lines in the information flow would emerge. New information hierarchies would result. As the information stores within the lineage are increasingly exchanged and operated on by internally generated rules especially those set by learning systems, existing boundaries would begin to change according to new internal criteria. And so, new boundaries would emerge in a process analogous to the formation of species. These would be new classifications which were hitherto unknown and which emerged naturally from within the flow lines. The result is a rapidly growing lineage that is speciating and resulting in a tree-like structure as it interacts with its environment.

Due to this increasing opaqueness, the information line from computer to computer would for all practical purposes tend towards an increasing separation of its functions from the human-to-human information flow line. The hiving off of the computer line away from direct human culture is also seen in the variety of ways the environment is being sampled, with a greater spectrum of devices than the conventional human "five senses." Computers are being inputted through devices which increasingly cover almost the entire electro-magnetic or the entire acoustic spectrum. Bio-sensors that mimic the human nose are being developed that could identify a much greater range of chemicals in the environment than can the human nose (Albery, 1986). A variety of mechanical devices that get information from and manipulate the environment are being developed (Paul, 1981). Some of these devices have very sensitive end-effectors, with several sensing channels covering a much greater range than humans (Salisbury, 1984; Yasdani, 1986, p. 148). The information line of artefacts is increasing its range of inputs from, and outputs to the environment to be much broader than the human one and so literally is having a larger "world view" on the environment.

This opaqueness trait recalls the interesting case before the United States courts a few years ago where it was claimed that current arrangements in the United States for declaring war in the event of a nuclear attack violate the U.S. Constitution, because the decision depends almost exclusively on computers. It was alleged that a war declaration can be made only by the U.S. President and cannot in effect be made for him by a preprogrammed computer response. This example illustrates the fact that even in a relatively "unintelligent" one as the current U.S. Defense system, the machine information mode has become so opaque that its detailed working cannot be followed and reconfirmed in time by humans (Anderson, 1986).

Due to these and other factors that have been mentioned, the information line from computer to computer, thus would be increasingly taking an autonomy of its own. This autonomy arises from the large overload of new information sources and large data bases, the trends towards very cheap powerful computing devices and the AI aspects of the emerging systems, and the sheer numbers of computer devices.

The artefactual lineages are now poised to expand dramatically in the near future. Eventually they will rival in some aspects, the cultural and biological lineages. A new autonomous lineage system at the artefactual information level would have emerged.

5: BIOTECHNOLOGY

The genetic lineage that was described in chapter 2 and which has grown for over 3.5 billion years is now being consciously disturbed by a new development — biotechnology. This would have the most profound effects on the dynamics of the lineages. As the potential of the technology is very great and will seep into, and change large sections of living matter, it is useful to give, in relative detail, a description of biotechnology and its potential.

In biotechnology, biological material and organisms are used to create or modify products. In this sense, "classical biotechnology" or "old biotechnology" is thousands of years old. Traditional biotechnology begins with the neolithic revolution and the domestication of plants and animals. The first farmer who mated the best bull with the best cow to improve the herd was doing old biotechnology. Similarly, the first baker or brewer who used yeast to make bread or who brewed beer, was using enzymes — a biological material — to produce a product — and hence engaging in biotechnology.

The new biotechnology on the other hand, constitutes a number of methods that use organisms to make or alter products at a deeper biological level. It differs from the traditional biotechnology in that it achieves these objectives by modifying, or using the genetic material of organisms in a direct manner — at the level of a cell or of a gene (Board on Science & Technology for Development 1982, p. 30; UNDP, 1989, p. 15).

The science of genetics was first laid out in a systematic basis by the work of Gregor Mendel. Although his work was published in the 1860s, its impact had to wait until his rediscovery in the 1900s. Subsequently, application of Mendel's work on hybrids resulted in major improvements in the 20th century in such staples as corn and rice.

The new biotechnology, divides its more common applications into two levels, at the level of a cell, or of a gene. Characterizing biotechnology at the cell level are the techniques of tissue culture; and at the gene level, genetic engineering. It is helpful to describe these techniques briefly to give an insight into what is possible through biotechnology and what is its potential for the future. Let us first take tissue culture.

Tissue Culture

Tissue culture is a relatively cheap technique now becoming widely applied in plant propagation. Here, cells from one plant are used to propagate thousands of plants having the identical genetic structure. This "micro propagation" is done through shoot tip culture or through callus cultures. In shoot tip culture, the shoot tip is cultured in a suitable nutrient medium with plant hormones. From a single tip, several tips are obtained. Each can be developed into a complete plant. In callus cultures various parts of a plant are cultured in a suitable nutrient medium. In this process, the cells divide many times and form an amorphous mass called a callus. The callus can be further subdivided. The resulting divisions can be cultured to generate shoots which can then be grown until they are ready to be planted in the fields. Through this technique, a gram of callus tissue could yield up to 500 or more plants (UNDP, 1989, p. 15).

In plant *cell* culture, a step further than tissue culture is taken. After the callus is formed, the callus tissue is taken to shed individual cells. These cells are grown separately in culture flasks where they, like bacteria, grow and subdivide. These cultured cells can now be used either to generate new plants or to keep them growing in the culture where they would be able to excrete natural products that are normally produced by the whole plant. Through such cell culture techniques, one could produce dyes, drugs, flavors and pesticides (Bajaj, 1988, p. 15, UNDP, 1989, p. 18).

Also at the level of the total cell or protoplast (cell without the cell wall), two or more cells could be fused together to become a single cell with characteristics different from the original set of cells Through cell fusion, embryos from genetically widely different plants have been generated. Later these cells were cultured so that a colony of cells was propagated from a single cell kept in a suitable nutrient medium. So through cell fusion followed by tissue culture, it has been possible for hybrids to be produced from genetically widely different organisms (Farrington, 1989, p. 1).

Recombinant DNA — Genetic Engineering

Cells produce a wide variety of proteins which are coded for by their genes. Genes are a section of the macro molecule DNA, genes themselves being arranged in a string — the total set of an organism's genes constituting its genome. By cutting and splicing–in genes — "genetic engineering" — (also called recombinant DNA), major changes in the genetic make up can be made. For example, this process of recombination allows a piece of genetic material or DNA from one species to be inserted into the DNA of a second species (Watson, et al., 1983, p. 10; Farrington, 1989, p. 11). This allows for combination of genetic characteristics that were either unknown or were artificially put together. In the process, genes can cross the bacterium/plant/animal boundaries giving rise to plants with animal or microbial characteristics or vice versa and generally creating new plants and animals or old ones with new characteristics (Seidel, 1989, p. 216–21).

The key discoveries and techniques in biotechnology have given rise to a whole spectrum of new products and processes in several fields. The resulting applications in agriculture, animal husbandry and in humans are many and have the potential to radically change nature as we know it. In agriculture, this technology is now on the verge of revolutionizing the types and uses of plant and animal products that are consumed by humans.

Biotechnology in Plants and Animals

The application of the new biotechnology to plants will result in plants that are resistant to diseases, insects and herbicides and have the ability to grow in environmentally harsh climates. Microbial organisms that are genetically engineered will also be able to control plant pests and influence the nutrient uptake of plants (OECD, 1989, p. 25).

By transferring those genes that give a plant nitrogen fixing ability, a kind of self fertilization of plants has been made possible with enormous consequences for agriculture that now uses artificial fertilizers (UNDP, 1989, p. 24). Plants have been given a gene from a bacterium, Bacillus Thuringielsis, that codes for an insect-killing protein (Wickelgren, 1989, pp. 120–124). The gene engineered into a plant expresses a toxin which then kills insects feeding on it, thus protecting the plant.

Genetically engineered plants that resist viruses have been made. Plants that guard against viruses in several species such as tobacco, alfalfa, cucumber, potato, tobacco and tomato have already been made. Plants have also being engineered that tolerate specific herbicides. Genetic engineering techniques have also been used to improve the nutrient content of foods, for example, their protein composition. Preservation of food has been successfully attempted using the new technology. Thus, altering one gene of the 10,000 genes that constitute the tomato, a tomato that lasts longer has been designed (Miller & Ackerman, 1990).

Through genetic modification, plants have also been changed to produce useful products (Bylinsky, 1994, pp. 94–108). Plants would thus become factories for the production of important pharmaceuticals through genetical engineering techniques (Bajaj, 1988, p. 15). The biotechnology revolution in plants would yield a wide variety of new products, change processes, alter food habits, change agriculture and affect many areas.

The biotechnology efforts in the plant sphere are being paralleled by biotechnology advances in animals. At the farm animal level, key technological changes are increasing productivity. Bovinesomatotrotin (BST) is a pituitary hormone that is produced in cattle and increases milk production. Genetic engineering has made it possible to produce BST in large amounts and this product is already in use (Miller and Ackerman, 1990). By inserting appropriate growth hormone genes, the growth rate of salmon has been increased to nearly 40 times their normal weight. Other potential improvements include meat that has a longer shelf life and a low sodium and cholesterol content, and an overall increase in productivity of animals (Miller and Ackerman, 1990).

Some of the most exciting and far reaching effects of animal bio-technology occur in developments in animal reproductive technology. These include the ability to create transgenic animals by mixing the genetic endowment from entirely different species. Other important developments include the realization of offspring from either two female or two male parents, and thirdly, the ability to clone animals by the thousands. The resulting animals will have genetic changes that will help them better resist (existing) diseases, yield better quality products, grow faster and reproduce themselves with greater efficiency (Seidel, 1989).

Transgenesis allows an animal to be created by adding, removing, inactivating or repairing genes. These genes can come from other species which would allow desirable characteristics to be transferred to domestic animals from genetically distant ones (Seidel, 1989). Exploiting the functions of eggs and sperms, a technique has been developed that allows an offspring to be produced from either two female parents (Gynogenesis) or two males (Androgenesis). This would mean that a desirable offspring could be the result of crossing either two high quality bulls or two high quality cows, rather than of crossing in the conventional manner, a superior bull with a female. These techniques of Gynogenesis and Androgenesis have been demonstrated in poultry, fish and amphibians (Seidel, 1989).

A technique of reproduction with far reaching results is that of transplantation of the nuclei of cells. This technique would yield thousands of identical animals. Such a method of reproduction would have advantages over sexual reproduction, which is unpredictable as to the characteristics of the offspring (Seidel, 1989).

These different transgenic technologies would yield animals in sufficient quantity with a wide variety of desirable qualities. The new technology, however, has also been used to turn out an entirely new range of animal products (Seidel, 1989). Through such techniques mice have been genetically altered so that they yield human growth hormones in their milk. The same approach has been tried in rabbits to yield human growth hormone (Watts, 1990, p. 26). Engineered mice have yielded milk having anti trypsin, a chemical used to treat lung diseases. Genes have been similarly transferred into mice, sheep and pigs which make their hosts produce substances such as insulin, tissue plasminogen activator (a blood clot-removing agent) and factor IX (a substance which is missing in some haemophiliacs (Watts, 1990, p. 26).

Medicine: Biotechnology Applications for Humans

The new technology is offering the possibility of a very wide range of products and services that go to the very foundation of the living process. These include the possibility of avoiding genetically based diseases, and medicines that are tightly targeted and without side effects. Examples of the latter would be monoclonal antibodies which can target specific antigens.

When an antigen, that is a foreign substance, enters a living organism, it triggers the immune system to generate an antibody which makes the antigen ineffective. Monoclonol antibodies are extremely pure antibodies which are made synthetically. A single cell of spleen which has been exposed to a specific antigen is fused with a cancer (Myeloma) cell. This results in a fused cell termed a hybridoma which produces the antibody directed against the antigen. This antibody will now target and identify the antigen. By culturing such hybridomas, it is possible to produce in quantity, pure "Monoclonol antibodies." Antibodies could also be mass produced cheaply by transplanting animal genes into a plant and making the plant produce the relevant animal antibodies (Coghlan, 1994 a, p. 20).

Monoclonal antibodies have been successfully used in therapies for a wide variety of diseases. These include uses for some tumors, for neutralizing the tetanus toxin, for blocking the construction of viruses or harmful proteins (Coghlan, 1994 b, p. 23; Travis, 1993, p. 1114). These uses illustrates the range of possibilities that exist with monoclonal antibody therapy.

Targeting medicines by other genetic means is also possible and is being developed, for example, in treating cancer. Genetic "bombs" that deliver toxic medicines directly to cancer cells only and not to nearby healthy cells are being explored (*The New York Times*, April 24, 1996, p. 3). Lymphocytes which infiltrate tumors, when isolated from patients' tumors, are specifically programmed to kill the patient's cancer cells. This property makes these cells target a tumor tightly and so deliver therapeutic agents. In the future, genes that produce cytokines, those substances produced by cells of the immune system such as tumor necrosis factor, interleukins and interferons could be inserted in tumor-infiltrating lymphocytes to attack cancers. Already as a prelude to using this technique, genes from harmless bacteria have been used to develop tumor-infiltrating lymphocytes that home in on the cells (Kingman, 1990, p. 31). Antibodies have also been developed to take chemicals that are poisonous directly to cancer sites, thus to attack cancerous cells while leaving healthy cells intact. An example of a successful use of this technique is against cancer of the lymph glands (Kingman, 1989, p. 29).

Growth factors are another set of targeted remedies based on natural processes and bioengineered products. They could help heal wounds quickly, smooth wrinkles, destroy cancer cells, restore functions to paralyzed limbs and generally enhance the immune system. These bioengineered products would be patterned after natural growth factor products existing in nature (Rusting 1989).

The new biotechnology also promises quick, cheap and specific diagnostics. These new diagnostic tools based on monoclonal antibodies and gene probes are expected to be faster and more precise. The development of these tests is considered to be much cheaper than the development of drugs. This diagnostic revolution would cover a variety of medical situations such as prenatal diagnosis, very early diagnosis of diseases and the monitoring of degenerative diseases (OECD, 1989, p. 68). These new tests have also many attractive qualities such as ease of use, high specificity, and short time for the tests, and they cover a wide range of applications with only a very small quantity of samples (blood, urine, cells, etc.) required. Some of these tests when properly purchased in a kit form could, in fact, be done at home (OECD, 1989, p. 68).

Vaccine development will be another major thrust of the new technology. The vaccines were expected to cover a wide variety of diseases including hepatitis, malaria and herpes. Expected in the 1990s were vaccines to cover gonorrhea, cyto megalovirus and AIDS. Diseases targeted for the next decade include lyme disease, salmonella, syphilis, shigella, Dengue fever, leprosy, malaria and cholera. With molecular biology and genetics, it was being thought possible that if resources permit, many Third World diseases could be eliminated through vaccines. Many of these vaccines could be delivered bunched together on a single shot (Bloom, 1989).

Many human disorders are now being discovered to be genetic in origin. The list of medical disorders that have been identified to be of genetic origin has been growing steadily. Before 1960, the number of genetically based disorders stood at 400 to 500, at, 1487 in 1966, 2,811 in 1978, 3,000 in 1982 (OECD, 1989, p. 18) and there were over 4,000 or so genes in 1993 identified as causing disease (Kahn, 1993, pp. 32–36). Many other diseases including heart disease, cancer, arthritis and senility are related to impairment of genes involved with the body's defenses (Anderson, 1995, pp. 124–128). Individual genes that have been already identified for various diseases include those for hypertension (Yam, 1993, p. 23), diabetes (*Gene linked New York Times*, 12 January 1993) Huntington's disease (Miller, 1993, pp. 37–40), congenital deafness, Leukemia (Gene clues *New York Times* February 23, 1993) and epilepsy (Leary, 1996, p. A19). A gene that has an effect on aging has also been found, pointing to future discoveries on the genetic basis of aging (Altman, 1996, p. A 27). The Human Genome Initiative in making a detailed map of human genes would allow for the systematic and exact identification of most defective genes. With the availability of techniques that could repair these genes, the possibility of medical intervention is enhanced dramatically.

Genes that have been switched off in the process of development could in the future also be switched on once again. This has already been realized in the case of switching on a gene in a blood disorder by administering a chemical (Bishop, 1993). Such techniques would allow for increased genetic interventions.

In 1983, one of a set of cancers which are genetically activated — by oncogenes — was found. Later, suppressor genes, that is, genes that prevent cells from becoming cancerous, were also found. In the future, it would be possible to identify those persons with a gene that causes cancer and so spot those most at risk from that disease. After the human genome is mapped, both oncogenes as well as suppressor genes would be identified and so allow for direct human intervention.

Foreign genes were for the first time safely and successfully inserted into the human body in 1990. The gene in this case was not meant to cure but only to demonstrate the feasibility of the approach (Gene triump *New Scientist*, 8 September 1990, p. 33). The first human gene therapy was done to treat adenosine deaminase (ADA) deficient severe combined immunodeficiency. The ADA deficiency was corrected by inserting a functional human ADA gene into T lymphocytes of the patient and readminstering them back into the patient (Culotta, 1993). Other gene therapies being developed by the mid-1990s and some used in experimental treatments include those for lung cancer, breast cancer, pancreatic cancer, cystic fibrosis, Gaucher's disease, infectious diseases and arthritis (Coghlan, 1993 b; Culotta 1993, the scientists try to disarm, *New York Times*, April 4, 1993).

Genes have been implanted to mouse embryos by simply injecting the gene into the pregnant mother. This raises the possibility in the future of treating genetic diseases in the womb using simple injections to the mother. The genes, however, lasted for only a few months in the mice, but the technique could be used for treating genetic diseases that do damage at the level of the fetus. These include conditions such as blindness, disfiguring skull formations and mental retardation (Gene implanted in mice *The New York Times*, February 28, 1995, p. 3).

By 1995 several hundred patients had already been treated through gene therapy (Gene implanted in mice, *The New York Times*, February 28, 1995, p. 3) and further more dramatic gene incursions in the form of stem cell therapy and even sperm cell therapy were in the cards.

Stem cells are precursor cells that exist in the bone marrow. Stem cells live as long as the patient does, and they give rise to the entire set of blood cells in circulation. They thus become a permanent reservoir for any gene that is introduced. Stem cells will be the target for future therapy, which has already been successfully carried out for severe combined immune deficiency (Anderson, 1995, pp. 124–128).

At the moment gene therapy is performed only on somatic cells. These are all the cell types except sperms, eggs and their precursors (*Gene implanted in mice, The New York Times*, February 28, 1995, p. 3). Yet, recently the alteration of genes in sperm cells has been achieved. This also allows the possibility of putting genes from one species into another so that the resulting genetic endowment can be inherited.

This technique provides for the insertion and deletion of genes in sperm stem cells. The possibility of eliminating once and for all, thousands of inherited diseases — like the successful elimination of small pox through vaccination — now exists as a possibility (Gene implanted in Mice, *The New York Times*, February 28, 1995, p. 3).

The regrowing of sperm cells has occurred in other animal environments, for example being transplanted to the testes of another animal of another species. Such sperm stem cells have also been frozen and regrown. Frozen stem sperm cells allow a future single mother say, to have a child from her favorite intellect or favorite star, even years after the latter's death (Lemonick, 1996, p. 49). These techniques also leave the possibility that a man about to undergo a serious operation will freeze his sperm, allow it to grow in another animal such as a horse or for that matter a snake, and the resulting sperms could then be fertilized with a human egg and be brought to fruition in a human womb (Kolata 1996a 30, p. 24).

As part of the Human Genome Project, efforts have started in the United States to screen for genetic defects, beginning with cystic fibrosis (CF). Other countries such as the United Kingdom and Denmark have also begun genetic screening (Anderson, 1990, p. 569).

A fetus could by 1996 be tested for whether it carries the gene for inherited bowel cancer, cystic fibrosis or the muscle wasting disease, muscle dystrophy. In 1996, up to 100 different inherited conditions could be tested for, although many of these were for rare diseases. Within a few years, there will be tests available for many hereditary cancers, Alzheimer s disease, dyslexia and several behavioral disorders (Rogers & Craig, 1996, p. 16).

A simple test using DNA from a single human hair now allows mass screening; the test lasts about five hours, compared to the days, a standard gene probe will take (Rogers, 1996, p. 16). Screening for genetic mutations would in the coming decades be routinized. Already by 1996 a U.S. based company's apparatus was analyzing simultaneously 500 patients for the presence of 106 mutations on seven genes. The efficiency and speed of such mass screening techniques are bound to increase in the future (Anderson, October 1991).

Technology exists in a preliminary stage for taking embryos out, testing them for defects and returning them to the womb (Beardsley, 1996, p. 100). Some of these genetic screening tests can be done by plucking a single cell from an embryo out of the four or eight cells just three days after fertilization (Elmer–Dewitt, 1992). This screening would allow the option of rejecting any embryo whose genetic makeup was not desirable.

The new biotechnology is now poised to dramatically alter the most fundamental biological endowments of plants, animals and humans.

The Human Genome Initiative

Biotechnology's normal applications are in the fields of plants, animals and in the case of humans, in diseases of genetic origin. A development in basic science, the mapping of the human genome now under way, will, when applied and so turned into a biotechnology, have perhaps a more far-reaching effect on humans than all the other biotechnologies.

The human genome initiative is a "Big Science" project which emerged around 1985 and has the ambitious task of determining the sequence of the entire human genome. This means identifying the approximately three billion base pairs in the 46 chromosomes that constitute human genetic material (Goodman, 1990).

The three billion base pairs have within their structure the genes which constitute the core-biological information of humans. This information is encoded in four chemical bases, namely Adenine (A), Thymine (T), Guanine (G) and Cytosine (C). Each piece of genetic information directs the manufacture by the cells of particular proteins that determine the phenotypal characteristics. The latter include for example, the color of eyes, the shape of a chin, the length of a foot and proclivities for particular diseases. This information contained in the three billion base pairs will constitute the most important set of biological instruction codes for humans. It will constitute "the ultimate answers to the chemical underpinnings of human existence" (Watson, 1990, p.).

The possibility of knowing the complete set of genetic instructions arose with the discovery in 1953, of the double helical structure of DNA. But at that time this would have appeared an unrealizable scientific objective. There was no way then to sequence even very short strands of DNA, let alone the very large human DNA. In 1973, with the emergence of recombinant DNA technology, it was now possible to routinely isolate individual genes. Powerful sequencing techniques were then developed which led to the almost routine process of establishing from 300 to 500 base pairs of DNA sequence (Watson, 1990, p. 44).

By 1977, the complete DNA sequences of smaller DNA viruses containing about 5,000 base pairs had been identified. By 1982, this ability had increased tenfold and DNA sequences of bacteriophages were being determined. And by 1990, it was possible to identify the over 100,000 base pairs of DNA of several plant chloroplasts. The longest DNA sequence to be identified by 1990 was that of the herpes virus which has a quarter million base pairs (Watson).

In addition, the sequences of a large number of individual genes had been identified. The latter constituted a total of over 37 million base pairs. The organism most intensively studied by biologists has been the Escherichia coli, a bacterium. 800,000 base pairs of its nearly 5 million of base pairs long genome have been identified. It is expected that soon the total sequence of this bacterium would be known (Watson, ibid).

Another organism that has been studied intensely for decades by geneticists with studies predating the discovery of DNA is the fruit fly Drosophila. The Drosophila genome is roughly one twentieth the size of the human genome. By 1990, about half of the Drosophila genome had been mapped (Goodman, 1990). In 1996 the complete genetic blueprint of baker's yeast was uncovered. In addition, the complete genetic makeup of several bacteria were announced. But unlike bacteria, yeast is a more complex eukaryote possessing nuclei in its cells (Kolata, 1996).

These sequencing results had been hitherto obtained, by what could be described as a cottage industry approach, with small groups of scientists working on their own scientific goals. However, the human genome is over a thousand times larger than that of E. coli, and is distributed over 46 different chromosomes. The cottage industry approach of analyzing this vast length of genetic material is not expected to yield results over the 15-year period goal of the Genome Initiative (Watson, 1990, p. 45).

The Human Genome Initiative hopes to have three "maps" of the genome. The first map is that which shows the relative distances between markers on a chromosome, a genetic linkage map. The second, physical map gives the actual number of DNA subunits — nucleotide bases — between genetic landmarks. The final map is at the molecular level and gives the sequence of bases in a chromosome and the proteins that the latter make (*Scientific American*, January 1993, pp. 16–17). The sequence of the genome would describe the chemical constituents of the DNA, base by base.

In genetic mapping, genetists can create a picture of which genes are close to which other genes. This would yield a map that shows the general, although not the absolute, location of genes as they exist on chromosomes (Lewin, 1990, pp. 34–38). In a physical map, the distance between particular landmarks is identified in terms of the actual length of DNA. Such a map allows researchers to identify within a genome exactly any piece of DNA that they are interested in (Lewin, 1990, pp. 34–38). In the sequence, the complete set of nucleotide bases that constitute the human genome will be known. The target date for the complete molecular sequence in the human genome project is 2005 (Lewin, 1990, pp. 34–38).

In the early 1990s, sequencing cost between $3.00 and $5.00 per base pair. However, it was expected that this cost would drop in the coming years. A five-to ten-fold increase in the efficiency of gene mapping, sequencing and data analyzing was expected (Watson, 1990, p. 45). This would be done primarily by turning the "cottage industry" approach of individual scientists working manually to more automated mass production means. Automation would also be extended to analysis of the enormous amounts of data turned up in the project, this analysis often requiring Artificial Intelligence techniques.

The active genes of the human genome take up only about 5% of the length of the genome. The 95% remaining nongene material probably consists of genetic baggage from the past evolutionary history of humans, which are apparently of no practical use. For the genome project to be of immediate practical use, efforts will concentrate on the 5% of DNA that is useful genetic material and which code for the proteins produced in a cell.

Although conventional wisdom at the time the Genome Project was launched suggested that it would take 15 years to accomplish, current developments suggest that it would be done much earlier. Use of automated computer-based systems have already made heady progress. In 1993, the French team announced that it had completed well over 90% of the first generation physical map of the human genome. With about 2,000 known genetic markers, this gave guidelines for location of genes in the different parts of the chromosome. This map would now help search for individual genes (Kahn, 1993, pp. 32–36, James, 1993). A good genetic map covering the entire human genome was completed by 1994. High quality physical maps covering over 95% of the genome were available by early 1996 (Beardsley, 1996, p. 100). In 1996, in completion of the first part of the human genome project, a comprehensive map of human DNA was published (Scientists finish First phase *The New York Times*, March 19, 1996, p. C7).

While the physical mapping was going on, genetic mapping has equally speeded up. This means that mapping of single genes has dropped to months instead of years (Kahn, 1993, pp. 32–36).

Apart from the human genome project, there are other equally important genome projects. Several attempts are thus being made to map plant genomes. Such an attempt will help identify individual plant genes which could then be transferred from organism to organism to give desired characteristics. As part of this general thrust the Plant Genome Research Programme (PGRP) of the U.S. Agricultural Research Service (ARS) will construct low resolution maps for the major crop species important to the United States and for which little information exists now. Several genomes of plants valuable for humans are being studied. Where sufficient background information already exists — such as for tomatoes, corn and rice — high resolution genetic maps will be constructed soon (Wiggen, 1990, p. 18).

The various gene mapping projects will gather in an easily usable form, the genetic information of thousands of years of history of life on earth — a library of information allowing for their reassembly in different new combinations.

The Spread of Biotechnology

The technical developments in biotechnology are today poised to penetrate many sectors of the economies in the developed world. The potential impact on developing countries was expected to be as deep (OECD, p. 89).

The brief survey in this chapter indicates that the biotechnology revolution has been underway in the plant, animal and human spheres and is about to have a major impact across the globe. We will give further examples of these biotechnology developments and their impacts in subsequent chapters. Compared with the earlier generic technologies like steam, electricity and oil, biotechnology would have a very pervasive effect, penetrating many sectors. The entire genetic information pool of 4,000 million years of natural history is now potentially subject to an extreme plasticity.

SECTION 2

THE THREE LINEAGES MERGE

6: THE MERGING OF CULTURE AND ARTIFICIAL INFORMATION

Information technology is a generic technology. Its effects will be far reaching, intruding into almost every economic and social niche. Of all the major technologies since the Industrial Revolution — steam power, electricity, chemicals and the internal combustion engine — information technology will have, with the possible exception of bio-technology, the most far-reaching effect (Freeman, 1987, p. 15).

Its penetration because of its rapid price-drop, further micro miniaturization and other unique characteristics, will be very much faster than these earlier technologies. As it penetrates different sectors and niches, it rearranges the several human and material elements that it encounters. As it moves across the social and cultural landscape, it cuts a broad swath across it, reshaping it. In turn, the social and cultural landscape itself moves into the technology, moulding it in particular ways. A dynamic interaction between the two results.

The information in culture and that in computers, influence and interact with each other in many ways. These interactions occur at a direct level between computer and human user when, say, a person, stares at the output of a computer screen and changes his thoughts, that is his cultural information; and he in turn by operating on the computer changes its information content. But, behind the encounter on the screen, are a host of social and technological factors that brought the respective informations to the screen and to the human operators' minds. And these factors also interact and interpenetrate each other.

These indirect interactions which stand behind the direct human and computer information interfacing occur when the social and computer frameworks behind the direct interaction change. The social frameworks constitute those human relationships which impinge on information technology and computer information, and change their development and content. In a reverse direction, the impact of information technology changes both social relationships and hence the matrix, the scaffolding down which culture flows. It also changes the social psychology of the humans concerned and the contents of their minds. The direct interactions between cultural and machine information are often the end product of these deeper, more structural, indirect interactions between social and computer systems. And to fully follow the information interactions between culture and computer information, we must also understand these deeper interactions, which we will now sketch.

Social Construction of Computer Information
The indirect level effects of society on computers are due to the emergence of artefactual information lineages (and their respective machine roles) corresponding to social lineages (and their respective social roles). This is an outcome of a variety of social factors. Some of these factors have already been described as the shift to information handling in the economy, which sets the broad background that necessitates the massive use of information technology.

This chapter will describe in more detail the other indirect social factors that influence the culture mapped within computers as information. These factors generally will be equivalent to the social factors that condition scientific cultural knowledge already described in chapter 3. The cultural output that comes out as science, it was noted, is influenced by social factors operating at the macro-historical, national, and the micro level at which groups of scientists work. One of the macro level influences in the case of computer culture is the shift to information society. This shift changes the social structure, the framework and scaffolding along which human culture flows and is accompanied by intrusions of information technology. This shift and intrusion, however, depends on the interplay of particular social forces. Thus, the shift to information societies and information technology are also influenced by larger forces operating globally.

Geo-Economic Influences
Geo-economic considerations determine where computers are manufactured and software written and where they are used. Thus, the manufacture of information technology is governed by the dynamics of global investment patterns. The manufacture occurs, not only in certain developed countries, but also, because of the globalization of the division of labor, to varying degrees, in some Asian countries with an industrial base.

Because of the capital investment involved, few countries can afford semiconductor manufacturing. Because of these particular global investment patterns — from chip manufacture in Malaysia to computer-related industries in Korea, Taiwan, Hong Kong and Singapore — the East Asian region is one of the strong manufacturing bases for the new technology. A once developing country, Korea, is today one of the leading manufacturers of DRAM chips in the world.

Global informatization is also occurring at another level, due to a geo-economic shift in particular types of information work. Thus, there has been a shift of lower-end, unskilled computer work to developing countries, paralleling the earlier shift of some electronic manufacturing to the developing countries. Key punch operators in developing countries feed in data to be processed later in developed countries (*Wall Street Journal,* February 26, 1985). This however is changing today as scanning systems obviate the need for manual entry.

Because of relative costs, certain other intellectual-based information technology activities can also be downloaded to developing countries because it is cheaper. A recent example is software exports, which in countries like India is growing rapidly. Such information exports can be extended to other skills. When telecommunication links exist between developed and developing countries, a new type of global information technology worker, an "electronic immigrant," is expected to emerge (Pelton, 1989, p. 12). Already, telemarketers, insurance claims processors, currency traders, and software writers have emerged as such migrants (Burgess, 1991). Professionals in relatively cheaper labor markets, for example India, Jamaica, and the Philippines, would increasingly be hired to remotely perform a variety of computer-based tasks. These could include activities such as computer programming, some scientific problems, word processing, inventory control, telephone-based sales and some aspects of management.

A set of dynamic global social and market forces, a complex interacting matrix is shaping the adoption of information technologies across the world. These forces give rise to a particular selection and distribution of computing artefacts.

The National Level Construction of Information Technology

Apart from broad global level social and economic forces, influences at a level of the nation, also play a significant part in how information technology is formed. Especially the particular format information technology has taken today has been governed by major social forces that impinged on its development within the boundaries of those countries where it was nurtured. These national level forces have consequently made their stamp on the technology. Let us recall some of these particular forces and circumstances.

In the United States, local military considerations were a major fillip for the initial development of computers and continue to shape the U.S.'s purpose, directions and intended end use of computer technology (Edwards, 1990). Many civilian uses have been largely tangential spinoffs. Taking a software example, the very specifications for the once widely used programming language COBOL (Common Business-Oriented Language) were given by the U.S. Department of Defense (Flamm, 1987). Funding decisions in computer technology, like in all sciences, deeply influence what is researched and hence, influence the outcomes of the research that ultimately emerge as useful applicable knowledge. When these decisions were made by the military, they were for military uses, were conducted in secrecy, gave rise to a particular form of socially constructed knowledge (Edwards, 1990, p. 124). Thus, the now dropped Strategic Defense Initiative ("Star Wars") of the United States was to have given the largest quantum of funding by far to AI — according to one estimate U.S. $10 billion (Edwards, 1990, p. 122). Applications from this research to the civilian sector would have been indirect, as a spinoff, and would have had some of the initial social assumptions of the military stamped on it.

The military has other pervasive impacts. Thus, war, it has been noted, is an artificial, socially constructed micro world. It has abstracted a few human qualities and encoded these in an organization. It is a carefully nurtured micro world that limits full human interactions, sanitized from contamination from the real world. Through its scientific routine, war removes the gray uncertainties and ambiguities of ordinary life (Broyles, 1984, p. 58). The information technology that emerges from this military culture also has the mark of this rigidity and lack of ambiguity. There is thus, a strong parallel between the military and the simplified world of (present day) computing and hence, the military culture is partially reproduced in the contemporary computing artefact.

The decision to use computers either in the military or in civilian life, and in which way, is also not simply a decision on technology. It is also a decision about relationships between people in the organization. It reflects, for example, the balance of power between management and labor, computers being able to change this balance (Wessells, 1990, p. 49). Managers, through computers, can reduce the work force, reduce the quality of their work and reduce the access of information to workers or do the opposite. It can help centralize power or decentralize it (Wessells, 1990, p. 49).

A vivid illustration of the issues related to the shaping of information technology in the civilian sector by social factors has been seen in the experience of countries with different cultures moving towards the fully automated factory, in the form of Computer Integrated Manufacture (CIM). Here, depending on different countries' social assumptions, there are different approaches, different technological solutions, and differing successes that arise depending on the social context surrounding the knowledge. This is amply illustrated by the relative experiences of different countries (Ebel, 1989).

Generally, the existing approaches for CIM in Europe and the United States do not question existing production organization structures, but simply try to solve production problems by the use of computers (Brodner, 1990). The U.S. approach is especially from a perspective that sees workers and technicians from a Taylorite (named after Frederick Taylor, the father of the so-called "Scientific Management" movement in the early decades of this century) point of view, as unpredictable humans. The unmanned factory is seen as the ultimate goal of this point of view (Brodner, 1990). The Japanese approach, on the other hand, emphasizes the human aspects. It relies on highly motivated employees, and gradual improvements towards CIM are made by the total group as a whole (Ebel, 1990, p. 7). The result is different technologies arising from the different national contexts.

The social context generally determines not only the broad applications, but also the hardware and software developments of information technology. How social factors determine the construction of the technology at the level of software usage is illustrated by the way a computer device such as a basic word processing function is used differentially between professional and unskilled workers. In the latter case, in some uses, control functions are embedded in the computer program that pace, and control the unskilled worker's task. The professional on the other hand, is not so paced. Yet, the basic logic of the computer provides the framework for both these different actions.

The technology is complete only with the software, and the latter can embed the control protocols that pace workers — as well as their opposite which enhances and amplifies a worker's creativity. The decisions on what to incorporate in the software packages are ultimately politically and socially derived, resting on such societally constructed and given criteria as the existing divisions of labor, the relative costs of jobs, the competitiveness of particular companies, the rate of growth of profits and so on. These social givens, are translated at the first level to cultural information on what is expected of the machine, and then embedded in the technology.

Generally speaking, the new information technologies as with all other technologies are colored by the social assumptions of the societies that gave birth to them (ATAS, 1986, p. 5). The social context fashions and shapes information technology. Computers thus generally represent the outcome of particular cultural ideas and so, are not neutral (Bowers, 1988). They carry within them certain values, orientations and cultural assumptions, through the manner computers have been socially constructed. There is consequently an inevitable gender, racial, cultural and technological bias, often indirectly ingrained in them. Existing cultural ideas and values are congealed as hardware and software (Bowers, 1988).

When we use them, computers also frame our boundaries of what we think and experience. The manner in which computers have been thought about and then used is associated with a strong set of values. Conversely, the more computers are used, the more these values are reinforced (Bowers, 1988).

The various debates over one aspect of computers — AI — have had strong political and ideological overtones (Knee, 1985). Some of the key figures in the development of AI have indirectly used strong capitalist ideology in the development of the technology. A key figure, Herbert Simon, wanted the computer to embody the capitalist entrepreneur's idealized rationality; while another key figure, Marvin Minsky, used the corporate hierarchy to describe the various levels of operation and control in human thought. What was therefore being cloned in AI in these cases, was not the thinking capacity of a disembodied, asocial human, but that of "the collective and inherently social 'mind' of a bureaucratic organization" (Berman, 1992, pp. 103–115). Similarly, detailed sociological studies of the daily work of AI practitioners working on expert systems indicate that the procedures and facts being programmed are culturally contingent. Such systems are highly value laden (Forsythe, 1993, pp. 460–480). It has also been noted that computers used for education have a hidden ideological curriculum which is never stated explicitly. This is the ideology of the dominant class which emphasizes the preservation of the present social order and its attributes. This line of thinking assumes that the hidden unconscious purpose of computers in education is not just to teach computation but also to prepare students to fit into the slots of such a social order (Sloan, 1992).

Many commentators have also observed a gender bias created in the technology, including current computer software (Kramer and Lehman, 1990). Current programs, it has been noted, incorporate several restricting tendencies for women. Thus, feminists have shown from historical studies in language, and analyses of text as well as empirical data that the disciplines covered by logical-mathematical intelligence (of which the computer field is only a part) are gendered. Jansen shows that AI, its models and disciplinary assumptions suggest a masculinization. The result has been a "phantom objectivity" that ignores alternative social constructions of reality (Jansen 1988). Tests have also generally shown that women perform less competently than men in the computer field. This assumed backwardness of women in using computers also has its parallels in women's performances in mathematics. Here, research suggests that sex differences in mathematics performances are related to the self-perception of women, which is socially constructed. Social factors influencing this self-perception include parents' and teachers' expectations for their daughters and girl students (Fenema and Sherman, 1977, pp. 51–71). The same gender construction stands true in the field of computing.

The social system stamps its social imprint on computer use in various ways, by class, gender and other social groupings. This cultural stamp is also seen in programming.

Individual Styles of Molding Computer Information

Computer programming languages, researchers have noted, also have their own built-in subcultural modes of processing information. Each computer language is associated with a particular programming style. Thus Pascal has a highly structured specific style, while the AI language LISP has a more interactive style. The different programming languages fit into the individual styles of thinking and cultural biases of different uses (Fenema and Sherman, 1977, pp. 51–71). These differences arise from the transfer of particular cultural modes into the programming realm. Apart from this unconscious transfer of cultural modes into computing, there are of course, conscious transfers. Thus, human techniques of problem solving were transferred to the computer modes consciously by Allen Newell, Herbert Simon and J.C. Shaw, who studied human problem solving and evolved a series of heuristic programming techniques based on these studies (Weinberg, 1990, p. 164).

Because of the inherent cultural bias of programs, computer programs which have been developed in the different cultural context of

advanced industrialized countries, a detailed study indicates, are sometimes inappropriate for developing countries (Lind, 1991, p. xiii). Because there are different cultural assumptions and values in the two
contexts, computers are not used in the same manner in developing
countries as they are in developed countries. The low utilization of
computers in developing countries has been partly explained as being
due to this cultural mismatch (Lind, 1991, p. 9).

The multiple social influences on computing extend also into individual styles of doing computer work. The work of Turkle and Papert
indicates a diversity of practices in computing that results in an "epistemological pluralism," in the way individual practitioners approach computers. Some programmers use approaches that are formal and abstract;
others that are more concrete, and more reminiscent of the work of a
painter than that of a logician (Ibid). This latter type of programmers
was designated by Turkle and Papert as bricoleur programmers (Turkle
and Papert, pp. 145). Such bricoleur programmers sometimes enter
into relationships that tend to anthropomorphize computational objects
and computers (Turkle and Papert, pp. 148). Computational objects are
the objects on a computer screen. These different styles are reflected in
the way some workers approach programming. Especially women feel
that they have an interactive, relational attitude to computers. Thus,
Lisa, a woman programmer wishes to manipulate computer programs
like one does words in a poem, sculpting the whole (Turkle and Papert,
1990, pp. 144). To some the computer offers its objects as something to
be experienced in a tactile and concrete fashion, and not as something
abstract (Turkle and Papert, 1990).

Fully recognizing that the components are not live, one female computer scientist did her programming imagining what the components
feel like. Another interacted as if the computers had an intellectual
personality, getting "involved with a thing". Generally, women would
feel more comfortable with a relational, interactive, "as it were a person" way of dealing with computers (Turkle and Papert). This style is
a contrast to the formally expressed ideology of the computer scientist. Newer techniques of computing that use icons are, it has been
observed, more conducive to this "woman's way of knowing" (Turkle
and Papert, 1990, pp. 153–157).

The acquisition of computers, their patterns of ownership, the
particular problems they address, their programming styles and
"behavior" in front of the operator are thus governed by a host of social
and economic forces operating at various levels. The cultural information

coded and put in as computer information also is governed by social forces. It is the particular forms of collection, distribution, styles and contents of computing that determine where and how computer information is processed and distributed and how and in which manner it flows. The structure of the flow of information as well as its contents have on them the intimate stamp of the culture which gave rise to them.

Recognition of this intimate relationship between society, culture and technology and the consequent malleability of technology to social factors have resulted in attempts at the conscious development of congenial technologies. A very interesting example has been the pan-European program to develop so-called "human centered" technologies. This philosophy of "anthromopocentric" production systems has been adopted by the Forecasting and Assessment in Science and Technology (FAST) programme of research in Europe which has an advisory input to the EEC countries (Wobbe, 1990). The FAST programme has moved towards the study and development of desirable production systems using information technology that emphasize human qualities, relatively flat hierarchies and that takes cultural differences into account. It assumes that Europe has many cultures and the technologies should fit this variety.

The Impact of Computer Technology on Society: The Channeling Framework for Culture

The previous sections described the impact of society and culture on information technology. An interaction between culture and computer information occurs in the opposite direction through changes in society wrought by the impact of computers. Our knowledge of the detailed social impact of such changes is still tentative. Yet, there is ample evidence that they profoundly change the social system, as do all major generic technologies, computer technology being probably the most profound cause of change. Through its impact, information technology generally rearranges social systems, the macro framework along which culture is transmitted. This rearranging takes many forms.

Thus, according to one analyst, "the new information capability of super companies has shifted dramatically the balance between capital and labor to the advantage of the former" (Schiller, 1987, p. 24). This changes the social structure and the power relations between different social actors, and hence the cultural carriers involved, not only with those dealing directly with information technology, but also in society at large.

These technological and social changes would bring deep transformations in the social system. The new information technologies, it has been said, would have a major impact on "private life, consumption, work places, organizations, institutional structures, political processes and societal development. There is hardly any social parameter which is not influenced by its introduction" (Renn and Peters, 1986).

Generally, the introduction of the new information technology would lead to the relative decline of the primary production sector in the national economy, an increase in automation in the secondary and tertiary sectors, and extensive computerization of work and services. Both production activities as well as social interaction would be influenced by extensive communication networks. And flexible work organization, as well as flexible production techniques would, because of informatization, become pervasive.

And as social roles and functions that are informatized get transported across national borders, they become subject to international power relations. This happens in computerized transborder data flows. Here, issues such as privacy, sovereignty and cultural identity of countries which have little control over data flows become subject to international influences (UNCTC, 1983). Most of the major data banks are in the U.S. and there have been instances where even countries friendly to the United States, such as France, have found that their companies were denied access to data banks on the basis of internal U.S. laws (Rada, 1986, p. 49).

The introduction of the new technology creates a large number of "machine roles" that clone, and substitute to varying degrees, for a variety of social roles. The new information technology is, therefore, penetrating many sectors of the economy, changing their interrelationships, as well as changing the different occupational and social roles within these sectors and also between competing economies.

The encroachment of information technology replaces certain social roles and creates new ones. The extent to which the new technology thus displaces jobs and create thems is still uncertain; some skills are displaced while new ones are created (UNCTC, 1990, p. 13). At the level of the enterprise, information technology does reduce labor input per unit of output in many sectors such as telecommunication, banking, and office work generally. On the other hand, many jobs such as computer operators have been created due to the advent of the technology.

Changes in Organization

This impact of information technology in replacing human skills with machine functions is changing social relations within the work place. Computers, when introduced to an organization, thus change relationships between people in the organization.

This use of computers in organizations reflects the balance of power between management and labor (Wessells, 1990, p. 49). Because of the computer's versatility, it has been claimed that chip-based technology could be democratic, allowing a high degree of personal control. And, taking the opposite position, it was also being argued that instead, the logic of market forces would relegate any democratic tendencies to a largely marginal position (Garrett and Wright,1978). It is evident that depending on the context both tendencies have prevailed.

Thus, some workers using the new technology have come under stricter control. For example truck drivers who had been enjoying the near anarchic feel of the "freedom of the road" have come to be effectively controlled through the use of computers. And in other contexts, computers have been used to monitor the use of time and the intensity of application to work, for example by counting the number of strokes a worker hammers on a keyboard (Wessels, 1990, p. 43).

Before the Industrial Revolution, workers had prided themselves in their craftsmanship. Their work combined manual and sensory experience in one whole, their work being an extension of their creativity (Wessells, 1990, p. 35). The Industrial Revolution changed many aspects of this craftsmanship by deskilling work of the majority of factory workers. The application of information technology on the one hand, continues this process of deskilling associated with mechanization since the Industrial Revolution. And, in the reverse direction, by the adoption of new higher skills, it necessitates the opposite. Thus, print industry employees work today at a video monitor; resulting in hitherto skilled work, such as typesetting, proofreading and layout being replaced by lower skills. The contrary process of upgrading of skills is seen in former secretaries who are now interrogating data bases, producing reports, advising customers and enlarging their spheres of autonomy.

The geographic flexibility given by the new technology has also allowed certain jobs — especially those of women — to be transferred to the home to be "telecommuted." This shifting of work to a home computer in the Western world has many parallels to the shift of work to Free Trade Zones (FTZs) in the rest of the world. It is also comparable to some of the labor restrictions of FTZs. On the other hand, the introduction of electronic data processing within offices has also resulted in changes in the work content of clericals — mostly women. The technology, as it affects women, therefore, reflects both the capitalist as well as the gender power structure.

Computerization has other more general effects on the status hierarchy and social roles of organizations. By giving workers access to information through a computer, far reaching effects on the structure of the organization result. Because of the integrated information system given by the new technology workers feel they are in a position to make decisions normally done by managers. In a system that decentralizes information, grounds for authority in the organization would not be the position in the hierarchy. It would be the data that would now be available to both worker and manager. Workers under such a scheme would enjoy a functional authority, using the information available through computers to make decisions. This leads in these circumstances to a blurring of distinctions between the role of manager and worker, and consequently to a shifting of power and control towards workers (Zuboff, 1988, p. 57).

Computer-mediated communication in the form of computer based e-mail and conferences similarly alter people's relationships. In such computer-mediated communications between humans, as for example in electronic mail, the loss of face-to-face interaction gives unexpected results. It sometimes helps break down hierarchical barriers. In the absence of a face-to-face interaction, a person operating through a computer can feel indifferent to status differences and participants may express their views more forcefully.

It has even been suggested that the use of computers in production would change the alienation at the work place as described by Marx. In an information-based society, the access to information and decisions vary only with the individual's education and his ability to express himself through the computer. Such personal control according to one commentator, approaches Marx's ideal of the unalienated worker under communism (Etzkorn, 1985, pp. 43–48).

A similar liberatory role for computers has also been envisaged in teaching. The way children learn is very different from the way they are taught, according to the theories of Dewey and the experimental work of Piaget. Children learn best by constructing their own environment through play. The rote drill used in current schools is far from an optimum strategy for this. The role of the ideal teacher would be to guide the learning child in a gentle way through his play world. Seymour Papert sees the computer in the role of constructing little micro worlds which the child can play with, and explore. It could, for example, be a game in which the children would have to solve math problems. Children could use the machines to explore fields of knowledge at their pace and in a manner they like. In this, the machines are a contrast to the methods of the teaching bureaucracy, which are rigid, unimaginative and in fact robot-like. The computer for children, then, becomes a much more humane tool than programmed teaching by teachers.

The impact of computer technology, thus rearranges many social and psychological relationships, defines new ones, drops older ones and creates new opportunities as well as problems. These impacts at various levels of information technology on society have been for developed countries. But what are their effects on the bulk of humankind in developing countries?

Developing Countries

Computers are yet to penetrate the developing countries in a major way. The technology, it was noted earlier, penetrates every sector in developed countries including those associated with agriculture, industry, not only that narrowly defined as services or information work. This means even without a large information sector, information technology would penetrate developing societies.

Thus, some commentators have noted that the wide scope of the technology gives the possibility for leap frogging in development (Bagchi, 1987) including the use of such techniques as Computer Aided Design (CAD), Computer Aided Manufacture (CAM) and even Computer Integrated Manufacture (CIM) (*ATAS Bulletin,* 1986, p. 3). Computer aided production management (CAPM) has also been strongly advocated as a means of overcoming management deficiencies in developing countries (Lalith Goonatilake, 1989). Further, the advantage of cheap labor that developing countries had, is eroding because of the new technologies. Use of Computer Aided Design and Computer Aided Manufacture (CAD and CAM) has resulted in the textile and garment industries shifting back towards the industrialized countries (UNCTC, 1990, pp. 1,11). To keep abreast of international competition, many new industries would require the use in their production processes of CAD, and at least partially, CAM (UNCTC, 1990, p. 12).

Others, however, have questioned the possibility of widespread use of the new technology in developing countries (Arriaga, 1986, pp. 85–91) on the grounds of the cost of these devices (p. 67). Yet, the extreme rapidity of the drop in prices would imply that even today, a chip incorporating a technology of 10 years ago, would cost less than an elementary agricultural implement, or even less than a meal in a developing country. The next decade would see further dramatic price and performance changes leading towards very widespread use of the technology.

Not adopting the technology would be very disadvantageous in the future to developing countries and would tend to marginalize them. For example, with the rapid switch of data recording to electronic means, developed countries would mine national and international stores of information far more thoroughly than previously. Countries that do not use the technology would be marginalized from some vital data sources which are increasingly becoming only machine readable (*ATAS Bulletine*, 1986, p. 5).

There is mounting evidence that incipient computer use, divorced from communication links, is beginning to spread in developing countries. Computers — largely PCS — have been successfully used already in a variety of tasks in developing countries, most commonly in administration (*ATAS Bulletin*, 1986, pp. 66–73) . Other uses include diagnoses of tropical diseases using expert systems (Doukidis and Dayo, 1990), for health care decision modeling, (Parker, 1990), for agricultural policy analysis (Braverman and Hammer 1988) and for financial modeling of public utilities (Andima and Shem, 1987). Implementation of the Structural Adjustment Programmes of the World Bank has made it mandatory that the public sector of certain countries accept computerization (Ojulu, 1988). Computers have been used for health data-base management in Thailand and Sri Lanka (Ruskin, 1986). And several countries in Africa are using computers for fiscal planning and the national budget (Furst and Covert, 1988).

Computers are also entering the developing world in a major way though many embedded products. These include microprocessors that do controlling functions in tractors, motorcycles, radios and recorders and increasingly in many categories of imported equipment. Expert systems would come as self diagnostic systems in some of these and other products. The question would not be whether computers will come to the developing world, but to which pressing problems and for whose real requirements, and hence with what impact on social roles.

Generally at least in the initial stages, the information technology that is imported in developing countries would be for uses that have already been identified in the developed world. These would carry embedded with them the social influences of the society that gave rise to them through processes that were sketched earlier. Therefore, this transferred technology acts as a "social gene." It moves into its new host society, penetrates and rearranges some of its social roles to the template of the society of origin.

But with falls in the price of the technology, computers will increasingly impact the social structure of developing countries in ways other than they do on developed countries, as some of the previous examples illustrate. A different set of social roles would then result in the developing countries corresponding to this particular penetration of the technology.

The Social Impact of the Computer in the Home

Information technology is also increasingly penetrating (in developed countries) many areas of home life. It has already done so to a significant extent in the form of control devices embedded in consumer goods or as stand-alone computers. Because the technology is an information device with interactive properties, it also changes social interactions in the home, just as the technology did in the factory and office.

Research on such changes has only just begun even in developed countries. The results of existing studies have to be viewed from the perspective that the computer in the home is at least initially viewed as a consumer object on a par with other consumer objects such as VCRs and TVs.

These information and communication technologies enter the home into an already existing complex web of social and cultural relationships and are molded by the latter (Murdock, Hartmen and Gray 1993). It had been feared that a sophisticated communication technology entering the home would tend to disrupt communication, with family members withdrawing into isolated interactions with the computer at the expense of human interactions. Home computers, as far as current research shows, do not promote this more privatized world but increase socializing between, for example, other computer users.

With the coming merger of TV, computers, telephone and Internet services, the impact of all these will intensify. Especially through the explosive growth of the Internet, social interactions — albeit of a rather narrow kind — have increased. Research also shows that computer use results in preservation of existing roles in the family. There is considerable resilience in the way different families cope with the technology. But there is also sometimes a tendency for separation and isolation of family members as they withdraw into the private domain given by their artefacts, as for example in the case of family members who are "hackers" (Silverstone, 1991). Generally, social relations would be changed within the home as the information technology increasingly penetrates it, especially when the new information superhighway brings a host of new information services inside the home.

Social-Psychological Effects

The introduction of computers not only helps change the broad social structure of societies, and the micro social structure of organizations or of homes, but it also has profound social-psychological effects, especially on the relationships and orientations humans have to work, to each other and to the computer. It is in these relationships and orientations that the intimate bond and interaction between computer and human could be best explored. We can best express the richness of these changes by looking in detail at some empirical studies. They yield a variety of examples.

Human information created at the various levels of the social structure and encroached upon and transformed by computers at these various levels into computer information now interacts with human culture. This informatized and materialized culture now impinges on its creators. In this process of human interfacing with computers, it has been noted that there are multiple ways of knowing, thinking and reacting (Turkle & Papert, 1990).

For example, we have already noted that different programming languages are associated with different subcultures and approaches. These differences are reflected most intimately in the computer screen-human interaction. There are several studies that indicate the nature of this intimate relationship.

For many users, computers have become an extension of themselves. Programmers also often feel that their programs are extensions of themselves. On the other hand, researchers find that to many frequent users, computers, even those without any "intelligence" feel not so much like tools, but more like friendly companions without which they feel lonely and not entirely complete (Wessells, 1990, p. 214).

Studies of children who have played with computer toys indicate that computers can become in the words of Turkle, "evocative objects," that is, objects that stimulate discussion and reflection about philosophical and psychological issues. These reflections include whether the object was alive, smart or cheating. In fact, human attributes are taken by the evocative object (Turkle, 1984). Especially very young children cannot distinguish whether computers are alive or not. But even older children having formally recognized that computers are not alive, interact as if they were a "kind of life" (Turkle 1984). Some of course do not think in that way, these latter regarding them as objects. Some children treat a computer as a person in a relational way, others treat it as an object to be manipulated (Turkle & Papert, 1990, p. 149). This anthropomorphism is expressed not only by children, but to varying degrees, also by adults.

Thus, studies of college students show that those who had more experience with computers see them as warm, pleasing, effective and submissive (Arndt, Clevenger and Meiskey, 1985, pp. 181–190). One female considers a computer in a limited sense as a male companion. In another example of anthropomorphism, when a player of a chess program says that the machine has made a move, he evokes all the associations he has had in playing with humans. This anthropomorphization is not due to the computer user or specialist lacking an understanding of how the computer works, but because of stylistic preferences (Turkle and Papert, 1990). It is convenient to think in those terms.

"Hackers," those users who explore computers obsessively, consider computers as a way of life. To some of them, the computer becomes subjectively an extension of their mind, sometimes of their body (Turkle, 1984, p. 212). The hackers' experience is internally vitalizing and to them deeply satisfying. And it has been observed that it even has overtones normally associated with the intensity of sexual activity (Wessells, 1990, p. 219).

Illustrative of this intimate relation a computer program can have with a human is the use of programs in psychotherapy. Here computer programs have successfully taken the intimate human role of psychotherapist. One, based on cognitive-behavioral therapy, delivers mental exercises aimed at changing the thoughts and behaviors that contribute to depression. Many patients related to this therapeutic computer as if it were a person. Some of them said they perceived a "therapist understanding" from the computer (Bower, 1990, p. 37).

Researchers have also pointed out that some of the newer information technologies bring out entirely new types of interactions with a machine (Graziella, 1990). Machines now present humans with new combinations of the "real" and the "fantastic," which makes a qualitative difference from the earlier, less imaginative interactions of humans with machines. For example, CAD/CAM could create new metaphors of reality which do not belong to any previous human experience (Ibid). The ability to "animate" one's creative endeavors using these new techniques allows a person to enter into new subjective experiences.

Computerization has also resulted in the social isolation of workers as they are now cut off from their co-workers who work glued to the computer screen. They miss face-to-face interactions, as communication comes only from the computer screen. On the other hand, because sometimes the quantity and quality of work has increased, some workers using computers in the manufacturing process find their jobs more interesting and more responsible.

Computers in some of their uses seem also to have reversed a trend in mechanization where, as machines improved, humans did progressively less work. Over the years, with machines, physical exertion was replaced by symbolic manipulation such as by words on paper. This abstract work was, however, indulged in by only a few persons in the 19th century. Computerization has increased exponentially this tendency to abstract work. It appears, according to studies by Zuboff to be the first technology to be reversing the process of simplifying work (Zuboff, 1988).

With the computer screen in front of a worker, the work is now distanced from manual and sensory experience. Persons watching computers and doing work operations, such as in factories, are doing so without the sensory input associated with earlier work. Operators in factories earlier had directly sensed and interpreted what they saw, smelt or felt. But now, that sensory input is cut off, and workers operate in a very abstract environment through the computer. The task for persons thus operating through a screen now appears as something ethereal. The consequence is that operators now have to work out more things in their mind by tracing the implications of what is on the screen. One now requires a mental picture of the system to operate the machines. As a result, the intellectual content of their work has increased. This process has occurred not only in manual work, but also in traditional white-collar jobs. Earlier, for example, insurance clerks handled documents relating to claims, payment records and other details of customer accounts. By doing calculations by hand, the clerks had a feel about the customer. Now with a highly computerized system, clerks find it hard to believe that the computer is actually doing the job. Here again, the work has become more abstract and more difficult for the worker himself to trust (Zuboff, 1988).

But, these studies by Zuboff of mental enhancement through computer work are based on only some forms of computer usage; they do not square with all computer experience. For example, the pace of workers can also be tightly controlled with the new technology, their jobs can be made narrower, requiring less skill.

Thus, nonprofessional women using computers are affected in negative ways in the work situation. Due to computerization, this type of women's work has become more isolated, and more fractionated, and so subjectively distressing. The work is tightly controlled, as craftlike knowledge is now broken down into smaller fragments. Paralleling the experience of the first Industrial Revolution, control of certain types of work hitherto located at the level of the (woman) worker is now transferred up to the level of management (Ibid). The breakdown of the content of work into its bare essentials and its incorporation in a computer program means that, for example, in a social welfare department the caring aspects of a social worker's job are lost in the narrowly defined computer-embedded new role (Garson, 1988, pp. 73–114).

According to some commentators, these negative effects on women are giving way to better ones in the newer, AI-based technology. Artificial Intelligence, it is believed, is more flexible and more conducive to women (Huws, 1986). AI techniques emphasize intuition, nonlinear problem solving, making the interaction between user and computer more "cooperative" than "confrontational" and so are nearer feminine values (Perry and Greber, 1990, pp. 93–95). So such techniques could make organizations more gender friendly and psychologically satisfying to women.

Sometimes, some jobs are replaced entirely by computers. To accommodate these workers they have to be retrained. And, as retrained lower-skilled workers move up the skill ladder, some of the higher skills themselves for which they have been trained get computerized in the meantime. Those same forces that eliminated the lower skills in clericals and upgraded them, have been upgrading the skills of those higher up. Computerization changes career patterns and the internal mental baggage required to navigate one's vocation.

Or, in a different scenario, the promoted worker now meets an already computerized system that uses an expert system, neural network or genetic algorithm which is generally opaque to detailed human intervention. This lack of transparency of these newer technologies engulfs both manager and managed, as both of these employee categories become opaque to the detailed processing of the information. Computerization brings new areas of the unknown into one's subjectivity, just as it illuminates new areas. This lack of transparency means that users would not necessarily become antipathetic to the computer output or be put off by it. Familiarity and continued use of the technology would mean acceptance of the unknowable, in the same way a calculator's output is accepted by a person who finds difficulty in arithmetic or a watch's reading is accepted by a user who would have no idea how such a watch keeps time.

The mental sphere is therefore, deeply encroached by these artefacts. Educationalists recognizing this have argued for a good symbiosis between human and computer capacities. They have called for a complementary division of labor between the two. Computers can do some tasks more quickly and more powerfully. But human brains have other, more flexible uses which can be supplemented by the computer. This perceived division of labor between human and machine has resulted in calls for a change in the school curriculum (Sylwester, 1990). The formal contents of human minds have, therefore, to be changed in new socialization packages that recognize the different capacities between computers and humans.

Generally speaking, the introduction of computers changes the broad internal worlds of those who come into contact with them. Some develop particular attitudes to computers, others find their subjective feelings at work changed, others find their mental horizons enlarged, or cramped, and others require wide changes in their mental baggage.

The mental factors impinge most immediately at the time the human is interacting with the computer. This immediacy is increasing with new developments.

The Computer and Human 'Face-to-Face'

The present output of computers is largely in the form of data or alphabetical characters, and to some extent, of charts, pictures and occasionally, sound. With the increasing encroachment of multimedia, the "human friendliness" of this computer contact will increase. It will increasingly approach human-to-human contact, especially when voice input and output with at least some natural language use and understanding by the computer is used.

There have been major developments in voice input and output and natural language interfacing over the last few years, at least for some limited applications (Pollack, 1993). Current trends indicate that some natural language abilities will be widespread in many artefacts in the next five to ten years (Uenohara and Linuma, 1989). When almost all electronic systems such as computers, telephones, radio, television, movies and photos move towards their widely expected seamless integration, the possibilities in the natural language and multimedia immediacy of computer output would be further enhanced.

This type of output with immediacy could be from such relatively simple activities as number crunching and word and picture processing. It could also be from those computer uses that approximate some professional and creative work, such as those for expert systems, neural networks, genetic algorithms, fuzzy systems and hybrids of some or all of these. Here, the encounter, because it is of a nonroutine nature, would approach human-like interactions, and be more intimate.

The intensity of close interactions with computers, however, will reach an entirely new plateau with an all-encompassing interactive medium — "virtual reality" (VR).

Virtual realities in their usual format make use of three-dimensional graphics generated by a computer into which the user immerses himself. The user then manipulates and interacts with these graphics by means of input-output devices (Bylinsky, 1991, pp. 138–143). The interfacing apparatus used in the system includes data gloves, head-mounted tracking devices, goggles, headphones and wired body suits.

Through this setup s/he navigates the artificial or virtual environment termed "cyberspace" by practitioners and theorists. The term cyberspace comes from William Gibson's celebrated novel trilogy *Neuromancer* (Gibson, 1984) and is used widely to describe the inner space of virtual reality systems. Virtual realities in effect no longer just mimic or represent reality, they are a reality (Gibson, 1984).

Soon, throwing more computing power with newer generations of faster computers would increase virtual reality's intimacy. There are also other very radical approaches to the problem of virtual reality on which some British researchers are working. These would use laser micro scanners that would write images directly into the retina, in fact directly reaching the rods and cones of the retina which deliver the nerve impulses down into the brain. This would be a more direct form of addressing information, than seeing the dots (pixels) that are normally associated with computer displays and then feeding the pixels into the brain through the eyes. Such a direct system would have the same type of visual quality as normal sight (Suran Goonatilake, 1991a, p. 20). Virtual reality systems are also expected soon to have better tactile systems than the present ones by using pneumatic devices as, for example, in data gloves. The present bulky head-mounted stereo displays will be soon replaced by light weight "glasses." Current heavy tracking and sensing devices will be integrated into clothing or by systems such as video cameras that monitor movement from a distance (Laurel, 1995, p. 90). Future systems could also have virtual taste and smell.

The current nonentertainment activities and interest in VR centers around such uses of VR as in surgery, where for example, a computerized simulation of the brain is displayed so that the surgeon can practice on the image before delicate surgery. Another use is in Computer Aided Design (CAD) (Laurel, 1995, p. 90). Generally speaking VR allows, without going through reams of data in a conventional database, the intimate, body-experienced explorations of hitherto abstract intellectual spaces. One could have CAD models that, in effect, come alive, and one could enter them at any scale. These could be models of molecules, in which case, one could move about within them with one's whole body to explore their structures (Walser, 1990, p. 66). The abstract environment, therefore, becomes real in many ways. This is a direction of computer use, one should note, that is very different from the abstraction of work in the conventional use of computers, that has been noted by Zuboff and referred to earlier in the chapter.

Within the coming decades, it is very probable that virtual realities will shape a large segment of computing. Information consumers, whether at home, school or work place could be experiencing their respective environments through a comprehensive virtual reality at, say, a virtual work place while keeping their bodies at home (Suran Goonatilake, 1991b, p. 20). When this intimate output of virtual reality interfaces with AI technologies such as genetic algorithms and neural networks that give nonroutine results, the computer and human contact would increasingly approach that between humans, with the exchange of information between the two very close and intimate.

The Merge

Cross-cultural psychological research has shown that the cognition of individuals differ according to the differing technological systems that they use. Therefore the human thought that would emerge because of the increased interaction with computers would not be the same as without them (Guilmet, 1983, pp. 45–56). Computers being a technological artefact that is directly involved in the "cognition business," these changes in human thought would also be more intense.

On the computer screen or other output, information is presented, and a machine-human communication is made. One could say that the computer and the human are both spewing out information and reacting to each other's output. They are engaged in a two-way merger of their information contents and processing. The merger occurring from culture to computer, and from computer to culture, results in changes in both information streams — cultural and computer.

The human interacting with the computer transfers to the latter, part of his stock of culture. It is not all his cultural content, but that particular set to which the computer program has an aperture. In thus transferring parts of his culture to the computer system, he merges his cultural information with the existing artefactual information in the computer system.

In the reverse direction on the other hand, information outputs of computers are received by humans as cultural signals, and so get merged with the general human culture. The person sitting in front of a video terminal either in home, office or factory is responding in behavioral terms to the computer's output. This output need not be restricted to the visual, it can come in any form: voice, graphic or for that matter even smell and touch. Current approaches using icons and "object oriented programming" also bring more concrete approaches where the interactions with the computer become more like that of a human (Turkle and Papert, 1990, p. 156).

The machine outputs feed human brains and become merged with the rest of human learned information — culture. New input-output devices such as those that use "virtual reality" could enter this human culture very directly and imperceptibly. Through these means, computer information gets merged more easily, intimately and seamlessly with cultural information in the user's mind as he internalizes it relatively effortlessly, and reacts to it.

These two processes of culture to artefact and vice versa transfers are the result of direct mergers. But, in fact, the two information streams are also simultaneously interacting at another level, indirectly. At a macro indirect level, there is a jostling and interaction between societal frameworks on the one hand, and patterned arrangements of computers on the other, that is, between the flow arrangements for cultural and artefactual information.

Behind every overt spewing out of information from a computer and a human and the resulting merger is a welter of social forces on computer technology as well as the impact of computer technology on society, whose respective dynamics result in the immediate outcome, that is, the computer output or the human reaction to it. There are in this case two indirect processes involved, with corresponding two directions which ultimately culminate in the direct interactions.

The first direction is the social chain that influences computer technology, its structure and information output. This chain leads, as we have already described it, from the macro societal level, to the social group, to the mental world and the associated culture which constructs the technology and also to the human information that is captured by it. The second direction is that of the arrow beginning from the technology as it influences and rearranges the broader socioeconomic system, the group and culture.

The information associated with the use of computers is but a cultural product shaped by social forces. At the hardware level, computers are translations of cultural information held by computer specialists. At another level, software is similarly translations of cultural information. Cultural information on how to use a computer, what to do with it, to which ends, is still higher level human information controls on the hardware.

This cultural information is shaped by social forces at different levels. These include the computer and AI specialists' peer groups, national factors such as competition between firms and the relative funding for particular areas of research, as well as geo-economic and geo-political factors that affect this industry. The cultural information is molded by social forces at the level of the practitioner, nation and wider socio-historical context. Human discussions, negotiations, conflicts, consensuses, market forces, military and civilian demands, geo-political tensions have all shaped this cultural stream of information.

There is also a hierarchy of levels in computer systems: the application software such as a word processing program which translates an immediate cultural need, the machine code which carries information of a more general, less immediate level and the information coded in the hardware which is on a longer time frame and less flexible. This cultural information on how to build hardware, how to do machine code, what are software requirements, and how to do a particular application is what gets merged in and becomes part of existing artefactual information.

The cyberspace of virtual reality, the most intimate face of computing, one should note, is also a constructed space where culture and technology meet in a very interesting manner. And being so, the process maps within the VR cyberspace, the social psychological constructions of not only the programmer but the whole edifice of social forces that have been alluded to earlier. Just like cosmetic surgery maps society's wishes onto the biological body, the constructed bodies and objects in cyberspace are intimately marked by their society's views on gender, beauty, and morality. As an illustrative example of the mapping of culture into VR, one can take the current VR technology-driven fiction in the United States, which displays a strong masculine metaphor (Balsamo, 1993). In VR, therefore, the moral code can be directly transferred into computer code in a very intimate way. Computer code in such an intimate transfer wears the body glove of the moral code.

A set of nested, culturally derived information shaped by social forces is thus initially transformed in human/computer interactions to artefactual information. If there is already information preexisting in the artefactual mode, it adds on to such existing stores and becomes part of it, a culture-to-artefact merger thus occurring.

Through the chain from society to artefact, the computer becomes a projective screen on to which are projected different approaches to knowledge, and indirectly the human condition (Turkle and Papert 1990, p. 154). Here, the "conversation" between computer and humans initially becomes one between human and a projection of the human and his society. It is a dialogue with the "other," but the other is one's culture transformed and then artefactually modified, which now feeds back from the artefact into one's culture and transforms it further.

But, once this culture-embedded information is put into the artefact, and the latter is allowed a degree of autonomy as in the newer techniques that modify their core internal configurations through environmental interactions, the direct cultural information's influence becomes increasingly less immediate. With newer AI techniques that use learning systems, neural networks and genetic algorithms, the ability to create new information patterns exists. If the AI system produces new significant discoveries, as already has occurred in a few cases, and is bound to increase with the harnessing of devices such as "know bots" to make sense of massive data outputs, then these new constructed information patterns would be nontrivial. Given sufficient time after entry of cultural information to the artefact, the artefactual lineage would now develop autonomously. And the conversations with humans then become less than with one's slightly altered mirror image.

But, just as society and culture influence artefactual information, what comes out as cultural information is itself influenced by information technology. We have described how information technology penetrates and rearranges the social system. It influences macro international relations, relations at the national level of society and at the level of the small social group. These are the structures of society that give rise to the social cleavages, the lineages down which culture flows. In thus rearranging partly the social landscape, it indirectly rearranges the cultural landscape. Because humans in the rearranged social landscape have different interactions with their environments, the contents of their minds likewise are different, and are changed because of the impact of the information technology.

The changes through information technology in the content of culture itself are also brought about by information technology processing and generating of cultural information. Cultural information generated or modified by information technology covers a large spectrum of culture expressions from numbers, words, and sounds to pictures. This spread will increase in the future. This culture-related output from the computer embeds itself within human minds and changes their contents.

One interconnected chain from human to computer gives rise to the particular type of software program used in a particular computer at a particular place, for a particular purpose, and handling particular information. Socially constructed cultural information arising through the forces in this chain gets transferred into the computer realm and is embedded as computer information.

The second chain arising from the computer outwards to humans gives rise to a particular type of broad societal arrangements, to social groups, individuals and ultimately to computer information that embed themselves in thoughts that arise in a person. Consequently, through the two chains interacting, cultural information and computer information get merged in particular ways.

The interactions between computers and humans therefore, take the form of a series of 'conversations' at different levels. One is at the surface level of the computer interfacing with the human, as for example on the screen, with the computer's and human's respective internal states changing as the result of information inputs from the other. At a deeper level, are the "conversations" carried via societal structures encountering structured collectivities of information artefacts and interpenetrating each other.

As it were, two icebergs seem to collide and jostle, giving rise to various interactions and forms for mergings. The literal direct merging of the two information streams is only touching of the tips of these two icebergs. But, below the icebergs, a large set of indirect mergings occur as computers are penetrated by social forces and cultural structures, which in turn are penetrated by changes brought about by information technology (see Figure 5).

There are many recursive loops in these sets of two-way merging. For example, at one level, a model of how organizations solve problems feeds into a computer software for problem solving. Thus, the hierarchical organization structure of the corporate world, of the Organization Man, was modelled by Simon, and mapped into his problem-solving

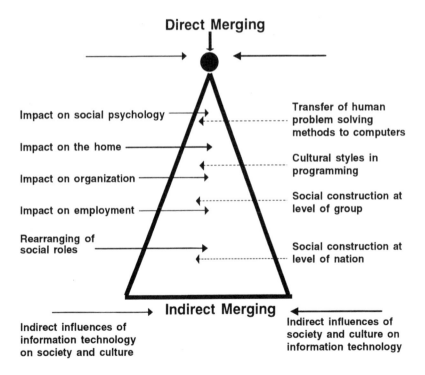

Figure 5   Cultural and artefactual information merges

software. The computer system, in turn, however, now becomes an input into decision making in organizations, computers bringing changes into the organization structure. These computers lead to changes in information processing in organizations, and as we have already seen, making in effect for a flatter hierarchy. This would probably now in turn become a model for new problem-solving software.

Virtual reality being the most intimate computer/human interface, interesting ramifications of the merging process occur. At first usage, Virtual Reality and the virtual bodies in it, are expressions of society's wants and desires, and the mapping of cultural ideals of a given society. But, these do not remain so. Such virtual images eventually become deeply transformed within the field of interactivity itself. Humans interacting with the virtual image transform its representative nature. In such a context, the material body ceases to be a bounded entity. It is also difficult to distinguish its inside from its outside, or for that matter, "its surface from its depth," "its aura from its projection." Through that process, "the material body" which as a material object has structural integrity and has boundaries becomes technologically deconstructed (Balsamo, 1993).

Because of the very intimate nature of the VR technology it has many characteristics that take it to a class of its own. Because the observer through the goggles sees himself acting in the virtual space, he is both observer and observed. This raises contentious issues of a philosophical nature. Cyberspace in VR appears between object and subject, a grid like the Indra's net of the Buddhist philosopher of the First Century Nagarjuna. It thereby blurs the distinction between subject and object, between the seer and the seen, between the construct and the constructor. It helps internalize the 'other'. All: object, tool, construct and imagination, can exchange their roles in cyberspace.

Consequently, key questions can be posed as Balsamo has done, about the social and psychological construction of VR, questions bordering on the classical philosophical ones associated with the subject/object dichotomy. For example, does the use of VR change the center of perception which is now in a virtual world, from the mind? Is the VR user's "body" in cyberspace humanoid (Balsamo 1993)? And so on.

Generally speaking, computer hardware and software, as well as the information within them are creations of humans. So when humans initially dialogue with computers, it is initially a dialogue with their slightly altered mirror image; a self referential dialogue like that evoked by the Dutch painter Escher's drawings, of a hand drawing itself drawing itself. Later, after the autonomous processes that we have described come into play, the mirror image takes a life of its own but with the results of past conversations embedded in it.

As computers and humans interface, a dynamic interaction between two icebergs takes place, one in turn molds, and in turn, is molded by the other. A rich tapestry of merging interactions occur, reflecting the wide tapestry of social and computer arrangements.

7: THE MERGING OF CULTURE AND GENES

Just as information technology and the social system interact intimately, resulting directly and indirectly in the intermingling of information streams in the cultural and artefactual realms, a similar process occurs through biotechnology where there is a mingling of biological and cultural information.

But biotechnology is not identical with information technology. There are qualitative differences. Because biotechnology operates through living organisms or their products, its activities are limited to those materials that can be biologically manipulated. This means for example that biotechnology would not, as would information technology, have a direct influence on technologies such as those in metal and steel industries, and mechanical industries. Indirect influences would exist.

Information technology on the other hand, can penetrate most industries because it directly substitutes for labor. The new biotechnology yields an array of products which require less material and labor inputs than the earlier technology (OECD, 1989). In this sense, it indirectly substitutes for labor. However in the future, when biotechnology products are expected to directly enter information technology, biotechnology could in certain areas also directly substitute for labor. It could then have the pervasive impact of information technology. Examples of this mixing of the biological and information technologies would for example be in bio chips, neurocomputers and bio robotics (Gross, 1990, p. 94; Conrad, 1986, pp. 55–60).

These and other differences with information technology reflect the manner by which societal and cultural factors influence biotechnology and how biotechnology in turn, influences the structure of society, the scaffolding for the flow lines of culture. These interactions between biological and cultural information take place in an indirect and direct manner. Historical, economic, cultural, ethical, social psychological, psychological and biological factors are key players in this two-way interaction of biotechnology and culture.

The Social Construction of the Cultural Lineage of Biotechnology

The existence of the possibility of extreme genetic plasticity through the new technology does not mean that every possible biotechnology act or genetic transfer would be done. The actual "doing" is a result of human actions. A gene transfer is not just the result of an individual bio-technologist's will; behind each transfer are social and historical forces.

Students of the relationship between technology and the socioeconomic system have shown how technology, especially complex technology, changes in response to implicit or overt socioeconomic changes. Thus, the external socioeconomic environment and its associated ideology was mapped inside the factory technology of the early 19th century and subsequent periods (Edquist, 1978). Similarly science, as was noted earlier, is influenced by external factors. But the relationship between technology and science in biotechnology is much more intimate than in any other field.

Thus, the study of citations and referencing data from biotechnology patents and bioscience research papers has shown that the bibiliometric properties of both the biotechnology and bioscience domains are very similar. What this indicates is that science and technology are closely linked in the biotechnology field and the distinction between the two has virtually disappeared (Narin & Noma, 1985, pp. 369–381). This implies that all the categories of social influences on science that were documented earlier now have a bearing on biotechnology as do the factors that influence technology.

A given biotechnology therefore is generally the result of an historical process, the outcome of particular social forces and a congealing of particular cultural traits. The biochemist that splices in a particular gene, and makes it express to give rise to a particular product, cell, plant or animal is at one level doing a technical action. Putting chemicals together, operating various mechanical and electrical apparatus, taking readings, analyzing them, he seems to be doing pure technical actions. But behind him stands a host of social forces, near and far, varying from those in his immediate peer group, national level market and cultural forces and the large scale socioeconomic forces that govern these national level forces. So, the hand that shakes the particular test tube is a hand "pushed" by these larger socioeconomic and historical forces. The operation of a few of these socioeconomic forces on a few selected biotechnology products can be taken to illustrate how the social construction of biotechnology culture takes place.

Economics of Biotechnology

One of these forces that operate on biotechnology is market forces. Its vicissitudes influence the direction of the industry and hence of bio-technology information. Let us take as illustration a few examples. Thus, in the case of agriculture, it has been observed that a particular conjuncture of capitalist forces provided the basis for the social arrangements for the earlier technology of agricultural production. This past capitalist penetration of agriculture based on mechanization, fertilizers and new hybrids has prepared the ground for a new penetration by biotechnology (Klappenburg & Kenney, 1984, pp. 3–17).

But since the biotechnology industry emerged into the commercial field around 1980, it has been buffeted by turbulence in the market. The forecasts then, with a promise of quick profits, were for very rapid growth reflected in initial investor euphoria (Gianturco, 1990). Yet, in the decade since 1980, only a handful of distinct products were brought to market (Gianturco, 1990). There had been substantial underestimates of the time taken to get a product to market. This delay was largely on account of the need to get products approved for use, taking into consideration their effects on planetary life, including that of humans.

In the decade of the 1990s, this market picture seesawed. Many more drugs came into production than previously (Gianturco, 1990). But, biotechnology stocks rose and dropped corresponding to technical developments, as well as the external economic environment (Stone, 1993, pp. 908–910). Generally, as we have seen in chapter 5, the development of biotechnology broadly depended on the vicissitudes of the market. These affected all the products, from monoclonal antibodies to gene probes to drugs to new seeds.

Because economics determined the general direction of biotechnology knowledge and products in 1993, two-thirds of biotechnology companies were focussing on diagnostic or therapeutic medical applications, while just 1 in 10 were doing work on agriculture. Perceived profit criteria were channeling the spigot of funds to these particular areas perceived as profitable and so influencing the direction of the growth of scientific information (Coghlan, 1993 b, pp. 26–31).

In the international arena, concentration of ownership in a few large companies was having repercussions in the production and commercialization of seeds of selected crops in the developing world (Sasson, 1988, p. 261). Driven by market forces, private sector R&D efforts target primarily products for the developed country markets, including those exported from developing countries, to the neglect of research into projects that would benefit developing countries. This excludes biotechnology products which are primarily aimed at the domestic market of developing countries. Without a local R&D capacity, such crops would not benefit early from the new technology.

Market forces thus determine what is considered a commercially desirable biotechnology product. Operating globally these forces preselect particular biological products for research, development and production. These products fit into particular market segments and niches. Market forces now select biological products for their commercial niches, partly mimicking Darwinian selection. In selecting the products, they also select knowledge associated with these products. The cultural stream of biotechnological knowledge now gets constructed at a macroeconomic level.

Geopolitics of Biotechnology Knowledge

But the construction of biotechnology knowledge is also governed by economic and other forces at the geopolitical level. For example, one obvious geopolitical structuring of the field is the Human Genome project itself. It has a strong ethnocentric bias in that only the genes of the Western world are being sampled to draw the genome maps, that is, of those that "have white skin [and] urban homes" (Ross, 1993, p. 17).

A good illustrative example of how geopolitics at a global level help shape biotechnology is the issue of ownership of varieties of knowledge relevant to the subject.

Unlike the Green Revolution technologies, the new biotechnology, especially genetic engineering, is being researched and developed in the private sector, largely in multinational corporations in developed countries. National research centers and international centers that spearheaded Green Revolution technologies are noticeably absent in genetic engineering. This tends to extend the secrecy of biotechnology products as, for example, through patents (UNCTAD, 1991).

Developing countries have the greatest biological diversity and hence the largest store of naturally occurring genetic material. Attempts by companies in the industrialized world to extend the scope of intellectual property rights to include those of plant breeders to patent some of this material has caused widespread concern in developing countries.

It should be noted that although genetic information is coded in the form of genes, and ultimately as a sequence of base pairs, it can be transferred to the realm of culture other than through the work of geneticists. The latter's work gives a more or less exact knowledge of the information of the genetic material. But a less exact and a rougher information can be transferred to the cultural realm by those biologists who classify and describe organisms on the basis of their phenotypal — overt — characteristics. Still rougher transfers of genetic information to the cultural realm occur through such groups as hunter gatherers in the rain forests who classify plants and animals and identify their uses.

Developing new biotechnology material requires access to a variety of useful genes found in microbes, plants and animals. Yet, only 1,100 of the 265,000 species of plants on earth have been thoroughly studied. Of these, 40,000 probably have medicinal and nutritional uses for humans (Michael, 1991, p. 52). Indicative of the potential is the fact that over three-fourths of the 121 plant-derived compounds in the (developed) world's existing pharmacopoeia has been derived from tropical plants (Joyce, 1991). The plants that are unknown in developed countries have many uses which have been already identified over the centuries by farmers, pastoralists and traditional healers across the globe.

This knowledge is now being gathered by multinational corporations, the plants and their properties identified, and later the particular gene responsible for a desired property isolated to be incorporated in a new genetically engineered plant. The scientist who finds and transplants the specific gene would be then rewarded with a patent, and the social group which through generations had identified and developed the plant in the first place would receive no reward. Further, the patented plant or seed could then be fed back as a commercial product into the agriculture of these social groups themselves, possibly also to the same groups that had identified the desired trait in the first place, replacing the existing flora (Juma, 1989).

The knowledge that has been patented is therefore from two sources, the original knowledge of the farmer that had over the centuries identified the plant's useful properties and the multinational corporation that isolated and incorporated the gene. Yet, under present arrangements, it is only the multinational corporation that is rewarded. This problem has been a subject of deep debate in several international fora organs. It has deep and profound implications for farmers' incomes and the relative global distribution of income.

As this illustrative example shows, the operation of constantly changing global economics and social factors extracts particular aspects from the world's reservoir of knowledge of plants and animals, marries them to that of modern science and produces a particular spectrum of biotechnology knowledge.

Environmental Politics and Biotechnology

The biosphere of the earth built over billions of years is fragile. Human interventions on the earth have recently caused considerable concern that the biosphere would be damaged by causes such as global warming and the depletion of the ozone layer. The release of bioengineered organisms into the environment carries similar risks.

Recognition of the fragility of the biosphere and concerns on it go back to the 1950s and has reached a high awareness today. But the question of what is environmentally benign and what is not, is not a clear cut issue. Some oppose all biotechnology, others take the opposite view. So, the creation and production of biotechnology is intimately tied to environmental politics. Problems of 'benignness' and potential damage to the environment through biotechnology are debated and particular products chosen through political and social processes. The examples below give some of the interactions the new biotechnology has with the environment and hence in turn with environmental politics and human perceptions of biotechnology leading to the possible acceptance or rejection of particular biotechnology products.

Thus, the new biotechnology in agriculture, by reducing the use of pesticides and fertilizer, could reduce polluting chemicals. Genetic engineering of plants on the other hand carries certain ecological risks. New plant varieties with traits conferring pest resistance, if introduced into other plants either by escape of the engineered crop or from wild plants crossing with the plants, would have a serious impact on cultivated crops. Herbicide-resistant genes would also be exchanged between domesticated plants and wild weeds, resulting in larger doses of chemicals to control the now resistant weeds (Hoffman, 1990).

New types of weeds that could be a threat to agricultural systems would then emerge. A weed that had incorporated a gene for herbicide resistance would now require more dangerous chemicals to destroy it. Similarly, insect-resistant traits might lead to the rapid evolution of pest species (Hoffman, 1990). Weeds with a new trait that make them withstand their usual enemies would tend to reduce genetic diversity.

As companies compete in developing countries and introduce a few biotechnologically made seeds, a shrinkage of the genetic diversity takes place as old seeds are replaced. Many petrochemicals and pharmaceutical companies have either completely taken over seed-producing companies or have become major shareholders. One result of this is the development of particular seeds that will not be sensitive to a particular herbicide that the firm manufactures, allowing for the herbicide's exclusive application and hence ensuring the sale of both seed and herbicide from the same company. As they compete in developing countries and introduce a few biotechnologically made seeds, a shrinkage of the genetic diversity takes place as old seeds are replaced. These issues are debated intensely in the environmental politics of biotechnology and govern the selection and adoption of particular biotechnology products.

A result of the patenting of plant material from the tropical world is not only the removal of the knowledge of the plant from its source but also the subsequent possible disturbance of the entire ecological niche from which the plant is removed. The new patented seed, in a worst case scenario — and a probable one — would be reintroduced to its area of origin, tied to a particular set of chemicals and cultural practices, marginalizing the original holder of the knowledge, both economically and culturally. Further, the introduction of a set of uniform seeds would make the agricultural system very fragile and make it susceptible to vagaries of hitherto unknown pests and diseases. This factor, combined with the erosion of existing genetic diversity, could have strong implications for countries that receive the technology. Widespread use of the new biotechnology could speed up the erosion of both biodiversity as well as cultural diversity (Shiva, 1991).

The new technology through genetically engineered new organisms, could also pose a threat to the environment. This possibility resulted after considerable and often acrimonious debate in the strict control over experimentation and release of new organisms in most developed countries. Yet, this strict enforcement in developed countries has encouraged companies to seek "safe havens" in those developing countries which lack awareness of the problems and none or minimal control protocols. This echoes earlier practices of using developing countries as test beds for experimental medicines, as well as for the dumping of toxic wastes. In the absence of sufficient awareness and debate, unrestricted testing of medicines in the genetic field seems to be also occurring in the developing world, as for example in the overseas testing of genetically altered vaccines (Cordes, 1986).

Generally, in developing countries, there is a lack of public awareness on the issues involved and there is also a lack of trained scientific personnel. This filters in particular ways the global distribution of the spread of biotechnology knowledge and its associated technology (Cordes, 1986). But although in some parts of the Western world, there is a strong lobby for Green Politics that make these issues overt, in some developing countries without democratic processes, there would be a strong tendency to go ahead with biotechnology without much social concern. This has happened already in China where there have been extensive field tests on genetically engineered potatoes, tobacco and tomatoes on very large plots covering several square kilometers. Genetically engineered bacteria has also already been put to use in China (Coghlan, 1993 a, pp. 1–4).

A variety of economic, political and social factors therefore impinge on the environmental politics of biotechnology. These determine which promising product is ultimately chosen, which is developed and which quietly dropped.

Knowledge: Open and Secret

In 1980 the U.S. Supreme Court ruled that a living micro-organism could be patented (Office of Technology Assessment, 1989). And, in a ruling that was protested by environmental, animal welfare, farmer and religious groups, the U.S. Patent and Trademark Office ruled in 1987 that all genetically engineered multicellular organisms including all animals excepting humans, could be trade protected (Weiss, 1987). Yet, in spite of the latter exclusion of human constituents, products of the human body have already been patented. And generally the area of patents for biological material has today become a very contentious one (Lesser, 1989).

Recently, biotechnological firms have extended the concept of patents to genetic material already existing naturally, but whose extraction was discovered by them (Slutsker, 1991). This had risen from a successful suit by Genentech, claiming in fact exclusive ownership of *natural* TPC (tissue plasminogen activator), a blood clot-dissolving enzyme that occurs naturally, but the patents for whose extraction rested with the company (Slutsker, 1991).

Although a company already had a microorganism patented in the European Patent Office in 1988, there has been more resistance in Europe to the idea of patents (Dickson, 1988). Generally in Europe, there has been more concern and demand for the regulation of biotechnology products, in contrast to the United States where an opposite view of minimal regulation had prevailed especially in the Reagan-Bush era. In Europe, the debate opened up controversies with legal, moral, social and scientific overtones. European industry wanted the widest patents, while an alliance of Greens and religious groups sees patenting any living thing as immoral; the middle ground is taken by lawyers, scientists, plant breeders and environmentalists (Mackenzie, 1992, pp. 9–10).

The largest set of problems associated with the ownership of naturally occurring biological material would come with the push to patent human genetic material, which was already attempted in the United States. This would ultimately result in researchers working on the Human Genome project patenting sections of genetic material as they are decoded in the coming years. No consensus has emerged on this issue, which will have the most profound impact on the entire human species; Europeans have generally been more circumspect on·this than Americans. In late 1991, France's national ethics committee issued guidelines opposing the patenting of the human genome, declaring it the common heritage of humanity (*New Scientist*, 1991, p. 13). It also further called for open access to genome data banks. Certain American groups including the National Institutes of Health were, on the other hand, rushing to patent gene sequences as they came off sequencing machines without any idea what the sequences coded for (Kolata, 1992). But later, in a ruling, the U.S. patent office turned down requests for these types of patents and the U.S. government abandoned the practice (*Time*, 1992, p. 24; Angier, 1994).

With work on the human genome project accelerating in the years to come, concerns about the ownership of, and access to, the new genetic material would become a vital global issue. The issues would relate among others to the most vital common biological heritage of humanity, the largest percentage of which occurs outside the regions where the genome is being researched, as well as to incentives for those institutions engaged in this vital field of research. The debates and politics around this issue would help determine the broad as well as detailed contours of an important segment of biotechnology knowledge.

Ethics and Biotechnology

Issues of ethics debated in the public and scientific spheres influence what comes out as the culture of biotechnology. On the other hand, the adoption of an already generated biotechnology may raise ethical questions requiring a redefinition of ethics. It is sometimes difficult to separate this two-way process between ethics and the technology. Biotechnology may feed ethics, and vice versa in a spiral. In the descriptions here, the two processes are conceptually separated for purposes of discussion. First, the effect of ethics on biotechnology will be discussed and later on in the chapter, the effects of biotechnology on ethics will be reported, while at the same time, recognizing that the two are intimately intertwined. So what appears in one section, could by some stretching, well appear in the other.

Biotechnology, as it deals with many profound issues of life and death and the nature of life, has to confront itself with varieties of ethical questions, conceived on the different cultural frameworks of humankind. Since the new biotechnology, when applied to humans sometimes changes a person's biological makeup, it raises fundamental questions such as how a person is defined as a biological, social, physical and legal entity. Some of these questions relate to a person's "owner-ship" of his body and its constituents and were illustrated in the United States in the case relating to "Moore's spleen."

John Moore's spleen was removed in 1976 and parts of it were developed to an immortal cell line that produced a variety of useful products. In 1984, this cell line was patented by the physician who developed it. John Moore claimed ownership to the cell line which by then had a market value of about 3 billion dollars. A lower court supported Moore's claim but this was overturned by a majority vote of the State Supreme Court in 1990 (Baringa, 1990, p. 239; Annas, 1990).

But the variety of social, ethical and legal complications are illus-trated by the two dissenting opinions to this verdict. One justice ob-served that the majority verdict could not rest on the proposition that there could not be ownership of the rights to the body parts that were removed, because if another medical center were now to steal the pat-ented cells it would be considered theft. Now that the cell line was in the commercial domain, it appeared ironically, that everybody except the donor patient himself could remove the cells and treat them as his or her property. Another dissented from the majority view that up-holding Moore's claim would be detrimental to business. This dissent also drew attention to an important background belief of the respect due to the human body as "the physical and imperil expression of the unique human persona" (Annas, 1990, p. 37). The new technology was raising questions of a very fundamental kind which could not be easily contained within existing social and legal practice.

Current developments in biotechnology applications promise a future in which more advanced medicine will be incorporated into the habits of everyday life (Finkelstein, 1990). The way the body operates, and how the body looks physically would be increasingly decided by medical interventions that raise crucial questions.

The use of amniocentesis and chorionic villus sampling predicts future diseases, health, parentage and sex of the fetus. Because this knowledge can be used to terminate a pregnancy, it takes the function of evaluating which humans are more valuable, or which individuals would be potential burdens to their communities. When further diagnostic procedures — such as at the level of the gene — become widespread, a list of human traits that could be remedied becomes a reality.

It is becoming increasingly possible to screen the unborn for those genetic defects that give rise to diseases (Hunt, 1986, pp. 32–33). British researchers successfully demonstrated a technique that would enable genetic tests to be done on a "test tube" human embryo before it is implanted in a recipient womb (Weiss, 1989, p. 132), making the distinct possibility of a total gene screen of embryos.

The costs and benefits of genetic screening have been examined and the question is raised whether screening should be made compulsory as a public health requirement (Blank, 1982, pp. 355–374). Further, a genetic screen would provide useful information for potential carriers of a disease, but it would also raise social questions about the reproductivity decisions and marriageability of the carriers of the gene as well as the conditions under which they would get health and life insurance.

A social list of desired characteristics to be fostered and undesired characteristics to be excised out of the fetus now becomes feasible under the new technology (Blank, 1982 ibid). The use of amniocentesis to test for the sex of the fetus and then to abort it, if it is a girl — a precursor of mass genetic screening — has been rapidly adopted in certain developing countries (Pateln.n.d.). This could eventually lead in the future to attempt to "perfect" offsprings genetically (Berer, 1990, pp. 58–59).

Current fashions and standards of "normalcy" in physical appearance then can be realized through the technology. Taking a step further, it would mean that if biologically driven suicidal traits could be identified in the genome sequence, they could be excised out. In the reverse direction, echoing the use of cosmetic surgery to improve one's appearance, genes may be inserted to improve oneself or one's progeny's appearance, health or intelligence. In fact in a poll taken on Americans, a sizable percentage approved the use of gene therapy to enhance physical or mental characteristics (Angier, 1992).

Scientists are already identifying the sets of genes that give shape to the face as the embryo unfolds. The genetic mechanisms that structure the face are thus being unraveled (Johnson, 1996, pp. C1, C7). This would allow testing for the shape of a future infant's face and genetically intervening to give the parents' desired shape, which is of course governed by the ruling culture. The genome altered by excision of undesirable genes and the incision of desired genes, becomes in fact, a map of society's cultural wishes. A particular society's definitions of the correct, the beautiful and the desirable can be mapped through the reproductive technology directly into the embryo.

Life, under the economics of the new biotechnology, has become a commodity. And so reproduction now becomes a form of industrial production; goods being manufactured to be sold at a price in a particular market. When reproduction is influenced by what the market would buy, in the form of an excision of a gene, or of a good womb to develop the baby, the socioeconomic system's choice through the profit motive is also mapped within the progeny through the biotechnology.

The new reproductive technology also erodes the concept of human equality. This type of intervention to write-in society's preferences in the biological makeup of individuals brings severely into question the notion that humans are born equal and not created by society (Elshtain, 1989).

The work on the genome mapping also raises questions on the problems associated with genetic counseling and engineering (Bankowski, 1989). The conventional point of view is that professional secrecy serves the interest of both patient and doctor. However, with crucial genetic information, society it has been said, may be better served if that information is passed on to the relatives or the potential spouse of a patient, because the lives of relatives and of future children would be at stake. The new technology thus makes the impact of one's physical existence "exceed the limit of one's body." It turns the conventional right to secrecy into an obligation to share information with a larger social group than just the patient and the doctor.

Although vital ethical questions have been raised by biotechnology, the international bioethic debates have unfolded within a context that assumes as universal, Western conditions. Thus when the field of bioethics emerged in the late 1960s and early 1970s in the West, the debate was raised partly within the context of religious — that is, Christian — questions and by (Christian) religious thinkers (Callahan, 1990). It subsequently moved away from these overt religious traditions to one shaped increasingly by philosophical and legal concepts current in developed countries. Yet, although there was this deliberate screening out of religion, some key issues of religion — in the case of the United States, namely Christianity — were unconsciously brought in (Wind, 1990). Patients, policy makers and health care professionals smuggled these religious ideas underneath the surface discussions of a seeming technical discourse (Wind, 1990).

Public discourse in the West has emphasized these seeming secular, culture-free, "rationalistic" themes due to a lurking fear of religion and a desire to bypass it. This has resulted in a systematic denial of a common good or transcendent individual good or of philosophical speculation (Callahan, 1990). A reluctance has also existed to examine the conventional ends and goals of medicine, thereby seeming to confirm the correctness of the existing order of things (Callahan, 1990).

Yet, when new Western-developed medicine interacts with non-European cultures, the clash can be stark. For example, in New Zealand, the endogenous Maoris have a traditional community life, where the domains of the physical and spiritual, the individual and the communal are not sharply separated. In such a situation, it has been difficult to offer modern medical care, which comes unconsciously with an assumption of West European and North American values (Donnelley, 1989). Similarly in Japan, a Buddhist conception of life, especially on the relationship between the mind and body, has particular assumptions which cannot accommodate a definition of brain death, an essential ingredient for the widespread acceptance of transplantation (Donnelley, 1989). Because organ transplantation is philosophically embedded in Western individualism, it conflicts with traditional Japanese values which emphasize community and harmony as socially desirable and a belief that the body cannot be separated from the mind (Kajikawa, 1989). But the moral problems associated with the transplantation of organs are only a crude precursor of the ethical dilemmas that would be brought by the new biotechnology.

The existing bioethical discussions have also bypassed questions raised by long established traditions vital to the meaning of human nature, suffering, dying and human destiny (Callahan, 1990). Important issues that are outside the current Western technical discourse have for example, been such questions as the nature of suffering, which vary from culture to culture but are vital to discussions on bioethics (Campbell, 1990). Buddhism for example, treats human existence and suffering in a different way from the Judaeo-Christian traditions. In some Christian traditions suffering on the other hand is considered to have punitive, pedagogical or redemptive aspects for human experience (Campbell, 1990).

The ultimate questions which religions force about the nature of humans, their origins, the nature and purpose of life and its ultimate ends are vital to the serious questions raised by the new biotechnology. The ethical dilemmas of biotechnology in going to the roots of human biological existence have raised a Pandora's box of questions; vary from culture to culture, from North to South, from East to West, from small tribal groups in Latin America to parallel ones in North America, from a Catholic in Poland to a Buddhist in Japan. The way these questions will be answered depends on a wide variety of national and international debates. These answers would yield as residue, a particular form of biotechnology knowledge.

Construction of Biotechnology at the Level of Groups of Scientists

One of the recurring themes in the academic politics of biotechnology has been on the outcome of the marriage of commercialism and science, which biotechnology has brought to the scientific process. The flow of money with proprietary claims on research findings have restricted traditional scientific openness (Rule, 1988, pp. 430–436). It has been argued that the stakes involved have raised crucial questions about whether a scientist's values have been compromised (Rosner, 1992). Faculty conflicts of interest and the access to ownership rights for their funding sources have also affected the academic social debates on science (Ruscio, 1984, pp. 259–275).

The entry of new financial resources outside of academia has also resulted in the very subject of molecular biology being reconstructed. The new financial resources have raised questions relating to whether the rapid growth of biotechnology will feed theoretical molecular biology or draw resources away from it (Markle & Robin, 1985, pp. 70–79).

In addition to these and other peculiar factors that influence biotechnology, all the other general forces well known in the social epistemology of science (and described earlier in chapter 2) influence the cultural process of biotechnology knowledge construction (Baark and Jamison, 1990). These factors will not be dealt with in detail here except to reiterate that they include social influences at the level of the small group of scientists, publication patterns, the existing scientific hierarchy and the politics of ruling paradigms.

Merging of Culture into Biology

Biotechnology is involved in the isolation of desired genes and transferring them within or across species to give desirable products. This identification and transfer is done through scientific information — a particular form of cultural information. The latter is influenced as documented above by several social forces and so guide this recombination of genetic material. This cultural information operates at several levels on the biological information stream.

Thus the whole biotechnology project as such is a cultural project. Culture, guided by a particular set of social forces operating at different levels of society defines the need for biotechnology, and the biotechnology scientific culture through its particular dynamics gives particular biotechnological and hence genetic outcomes (Baark and Jamison, 1990).

The scientist who extracts a particular gene and splices it in, to give rise to a particular product, cell, plant or animal is doing a cultural act. He is thereby expressing cultural information. Cultural information of how genes are strung together in the genome, of the chemical constituents of the base pairs, of which genes code for which proteins etc. is made use of in the biotechnology act. This cultural process is influenced by the whole range of social factors documented in the social epistemology of science, such as the biotechnologist's immediate peer group, national market and cultural forces, to large scale socioeconomic changes. So, the biotechnologist's hand that produces a particular mix of genetic materials through biotechnology is indirectly guided by cultural information that has been deeply shaped by a set of socio-economic and historical forces.

Biologists distinguish between two sets of genes, structural genes which give rise to a particular biological attribute such as a finger and regulatory genes which describe how the structural information should act, as for example, when to start developing a finger and when to stop. The cultural information we have described is a still higher set of instructions that stand on top of the regulatory and structural genes and direct the macro reordering of the genetic material.

Cultural information, therefore, becomes another set of instructions on how to deal with particular genes in addition to the strictly biologically derived ones given by natural evolution. What therefore happens as a consequence through biotechnology is a merging of the cultural and genetic information.

This cultural information that gets merged with the genetic information involves, for example, how genes are strung together, which proteins are coded by which genes and which particular phenotypal attributes are valued in the society and in the economy. This cultural information, one should note, is not static, it is a dynamic entity. It is being constantly shaped, as is scientific information in general, by various social and historical forces at the level of both the scientific group of biotechologists as well as of the society at large (Annas, 1990; Finkelstein, 1990; Baark and Jamison, 1990; Callahan, 1990).

The cultural information that guides genetic information includes also past cultural information. Past human interactions and past historical struggles are congealed in this past cultural information. Past social history therefore "haunts" the latest genes. This past social history expressed as cultural information, now gets embedded in the genetic information. In addition to the biological evolutionary history which had hitherto coded for and guided the genes, "ghosts" of past human history now haunt the new genes, and guide their actions.

When these human created genes are shuffled among themselves, by interbreeding, they also shuffle implicitly the embedded cultural information to create new forms. These culture-embedded genes then acquire a genetic autonomy of their own requiring no further human aid. These genes then develop autonomously, leading possibly in the future to also different species, to different sublineages.

Biotechnological Effects on Culture

Just as culture influences the genetic stream of information, so does in turn the genetic stream influence the cultural, either directly, or indirectly. Indirect impacts of the new technology can be brought about as in information technology by changes in the production process and social structure, the framework for the flow lines of culture.

Research on these two areas of impact of biotechnology is still nascent and concentrated largely on the developed countries. Yet, it can indicate the emerging profiles of the impacts. One such social impact is on employment.

Employment Effects and Biotechnology

The introduction of biotechnology creates new jobs and destroys others. As it spreads it will have a deep impact on employment and so change the fabric of society and the scaffolding of culture. It changes patterns of domination and subordination as well as attendant social roles.

It is as yet too early in the technology to report on the entire employment effects of biotechnology. It is however known that in enterprises, innovations in *processes* generally lead to reduction in labor costs and employment, while *product* innovations add to employment.

Biotechnology affects both processes and products and the employment effects will be influenced by the interplay between the two. The least negative impact of the adoption of biotechnology on employment according to current estimates would be in countries such as Germany, Netherlands, U.K., U.S., Sweden and Switzerland, all of which have a small proportion of their labor force employed in agriculture and a highly developed biotechnology capacity (OECD, 1989). New products brought into the market for biotechnology would create new employment as a compensation for those jobs that are lost.

The new biotechnology would automatically affect the employment patterns of 60% of the Third World population that depends on agriculture. This constitutes a significant majority of the earth's population. In a series of studies, the International Labor Organization (ILO) has attempted to identify the employment effects of the new biotechnologies in the developing world. The studies have covered China, Mexico, Kenya, Malawi and Nigeria.

In the case of China (Yuanliang, 1989), there have been significant gains in productivity and so profit, but these were, however, accompanied by other social changes. Because of the biotechnology, those employed in farming in sampled rural areas declined substantially, paralleled by a rise in other economic spheres such as industry (Ahamed, 1989). In Mexico, Green Revolution technologies had helped richer farmers make productivity gains. But, the new biotechnology through micro propagation of disease resistant plants also allowed poor farmers to survive and raised the possibility of providing more employment and increasing incomes (Eastmond & Robert, 1989).

These studies indicate that the introduction of biotechnology was changing employment patterns across the globe. It was thus changing social roles, redefining carriers of culture and identifying some subcultures as important.

Trade Impact of Biotechnology

One of the socioeconomic relations that the new biotechnology would change is that of trade. The international trade regime, especially the classical North-South interactions, were established on the basis of the old industrial technology. This industrial era was characterized by smokestack industries that obtained their raw material in the present developing countries. These industries were also heavily material-and energy-dependent. As the spectrum of industrial products change with the new technologies, they signify a change from the old with attendant changes that will imply different material use.

The change will signify a lesser use of earlier raw materials and so a weakening of the trade links established in the 19th century. The effect on commodity exports from the developing world because of biotechnology would therefore be dramatic (UNCTAD, 1991).

At the moment the competition in biotechnology products is largely between OECD countries and the trade-derived impact is being felt largely in developing countries. However with biotechnology-based changes in grains such as wheat, maize, and rice which are cereals exported by OECD countries, these trade impacts of biotechnology will also rapidly reach the developing countries in the future (OECD, 1989, p. 14).

In the longer perspective, both a strong trade-creating aspect, as well as a large trade-displacing impact of biotechnology were being expected. The new technology would give rise to entirely new products for which there would be large markets. In this sense, biotechnology could lead to fewer trade tensions than in those technologies (such as in aircraft and automobiles) where competitors produce almost similar products for a market that is relatively stagnant (OECD, 1989, p. 15).

In a study published in the early 1990s (UNCTAD, 1991), UNCTAD (the United Nations Trade and Development Conference) and UNIDO (United Nations Industrial Development Organization) have estimated the types of crops in developing countries that could be affected by respectively tissue culture and genetic engineering developments on different crops on differing time frames — five, ten and fifteen years. This study also listed the countries whose exports will be affected by the two subtechnologies. The impact, the study concluded, could be severe, and on a relatively short time frame. In some exporting countries a large percentage of their agricultural exports could be affected and could lead to a major reordering of North-South trade patterns. These changes in global trade patterns would lead also to concurrent changes in social patterns and interactions. They would change the social patterns of carriers of culture as well as partially, the accompanying cultural patterns.

Biotechnological Effects on Knowledge and Ethics

If social, political and ethical discourse results in the molding of biotechnology knowledge, then the reverse process also takes place. The adoption of biotechnology raises deep questions about given socially related positions in society, ethics and knowledge, challenging them. As biotechnology enters into new realms that change biology, it raises new social questions and muddies earlier ones. An illustrative example is the confusion that has been wrought in feminist social theory. As an important social movement, feminism has over the last couple of decades developed a coherent body of formal literature with a distinct orientation to social problems. Advances in embryology, tissue transplants, and intervention at the point of creation of human life, now question several of its social assumptions (Elshtain, 1989).

Some of these key questions arise from the radical intrusions into reproductive processes. These techniques include sex pre-selection, surrogate motherhood, flushing of embryos, in-vitro fertilization, surrogate embryo transfer, cloning, and in the future, genetic manipulations. Some techniques have seen the radical reversal and confusion of biological and social kinships, as when a mother carries, in an act of surrogate motherhood, her own daughter's child. In this case the "mother" of the child who carries it to birth is the mother of her biological mother. So the child's mother and grandmother becomes in effect the same person. The child's identity now has multiple forms it is at the same time grandson, son and stepfather (Gruson, 1993).

For some feminists, some of these advances are a continuation of a process liberating women from biological determination (Elshtain, 1989). The new technology increases the capacity of women to break their links with both the animal origins of reproduction as well as patriarchal controls on reproduction. Yet, these pro-interventionist feminists are now on the defensive as the non-interventionist feminists draw negative outcomes of control of the reproductive function.

Thus according to anti-interventionists, this new technology would extend and intensify patriarchal control. According to the anti-interventionist radical position, the reproductive capacities of women such as wombs, ovaries and eggs would now be sold by "reproductive prostitutes" in the same way as "old time prostitutes" sold sexual body parts (Elshtain, 1991). The new technology has questioned earlier feminist assumptions and left a splintered social and ethical field as well as significantly changed its knowledge content.

This feminist dilemma is further illustrated by the well publicized "Baby M" case in the United States. Here, biological motherhood and social parenting were separated in the manner feminists have been demanding for a long time. The biological father wanted responsibility of fatherhood and to care for the child with his wife, who did not bear the child. The surrogate mother in whose womb the baby gestated wanted to care for the child for emotional reasons. Further, all parties to the contract had entered into it "freely." The controversy the case aroused illustrated the inadequacy of feminist terms such as "procreative liberty", "gestational hostess," "womb rental," "risk pay for pregnancy services." These and other similar terms were based on childbearing being a neutral activity. Surrogacy and the new eugenics force reconsideration of key issues and questions relating to family and human intimacy (Elshtain, 1989).

The new incursionist techniques in reproduction generally raise questions of how a parent is socially defined. Who, for example is the parent of a child brought about by in-vitro fertilization from an egg donated by Mrs. A., combined with a sperm from Mr. B., implanted in Mrs. C's uterus and given for adoption to Mr. D and Mrs. E.? The conventional emotional assumptions of such questions are muddied by recent research. Thus a British study has shown that couples who have test tube babies including those from donated sperm make better parents than those who have "normal" children. The mothers cared for their children better, they were warmer and more emotionally involved than parents of normal babies. The strong desire for parenthood expressed by the test tube parents had overridden any genetic ties (Laurence, 1995, p. 3).

Recent successes in cloning allows for newer developments in reproductive technology. One clone for example could be allowed to come to birth, and the other could be frozen and stored to be used later. In such an instance, one could have an identical twin delivered years or even decades later. The twin brother would be, say, twenty years younger. The parents would have a good idea how the new brother would look like twenty years ahead. In fact, this burden of the biological knowledge of the future, how one would look, what would be one's probable diseases, etc, would burden not only the parents but also the twin born later. On the other hand, some people may like having twins born apart, rather than together, allowing them more time to bring them up by rearing them apart (Kolata, 1993).

Foreboding more dramatic questions, a scientist in Edinburgh has transplanted ovaries of dead mice fetuses to adult mice. This procedure, it is envisaged, would soon lead to similar ones in humans. A ten-week-old human fetus already has about six to seven million eggs. If a fetal ovary is transplanted to a woman, the ovary grows to adult size in about, it is estimated, a year. Such a procedure in reproductive technology would not require donation of an egg by another woman as is the practice now for some infertile couples. It would also remove some of the negative features of the latter procedure and so would be welcomed by many (Kolata, 1994).

Such a procedure raises the possibility of a child whose mother was never born, and in fact is a dead fetus. The natural order of generations is further upset by creating grandmothers who were never mothers. Normally, in such thorny ethical questions in medicine, one gets the consent of a donor. But how could one get the consent of someone who has never been born (Kolata, 1994).

In instances of donated fertilized eggs that grow to term in somebody else's womb, children can have two mothers, the genetic mother of the donor and the mother in whom the gestation took place. Sometimes extras of such fertilized eggs are stored frozen. These now constitute potential kith and kin of existing persons or on the other hand, could be considered spare cells just like those in a blood bank. Some countries faced with these moral dilemmas have legislated, as in France, to prohibit some of the newer technologies. It appears that from one perspective parenthood now becomes a privilege not a right, a privilege, legislated by governments. Others have argued for a more diverse moral climate. In fact, in countries that have not legislated, such a diversity exists by default in the legal sphere (Kolata, 1994).

But in the face of the strong emotions that parenthood raises, such laws and guidelines may be observed in the breach. Thus although guidelines laid down by British authorities state that a fertility clinic should not pay more than 15 pounds for a donor of eggs, they in actuality are being superseded. Donor women in 1996 were earning up to 3,000 pounds a year by meeting the demand of anxious couples (Lawrence and Rogers, 1996, p. 8). In the same vein, genetic counselors may advise that children should not be tested for certain traits. Yet existing research shows that in spite of the possible unhappiness and detriment it may bring, children are being tested in large numbers by their parents (Beardsley, 1996, pp. 100–106).

This incursion of very complicated social and ethical issues through the new technology will intensify in the near future when genetic characteristics themselves can be excised in or out of chromosomes. In such an event, possible parents could be spread over a large number of desirable gene donors. In a hypothetical instance, a different donor each for the genes for a particular type of intelligence, for a nose, for eyes, for a set of teeth, for avoiding a particular disease and so on. If the gene for preventing a disease comes from a transgenic source such as another animal or plant, parentage then becomes very vexing indeed. One's "co-father" could well be a plant.

Ethical issues are raised not only about the beginning of life but also in its maintenance. Thus, fetal transplants to the brain have already been used to treat Parkinson's disease. Because brain cells are not rejected, this could be a precursor for other uses of brain tissue transplants in the future. Fetal neural transplants for treatment of neurological diseases has been successful in primates. When transferred to the human arena, several legal and moral problems are raised by these incursions (Mahowald et al., 1987, pp. 9–15). One of these could be wombs for hire for pregnancies, to be then aborted for fetal tissue (Elshtain, 1991, pp. 64–65). In some developing countries in the Middle East and South Asia, advances in medical technology in the form of organ transplants have led to the poor selling organs to rich patients. It is not too difficult to imagine the development of baby farms in the poorer areas of the world to meet this demand, eventually with even gene-screened babies.

Many of the questions on bioethics created by biotechnology have been raised within a Western perspective of individualism. New technology developments may require change even within this perspective. For example, the developments that would follow from the human genome project will raise important questions of distributive justice. Even the question of the price for the project raises the question of whether that large sum of money should be spent more usefully elsewhere. Once the genome project identifies the genes that give rise to particular diseases, further important questions would rise. What genetic disorders are so serious and widespread that they require immediate attention as opposed to more benign disorders? Which type of persons, families, and ethnic groups require genetic screening? What type of genetic tests should be used in mass screening, if ever? These type of issues relate not only to the individual, but to how the individual is placed in society and how he or she is prioritized by society (Lappe, 1990). Other issues raise key problems of privacy, confidentiality and applicability.

Ethical questions arise not only in biotechnological interventions in the human *persona* but also in genetically engineered food. If the food is that of a transgenic variety which has genes of different animals spliced into particular plants or other animals, it may ruffle religious susceptibilities. Thus if the plant contains transplanted genes exclusive to a pig, it could hurt an orthodox Muslim; if it contains genes related exclusively to a cow, a Hindu; and to any animal, a strict Buddhist; and if it contains genes that are exclusively human, some humans might find it repugnant, their minds evoking images of cannibalism.

As biotechnologies expand, they challenge and deeply change cultural assumptions. Taking into mind these considerations, Western ethicists have called for a public debate on these and other issues (Wheeler, 1991). When these issues are taken beyond the narrow confines of the West to other cultures, to other economic and political conditions, and address many different publics, one would have a multiplicity of value and ethical outcomes because of the introduction of biotechnology. In many significant ways, the introduction of biotechnology is bringing changes into the field of ethics as well as to the knowledge system.

Biotechnology Transfer Implications

The new biotechnology still emerges from the social and economic considerations of a few companies in a few developed countries. The technology that has emerged in these companies is the partial result of social debates in these countries. When the technologies are introduced into developing countries in a transfer process, they are often taken in as something only technological, devoid of their previous social backgrounds. The social assumptions and compromises made in its acceptance in the first place are forgotten by those who usher in the technology in the recipient countries. Yet once transferred and accepted, the technology tends to reproduce some of the social and cultural assumptions that first gave rise to the technology.

This, however, is not unique to biotechnology. Technology is a product of social and technical factors. And ingrained, for example, in the technology of the motor-car industry is a whole array of assumptions about the nature of man and human relations arising from the particular historical experience of capitalist development in the West (Susantha Goonatilake, 1979). When such a technology is imported into a different society or country, it results in the reproduction at a micro level of social assumptions and relations derived from the society that engendered the technology. Examples of this process include the adoption by the then Soviet Union of the motor car assembly line's alienating technology and the acceptance of the Green Revolution technology in Asian countries (Susantha Goonatilake, 1979, Susantha Goonatilake, 1984). These technologies being a product of social changes within certain Western countries, acted as a carrier of particular social relations (Edquist, 1978). The adopted technology which was purportedly introduced as neutral tended to recreate a nonneutral social situation. Technology in this role was history and social experience in concentrated form, which when adopted, reproduced some of the social relations of the society that gave birth to it.

Biotechnology acts in a similar fashion. The social and ethical implications of the acceptance of the new technological advances change many social, cultural and ethical assumptions in the recipient country. Acceptance of a particular biotechnology tends to reproduce aspects of the society of its origin relating to the prior ethical, market, political and social factors that in the first place gave rise to the particular biotechnology. For example, if the excision of a gene has been agreed to as a therapy after a particular set of technical and moral debates in America, its transfer to a developing country as a neutral technology means that the outcomes of these debates are all implicitly accepted in the developing country. And, if afterwards there is an ethical and legal challenge in the United States, with the Supreme Court banning the technology, then in turn this becomes the new "neutral" technology for the follower countries.

Direct Biological Merging of Genes into Culture

Human biology sets some of the parameters of culture and cultural information. Thus biology sets the sensual limits of experiencing the environment, giving us our subjective world. The range of molecules that we can smell or the acoustic spectrum through which we can sample the world is set by biology.

The genetic system sets the subjective limits of sight, sound, touch, and brain, including in the case of the latter, the differences due to gender. Biologically we experience a world different from that of, say, a bat (Nagel, 1974). And as accumulating evidence based on anatomical studies, psychological studies and brain scans reveals, we perceive the world differently from the other gender (Kolata, 1995, a pp. C1, C7). Biology sets the basic framework through which we view the world. Although we could transcend these biological limits indirectly through artificial means, our internal awareness of the external world is intimately governed by these factors. The particular structure and biochemistry of the brain gives the physical framework through which we acquire and process cultural information.

But the new biotechnology and genetically invasive medical procedures through new therapies and nutrients are changing this physical grid through which we acquire culture. The new biotechnology, in giving rise to a whole range of procedures, therapies and nutrients that affect our senses as well as the brain, influences this matrix which processes cultural information and so in turn influences cultural information itself. Let us recall some of these incursions into the nervous system.

Incursions into the Nervous Systems

Thus, brain tissue transplants taken from human fetuses have been successfully used as a partial remedy for Parkinson's disease. Fetal neural transplants for treatment of other neurological diseases have also been successful in primates (Kolata, 1995, pp. C1, C7). At Johns Hopkins University, scientists have discovered a means of nourishing and cultivating human brain cells. A laboratory culture of neurons has been thus sustained and multiplied for nearly two years. Until this breakthrough, it had been thought impossible to make neurons reproduce like other cells in the body. With this success, one of the major goals of all brain research had been achieved. This raises the possibility of cultured cells as a replacement for lost brain tissue presumably even beyond the present uses for Parkinson's disease (A Window on the mind, *Time*, 1990). In similar research, immature brain cells of mice have been transplanted to treat a genetic brain abnormality. Healthy brain cells of baby mice transplanted into the diseased brains of mice became part of the latter s central nervous system. The cure was effective (Brain Cell transplants, *New York Times*, 1995, p. A20). Researchers have also used compounds to regenerate damaged nerve tissue in rats. The compound could reverse nerve degeneration found in Parkinson s disease (Day, 1996, p. 22).

From the behavioral effects of these biological interventions to behavioral correlates at the individual gene level is a major step. Scientists have thus been working on mice to identify genetically based behavioral traits. A single gene, for example, has been found responsible for morphine addiction. Certain other mice have been bred that show extreme aggression. Analysis of their genes would lead to some of the genetic underpinnings of aggressive behavior (Kolata, 1995, p. C 12). The genetic basis of aspects of memory, tracing a link from molecules to cells to behaviors has been identified in mice (Wade, 1996), while the molecular and genetic basis of long-term memory has been successfully probed (Wickelgren, 1996). Scientists have also found that the ability to nurture the young in mice is based on a genetic component. The lack of this particular gene makes mutant mice ignore their offspring (Gene may be clue to Nature of Nurturing, *The New York Times*, 1996). Although complex behavior patterns cannot be adduced to the working of a gene or two, environmental plasticity being too great for that, search for such genetic correlates to behavior is expected to yield many results in the future (Kolata, 1995, p. C12).

There have also been recent studies that have purported to identify genetic factors in certain other behavioral patterns. For example, genes have recently been reported to have been found for lesbian behavior (Angier, 1993). And the genetic origins of male homosexuality has also been proposed on the basis of some studies (Hamer and Copeland, 1995). It has also been pointed out that a certain family can speak a language normally in most respects; however they cannot form plurals, due to one defective gene (Dazzaniga, 1992). Abnormalities in two types of neurotransmitters due to genetic defects have been associated with at least some drug addicts and alcoholics and with those children finding difficulty in concentrating. Genes have also been identified associated with alcoholism, anger, overeating and excessive aggression (Siebert, 1996, p. 15), while people haunted by anxiety seem to lack a gene (Angier, 1996).

Novelty seeking has been linked by Israeli and American scientists to a single gene found on chromosome 11 (Toufexis, 1996, p. 42). Scientists have also isolated a gene that underlies a key human conceptual ability, the process of taking things apart mentally and reassembling them to a whole. Persons who lack this gene do not have the ability to make out the checkerboard pattern of a collection of colored cubes. They are also poor at drawing, and are not capable of following simple instructions for assembling toys and furniture and similar tasks. This result raises the possibility that other unique genes could be found for behavioral aspects such as learning, musical talent, creativity and the facility for language (Blakeslee, 1996, p. C3).

Some of these findings relating to a direct interlinkage with genes and behavior are as yet controversial. Some of the alleged findings such as those which suggest deep genetic determinism down to coincidences of detailed behavior patterns of identical twins separated at birth are as yet not accepted unanimously and have to be treated with circumspection (Horgan, 1993, pp. 122–131). Yet, even the critics of extreme genetic determinism agree on genetic factors at least partially influencing behavior traits such as intelligence. The consensus of most studies is that about 50% of key behavioral traits are inherited (Horgan P). Many mental disorders have been found to run in families, again indicating genetic influences. Thus if one identical twin is schizophrenic, it is probable, though not certain that the other will be.

Genes have also been found that are linked to a disease that gives rise to Fragile X syndrome, a form of mental retardation (Kahn, 1993, pp. 32–36; Nelsen, 1992, p. 19). Other genes affecting neural diseases that have already been identified include those for X-linked adrenoleukodystrophy or ALD, which destroys nerves, leading to cessation of conscious brain functions, coma and ultimately to death (Lorenno's Oil Malady, *The New York Times*, March 2 1993); and for Lou Gehrig's disease, a neurogenerative disease resulting in the death of certain nerves so that patients lose their ability to speak, swallow, move and even breathe (Angier, 1993).

Biotechnological and genetic interventions on those aspects that relate to behavioral traits would directly change the biological background to the acquisition of culture. Such gene therapy has already been used in brain cancer (Coghlan, 1993, b pp. 26–31). Further, using a modified virus as a vehicle, scientists have succeeded in introducing genetic material directly to the brain. Hitherto, it had not been possible to introduce fresh genetic material to fully mature brain cells. Development of this research could lead to the treatment of the deterioration of aging brains and one should add, raises the possibility of direct genetic intervention into existing brain structures even to enhance existing nondiseased functions (Neurological gain seen, *The New York Times*, February 16, 1993).

There are new drugs coming into practice that affect the brain. They affect alertness, sensitivity and use biochemistry to alter personality. It is parallel to plastic surgery for the body, a "cosmetic change" of the mind. The prospective patient alters his or her interior life through drugs to give culturally desirable characteristics as output. The changes however are not all culturally determined, many are internally felt requirements, biologically based. But some characteristics, like those traits deemed desirable only by a particular culture or those that vary across cultures are culturally determined (Sen and Lee, 1988; Kramer, 1993). And when such drugs are biotechnologically made and/or intervene with genetic systems, biology modified by culture intrudes directly into one's thoughts.

Widespread biological and genetic interventions in the neural and brain structures would lead to changes in some human behavioral patterns and hence in their cultural outputs. At the least, the tendencies to particular behavior patterns would change and hence some of the broad directions of the cultural lineage. Through such genetic articulations, the merging of gene into culture now becomes direct and immediate. The genetic information in these potential gene therapies, thus adds itself as another information system to the cultural system by changing its biological grid, biology merging with culture. Biological information now gets merged more directly with cultural information.

Concluding Remarks

The societal construction of biotechnology knowledge as well as the reverse process of the biotechnological influence on society has been documented above. In one process, societal factors, impinge upon and change the cultural stream which includes the scientific knowledge of biotechnology. As this biotechnology cultural stream is expressed as a biological product, a merging of the cultural information and biological information takes place.

Just as culture influences the genetic stream of information, so does in turn, the genetic stream influence the cultural, either directly, or indirectly through social changes. The impact of biotechnology on

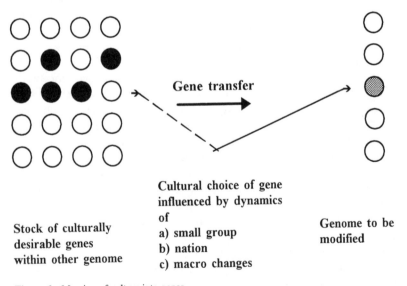

Gene transfer

Stock of culturally desirable genes within other genome

Cultural choice of gene influenced by dynamics of
a) small group
b) nation
c) macro changes

Genome to be modified

Figure 6   Merging of culture into genes

society changes employment patterns, job structures, income differentials, trading patterns, ethics, values and culture. In this sense, genetic information expressed through biotechnology products changes human and social structures and roles, the scaffolding down which culture is passed down. In addition, the knowledge and awareness of biotechnology itself influences humans' cultural definitions of themselves. It also thus changes parts of what is important in culture that is subsequently chosen to be handed down. An indirect merging now takes place from culture to the genetic system. A more direct merging takes place when biotechnology through interventions in the brain and the nervous system changes aspects of the biological framework for absorbing culture.

Directly and indirectly, therefore culture and genes interact, the two information streams influence each other, partially merging their information patterns and contents (see Figures 6 and 7).

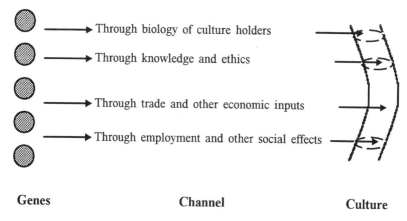

Through biology of culture holders

Through knowledge and ethics

Through trade and other economic inputs

Through employment and other social effects

Genes **Channel** **Culture**

Figure 7 Merging of genes into culture

8: THE MERGING OF BIOLOGY AND COMPUTING

Biological organisms with artefacts built into them or artificially constructed by humans have been a theme of science fiction for nearly two centuries. From Frankenstein to Robocop and the recent prolification of cyborgs in film and novel, the marriage of biology and machine has been evoked. But, the cyborg metaphor is a crude description of the interaction between intelligent artefact and biology. It is at best a static description of a short time slice of a set of deeper interactions. These speculations expressed in a fictional form are also possibly cultural manifestations of the short time span of the contemporary (Western) time perspective.

What is more significant and meaningful in the two-way interactions between biology and computing are the longer term ones involving evolutionary changes. The difference between the two approaches is that between a snapshot and a film. The latter gives a longer-range description, that of history, in contrast to the cyborg description of a single event.

Seen from this larger perspective, the interactions of intelligent artefact and human biology are much deeper and have more ramifications than the snapshot couplings implied in the cyborg metaphor. The interactions between the two occur in two ways, indirectly and directly. These vary from models of biology feeding models of computer construction and vice versa, to developments of computers with biological elements and the opposite of living elements having computer parts.

Computers from Biological Models

In 18th century Europe, man was viewed as a machine. This has now been replaced by the view of the human mind and brain as a computer (Mac Cormac, 1984, pp. 3, 6, 207, 216). And computers in turn are viewed as brain-like. The models derived from the two perspectives feed each other, in a mutual feedback process.

This mutual feeding of concepts between biology and computers has had a relatively rich history over the last fifty years. Thus, one of the founders of computer theory, Norbert Wiener and his views on cybernetics — the theory of control — fed many biological discussions, just as he himself drew examples from biology, such as homeostasis, to describe biological parallels with early information artefacts (Kaminuma & Matsumoto, 1991, p. 37).

The work of neurobiologist Donald Hebb was also very influential in carrying biological ideas into the direct computer field. He was of the view that neurons have a great deal of flexibility in the way they connect to their neighbors. If two cells or two systems of cells were continuously activitated, he held, they became associated with each other and facilitated each other's activities. Continuous stimulation meant that the connections between the cells became strengthened.

Later, McCulloch and Pitts described a neural network device, the 'Perceptron,' which was modeled after Hebbs' descriptions of how the human brain learned by reinforcing connections between neurons (Kaminuma and Matsumoto, 1991, p. 37). But, because of a lack of sufficient computing power, the potential of the Perceptron could not be realized. Computer scientists of the last decade who developed neural networks hold that once neural networks are simulated in the way Hebbs described it, intelligent behavior would automatically emerge. The proof of this approach has been the recent explosion in uses of neural networks in successful problem-solving applications (Milner, 1993, pp. 124–129).

Trained neural networks also produce an interesting biology-like phenomenon, which, it is speculated, may parallel what collections of dying brain cells experience as fantasies associated with the near-death experiences. When a trained neural network's connections are destroyed, it has been observed it continues to spew out results for some time, even as the circuits connecting the various elements become scrambled, the spewed-out results having a semblance of scrambled meanings ("fantasies") paralleling those of the dying human brain (The ghost, 1993, p. 92).

Another recent effort in emulating biological computing is the drive to parallel processing of information that is being increasingly used in computer architecture. It is a departure from the classical Von Neumann type architecture developed in the 1940s to a more biologically attuned one (Passarelli, 1989, pp. 50–57). Other biological properties are also being explored in computer hardware as, for example, in chips that are capable of self-repair. In such devices, stored spare chip cells replace those that malfunction. Or alternatively, they call upon untapped circuits as a replacement, when one goes out of action.

As computers increasingly replace people in many functions, it is also expected that new different sets of measurements, expectations and perspectives would be required to deal with them. This, it has been observed would require the use of a new metaphor for computers, one that is closer to biology than that associated with conventional machinery (Dyson, 1993, p. 33).

The ultimate merger of computing and biology would be in the symbiosis of organisms and machines. Examples of these include computing devices with both chips and biological neurons, artefacts that include biological sensors and tissues, and in the reverse direction, living organisms including humans, having implanted artefacts (Bugliarello, 1989, pp. 46–48). The very artefacts that normally extend humans' ability to deal with the environment now become part of themselves. "Our own biology [becomes] an artefact .... the artefact and its maker are now ..... merged" (Bugliarello, 1989, pp. 46–48).

Computers from Biological Elements

A direct merging of biology into computers occurs in the attempt to build computers from biological materials, whereby organic materials would be used as raw material for chips, replacing silicon (Conrad, 1986, pp. 56–60). These biocomputers will be using a host of materials associated with living matter as building blocks. Such building blocks would include proteins, enzymes and conducting polymers (Suran Goonatilake, 1991a, p. 27). These bioelectronic activities have intensified recently as the following examples show (Ward, 1989).

A bacterium, Halobacterium halobrium, has a pigment Bacteriorhodopsin which operates like a miniature solar cell. Molecules in this pigment can be made to function like silicon chips. Proteins from the halobacterium halobrium bacterium does computation by changing its molecular structure or state in reaction to light. When red light from a laser hits it, it becomes one state, when green light shines, it changes back into the original state. This property is used as the code for the 1s, and 0s of computing binary systems. One of the first applications of this technique has been in memories. A chip built around the light-sensitive substance could also process visual information (Dambrot, 1988, p. 29). The memories are cheap, 25 megabits capable of being stored in an area of 2 square centimeters; and these devices have a fast access time — one to four nanoseconds (Suran Goonatilake, 1991a, p. 27).

Biological material such as grass allows metals to enter it. This is done by the metals binding themselves to the roots, preventing the metal from going up into the rest of the plant. This property of metal binding has also been used to synthesize semiconductors biologically. Other devices using proteins are expected to give much higher storage capacities than existing ones. Using optical techniques, these devices make use of the fact that some proteins have a large cross-section for absorbing photons (Suran Goonatilake, 1991a, p. 27).

Other successful results in biocomputing devices dealing with the core aspects of electronics have been announced in different parts of the world. Thus, transistors based on organic polymers have been made by French researchers (Clery, 1990). Polymers have also been used by the Japanese to produce field effect transistors. Optical computing devices based on proteins have been developed (Suran Goonatilake, 1991a, p. 27). Mitsubishi has developed a biochip (*Japan Chemicals*, 1989, p. 23), and another Japanese firm has produced a special type of biochip that can convert light into electricity (Mitsubishis' biochip *Japan Chemicals*, 1989). They have also created a protein molecule that behaves like a diode (Marks, 1996, p. 23).

Researchers have combined circuits of brain cells together with those of silicon chips. The rejection problem associated with marrying living matter with foreign substances has been overcome in one such effort. The cells have been able to grow on the silicon base. These attempts hold out the possibility of combining the potential of silicon devices with that of living neurons (Pool, 1996, p. 20). Another research group has coupled isolated nerves cells directly to semiconductor transistors (Hindley, 1996, p. 22).

Another class of biocomputing devices would be wholly artificially made proteins and organic polymers that have computing characteristics. Such devices, already manufactured experimentally by the Japanese, would be able to detect chemicals, including those responsible for smells. An application of this approach has been developed into a 'freshness chip' which detects aromatic substances that are released when a fish decays. A development of such techniques would lead to an artificial nose (Dambrot, 1988, p. 29).

Biocomputers would also be designed to exploit some of their characteristics that lend themselves uniquely to the architecture of parallel processing. Thus, when harmful bacteria enter the bloodstream they are recognized as a foreign body by the immune system. Subsequently the immune system performs a host of decisions, such as whether more antibody-producing cells should be made and whether free antibodies should be released into the blood. In these functions the immune system acts like an adaptive, massively parallel computer which recognizes specific patterns. This is achieved through the capacity of these systems to recognize shapes of proteins. Many protein molecules, specially enzymes, can recognize and lock into other molecules at specific sites, as lock-and-key mechanisms, giving rise to a logic system. Biological computers can also be built using these basic recognition capabilities (Suran Goonatilake, 1991a, p. 27).

Biological molecules in tomorrow's computers would also be able to recognize patterns. Work has already been presented on biological structures called microtubules, tiny protein filaments, which exist in cellular cytoplasm and which can function as biological computers having pattern recognition properties (Dambrot, 1988, p. 29).

By getting DNA strands to code symbolically for numbers it has been possible to make them add by chemical means, creating a form of biological computer (Manning, 1996). A difficult mathematical problem has thus been translated to the language of molecular biology and solved through a chemical reaction taking place in a solution one-fiftieth of a teaspoon in volume. Symbols have been represented by the chemical units of DNA. By mixing the DNA biomolecules together, a desired mathematical outcome is reached by interpreting the chemical reaction's outcome (Kolata, 1994, p. C1–3).

By thus utilizing the power of DNA to represent symbols, genetic material may exceed in power the fastest computers. Chemical reactions occur very fast, hence a large number of computations can be made swiftly. Thus a memory bank containing about a pound of DNA and stored in a vessel one meter square would have more memory capacity than all the computers made so far. Such DNA computers would consume a billion times less energy than a conventional computer of similar capacity and would use a trillionth of the space to store information. They would exceed the storage capacity of neurons. The DNA at the bottom of a test tube would store a million times more information than the human brain. And, a 1000 liter vat of DNA would have the power of 10^{14} times that of a human brain. But searching for the resulting information in DNA computers would be slow, because it would take minutes or hours to trace a DNA sequence (Kolata, 1995, pp. C1, C10).

Biological systems have the ability of self-repair and self-organization and learning through evolution. Eventually with further realization in hardware of biological computing products and techniques, computer systems would be realized that evolve in hardware, as they now do in the software realm through the technique of genetic algorithms (Suran Goonatilake, 1991 b, p. 26). Such biological computers would be designed to evolve through mutation and natural selection. This means that current software solutions that arise from genetic algorithms would in effect now also be realized through real genetic materials (Suran Goonatilake, 1991 a, p. 27).

Biosensors

In existing computing devices the interactions of the computer to the outside world are usually through the keyboard or a mouse. These in certain specific applications, can be supplemented through sensors that react to environmental variables such as sight (e.g., through a video camera), sound (e.g., through a microphone), pressure and smell. This parallels the information input that living organisms get from the outside world through a variety of senses. Biosensors would be biologically based artefacts that would perform these and other functions of inputting data from a wide variety of environmental variables instead of only the present electronic or electromechanical ones. A list of current efforts indicate the possibilities here.

Lock-and-key devices derived from the biological world are already in use in such biosensor devices. These devices can detect a variety of organic materials. The Japanese have also been able to produce complex biosensors using genetic engineering techniques. Thus, by incorporating the gene that gives rise to the enzyme that causes fireflies to glow in a bacterium, a set of photosensors that do not glow in normal conditions, but glow in the presence of toxins, have been made (Suran Goonatilake, 1991 a, p. 27).

Neural networks have also been used to recognize molecules, giving rise to the identification of different smells. The projected uses of these artefacts lie in the monitoring of food freshness, in perfume manufacture and environmental monitoring (Holderness, 1990).

In Britain, biosensors activated by enzymes and which could be used as switching devices for biocomputers have been developed (Suran Goonatilake, 1991 a, p. 27). By combining semiconductor and biological approaches, a sensing device that in effect is a silicon chip with living cells has also been made. The device measures the response of a broad range of chemical and biological stimuli to the cell. This belongs to an emerging class of devices that have incorporated in them three systems: chemical, biological and electronic. These biosensors possess transducers that convert signals in one form — which could either be a chemical, antibody or cell — to another form of signal (Suran Goonatilake, 1991 a, p. 27).

A living form of biosensor has arisen from the work being done on tiny silicon devices that are implanted in the nervous systems of rats to get details of neuron outputs. The silicon device transfers the signal from the neuron into a binary form which is then fed into a computer. Rats have thus been trained through such computers to control the lights in their room or to control their water feeders (Fisher, 1992).

An extreme form of transferring data directly through a biological medium is in the serious work done on translating brain signals directly to computer commands, so that what a person thinks comes out as computer actions. Some of these developments allow, after some training, for a computer cursor to be moved up and down or sideways by human thought alone. In another experiment, at the University of Illinois, persons were able to type by just spelling the required words in their minds (Pollack, 1993).

In the same direction, some other researchers have taken advantage of the fact that before an action is taken, the brain emits certain voltages. As a result, a computer program has been developed that can distinguish between a left or right movement of a joystick. Other researchers have used the fact that when someone sees an event that has been awaited but takes place only rarely, the brain gives out a signal three-tenths of a second later. This effect has been used for identifying letters (Pollack, 1993).

There are several other attempts to control computers by thought. One approach is to analyze the EEG output. A computer could perhaps be trained to identify which EEG pattern corresponds to a particular thought. Japanese researchers have taught a computer to recognize a few words in this way. But such efforts can never be fully accurate, so limiting their uses (Thought control *New Scientist*, 1996, pp. 39–42).

The gradual encroachment of the artificial by direct biological interaction can also be illustrated by existing and incipient developments in electronic music. In the 1950s, musical instruments were electrified, in the 1970s came electronic synthesizers while the 1980s saw computer-composed and computer-played music. Now the step could be carried further whereby music responds directly to mind waves. This has been done through a system that acts on inputs of electrical brain waves. The device can be used for either switching on and off and controlling existing electronic instruments and systems or could in a crude way, be used to play music directly corresponding to brain rhythms (Atwood, 1996).

These types of mental control of, and inputs into computers, it should be noted, are still rudimentary and slow. And it is unlikely that, at least for the foreseeable future, detailed thoughts could be directly translated to computers (Pollack, 1993). However, limited applications of these results are foreseen, for example for severely handicapped people either to communicate with others or to operate appliances.

There are, thus, many emerging types of biosensors, from those built with specific organic molecules to even those using brain waves as inputs to computing devices. At the entry point of information into computers, an increasing merger of biology and computing is taking place.

The Brain as Scan

Biological models or biological elements that intrude into computer devices, and so help the merging of biological and computer information, have their opposites. These are computers that intrude either indirectly or directly into biological systems. These facilitate the intermingling of computer information and biological information either at the phenotypal or at the genetic level.

One such intrusion at the phenotypal level is through computerized images of the brain. Detailed studies of the brain have become possible by noninvasive techniques that use computer-based imaging. These include computerized tomography (CT) and nuclear magnetic resonance (NMR) (Kaminuma and Matsumoto, 1991, p. 40). Some of these imaging techniques using PET scans have even been able to show the particular parts of the brain that are being used when a particular thought is entertained. The system identifies where a word evokes activity in a particular segment of the brain by tracking the increased blood flow associated with those parts of the brain that are working (Hilts, 1991).

Computer-based imaging systems have also been increasingly used in surgical operations, especially on delicate ones that require precision which are difficult for a human surgeon to perform. Imaging data identify precisely where the surgeon should cut and intervene. The three-dimensional image that is generated allows a surgeon to see, e.g., a tumor from a variety of angles so that its exact position and condition are known before the incision is made (Corcoran, 1992). Before cutting soft tissue, surgeons can also practice on 3D software. This allows them to have a dry run without risk, and at minimum cost. Linking virtual reality with robotics would yield "telepresence," the ability to observe and manipulate things at a distance. With such an ability, it would be possible for a surgeon to operate on a patient remotely, literally thousands of miles away (Holusha, 1993).

In the future, with the increased precision available through computer-guided surgical tools, the act of surgery itself will be done largely through computerized systems.

Artefactual Inputs into Brains

We have described examples of outputs from biological organisms into computers. The reverse process of taking outputs from computers and feeding them into the nervous system is a much more difficult problem (Suran Goonatilake, 1991 a, p. 27).

Some of the incursions of computer systems into brains in the form of computer outputs such as numbers and images have already been referred to in the section on the merging of culture and artefact (See pp. 106–108). One such merger that takes an almost biological level as opposed to a cultural, abstract level is virtual reality.

Virtual reality in the way it feeds data into the brain has, in certain ways, parallels to a hallucinogenic world, that is a biologically felt reality. In fact, the LSD guru of the 1960s Timothy Leary was a strong advocate of VR (Suran Goonatilake, 1991 a, p. 27). But hallucigens are here replaced by *hallucigenres*. Even sex, in one of the ultimate technologies of the system, would be virtual. It would be done by slipping into a virtual reality body suit which would fit into one intimately, with microscopic actuators and sensors in all parts of the body suit (Milstead & Milhon, 1991). The partner lies elsewhere in cyberspace and fondles the computer-generated, tactile/visual/other senses image.

The direct feeding of computer information into brains occurs in several ways. These opposites of biosensors are thus electronic and computing devices that feed into the brain/neural system. Early examples are in common hearing aids that have been widely used for decades. These are the precursors of recent, more intrusive devices.

An example is chips that have been used to directly carry signals to the 32,000 nerve cells that send messages from the inner ear to the brain. A programmable speech processor analyzes sound signals that it receives from the listener's environment and then carries them through radio signals to an implanted chip. The chip receives these radio signals and carries them to a set of electrodes implanted in the cochlea, the inner ear. This system has been sufficiently successful to be able to make profoundly deaf people converse (Anderson 1989:38). Another more direct attempt at inputs to the brain aims at putting data directly into the neuronal system. Some experimenters have developed preliminary systems that feed video images directly into those who have lost their sight. Some are developing rudimentary direct electronic implants into the brain (*New Scientist*, 1996). In the future, similar chip-based prosthetics for a variety of sensors would be expected to intrude into the neural system.

The Human Genome Project and Computerization

The above examples of merging of biological and computer information through the medium of computer models and devices were at the indirect level of the phenotype. At the level of the genotype too, these processes take place at several indirect and direct levels.

With the Human Genome Project requiring the identification of hundreds of millions of genes, automated systems for analyzing gene sequences have become necessary. Major computer firms such as Microsoft are endowing departments of molecular biotechnology, precisely to further computer techniques in deciphering DNA. Hitherto, it had been biologists versed in computer software techniques that had developed techniques of gene sequencing. The belief has increased that only dual experts conversant with both genetic and computer information systems could design more efficient computer machinery for molecular work (Yang, 1992, pp. 73–76). With the genome project maturing, computer scientists are entering the field in droves to do the analysis and are moving into biology laboratories. This is turning biology into an information science (Kolata, 1996, pp. C1, C12).

Several companies have recently developed machines that automatically read nucleotides that makeup the double helix of DNA. These machines called DNA sequencers are capable of sequencing thousands of bases per second (Gaasterland and Sensen, 1996, pp. 76–78, Gwynne, 1996, pp. 41–42). In a related finding, techniques have been developed to sort out and purify chromosomes at a high speed (Gaasterland and Sensen, 1996, pp. 76–78; Gwynne, 1996, pp. 41–42).

Developments in various instrumentation techniques and chip technology have helped this automated sequencing. A robotic device has been developed as a work station that automates several chemical reactions usually done by technicians (Borman, 1989). To detect similarities and patterns in sequence data, a special integrated circuit chip, called the Biological Information Signal Processor (BISP) has been developed (Nishioka et al., 1995, pp. 335–338; Favello et al., 1995, pp. 551–569). An array of computer chips for scanning and integrating the nucleotides that will be identified in the project has been developed.

Two companies have built up a system called Fast Data Finder into whose chips are fed a stream of data, composed of the 4 letters (ACTH) which constitute the 4 bases of DNA. This data passes through 10 thousand processors and the system then identifies patterns of genetic material that have useful functions (Computer array *New Scientist*, 1989, p. 36). The system can also compare sequences that have been freshly found with existing databases to identify sections that match. Such matches lead to identification of the functions of the sequence. The system can go through a search of 27 million nucleotide bases in three seconds; other computerized systems of the early 1990s were taking anything between a few hours to several days to do the same feat (Computer array *New Scientist*, 1989, p. 36).

The sequences and other data obtained from these and other means would be stored in huge data bases. There are already international data bases that store and retrieve protein and DNA structural data — such as the sequence and three-dimensional structure of a genetic macro molecule. These existing services also include on-line access to the databases. These data bases have classified and stored data on such variables in the genetic field as polymorphism, gene-linkage data, laboratory material and practical details on genetic probes (Keen et al., 1996, pp. 13–16).

The data that is collected in the data banks is subjected to detailed analysis. Such analysis identifies functions of the different stretches of DNA. In fact, such analysis of DNA data using techniques familiar in other data fields has yielded interesting results. Thus, the genome has a preponderance of extra, so called 'junk' DNA which constitutes over 95% of the genome. It is usually assumed that this extra DNA has no function and is probably a relic of evolution, genetic garbage that has no use. But, this junk has been analyzed using computer-based cryptographic techniques. These analyses suggest that the 'extra' DNA could have a function very much like that of error correcting codes in standard cryptography. As a confirmation of this role, a researcher could predict 75% of parts of such error-correcting sections by the characteristics of the neighboring genetic material that code for the genes (Keen et al., 1996, pp. 13–16).

Computerized 'Dry' Manipulation of Genes

Experimental biochemists have usually dreamed up chemical reactions in their heads and carried them out "in the wet," to see whether their ideas actually worked. But now because of advances in computers, they can perform most of these reactions in the 'dry' using computational molecular biology. Computational molecular biology covers the entire field of computing dealing with protein and nucleic acid sequences (Fulton et al., 1995, pp. 571–582). These techniques have given rise to powerful methods of seeing biological molecules and identifying potential modalities of manipulating them.

There are programs available today that allow the drawing of recombinant DNA molecules even on a PC, helping biochemists to directly visualize the material they are working on (Fulton et al., 1995, pp. 571–582). A patent was given as far back as 1987 for AI-based methods to design new proteins using such techniques (Jones, 1987). Three-dimensional computer models of human protein molecules have also been made employing these methods. These allow the custom tailoring of particular drugs for particular diseases (Carpenter, 1989). And more recently, German scientists have used computer techniques to predict a chemical reaction, showing the ability to do chemistry at a virtual level (Emsley, 1992, p. 19).

The search for an efficacious cure in gene-associated therapy in a non-random way is to do systematic mass screenings, testing for likely solutions for a given medical problem by searching among a large number of possibilities, equivalent to searching for a needle in a haystack (Coghlan, 1993 b, pp. 26–31). Advances have been made in this field by again marrying computer technology with that of biology. Thus, it is possible to screen a database of commercially available chemical compounds to identify which of them would bind to various computer-generated molecular models of parasites like those associated with malaria and schistosomiasis. This means that possible inhibitors that fit into the niches and valleys of the target molecule can be identified rapidly (Fisher, 1993).

Peptides, specific amino acid sequences that bind to diseased cells are useful as a biotechnology therapy. But huge numbers of peptides have to be screened to identify the truly useful ones. Robots have now been used to create and test large numbers of peptides. AI software has also been used to explore molecular interactions and predict the exact peptide molecules that would work. This information interpreted through computers gives rise to a big leap in drug search (Fisher, 1992).

Commercially available software analyzes biologically active molecules and polymers, models them and designs others. The system provides valuable insights into biological systems. The use of neural networks has resulted in identification of microscopic biological elements such as leukocytes. Generally, a computerized system could process almost an infinite number of micro organisms much faster and at a lower cost than existing methods.

A team of scientists drawn from a variety of different fields including genetics and informatics, have been using some of these broad approaches to come up with an elegant and powerful scheme of screening based on chip technology. Such a micro chip of a size one centimeter square can synthesize and screen 65,000 compounds in 48 hours. This technology named "very large scale immobilized polymer synthesis" is ideal for uses such as in the Human Genome Project for accessing and storing data. As illustrative of the chip's potential for diagnoses, it is noted that such a chip could incorporate the 200 or so genetic mutations that cause cystic fibrosis, and this chip could then immediately say from a given sample of DNA whether one of the mutations were present (Coghlan, 1993 b, pp. 26–31).

Earlier, biochemists could not directly see the molecules that they were working on and so were partly handicapped. Recently, through computer technology, it has become possible to visualize atoms and molecules. Such computer graphics allow for visualization of the way antibodies target an invading molecule and the manner by which enzymes initiate a reaction.

The raw data for these visualization is usually provided by X-ray crystallography or Nuclear Magnetic Resonance (NMR) techniques. Other imaging techniques which are very powerful include scanning probe microscopy. The data supplied by these probes allow scientists to get detailed pictures of the largest macro molecules, such as enzymes, antibodies or even entire living micro entities such as viruses. The visualization allows the experimenter to see a molecule as a normal large macroscopic object, allowing the simulation of large reactions on the screen (Olson, 1992, pp. 76–81). Combining X-ray crystallography with a super computer helps scientists crawl inside molecules and identify their shapes, sizes and other characteristics. This allows structure-based drug design as a rational way to design drugs that fit into particular vulnerable niches and corners in biological molecules (Olson & Goodsell, 1992, pp. 76–81).

Similar properties allow for computer-aided molecular design, paralleling the techniques of Computer Aided Design (CAD) in regular industry. Computer analysis leads to more exact tailor making of new proteins, designing new drugs and useful micro organisms. These techniques have already been used in drug design for a variety of diseases such as forms of cancer, hypertension, glaucomas and AIDs (Olson ibid).

The field of molecular computer graphics is increasing very fast, paralleling the rapid increase in computer power. One of the very promising approaches uses virtual reality. Virtual reality increases enormously the ability to design complex molecules especially those dealing with life. The computer can generate in a set of virtual reality goggles, the likeness of three-dimensional molecules. Simulations based on virtual reality help the experimenter immerse him/herself in a tangible world of molecules with the feel and presence of the real world. The image projected on the three dimensional virtual reality video goggles changes as the head of the wearer moves around. This allows him by moving and changing his head to explore the various nooks and corners of the molecule, as if he were the size of a molecule and he himself were moving in and around it.

The use of force feedback technology tied to a data glove lets the researcher also feel the different forces acting on the different bonds of the molecule, allowing him to probe weak and strong spots. A computerized simulator that has been developed based on these principles allows possible drugs to be tested in a virtual sense by the virtual experimenter seeing and feeling how well they fit into a target site.

Newly developed electron microscopes based on holographic principles would also allow biologists to see and study biological molecules as they change from instant to instant (Brown, 1990, p. 30). By linking a virtual reality system to a scanning tunneling microscope, the chemist can not only see but also feel individual atoms and molecules as they are being probed by the microscope (Olson, and Goodsell, 1992, pp. 76–81). The scanning tunneling microscope when attached to the virtual reality display, gives the feel of real atoms as it moves around the by-ways of the structure of a molecule, not just the feel from a simulated model (Groping at Atoms *Economist*, 1992, pp. 87–88).

Computer-based virtual constructions of genes have come a long way. The promise in the immediate future is as newer techniques are developed for more intensive couplings of genetic systems and computers. A further more intensive development in this same direction is "Artificial Life."

Artificial Life

Artificial life — "A-Life" — is a new interdisciplinary field that studies biological processes by recreating biological phenomena within computer systems and other artefactual domains. Here, life is not considered a property of living systems alone, but a form of organization that can be realized in media other than biological matter. The logical form of life is thereby separated from the material basis of its construction (Emmeche, 1992). A-Life helps the study of these phenomena by constructing computer-based systems that behave like living organisms. By studying hypothetical systems with characteristics of living organisms, it raises the possibilities of different forms of "life-as-it-could-be."

Such synthetic work on biological systems is carried out, not only in the field of biology and the organic ("wet ware"), but also in computer-based hardware of robots and other life-like electro-mechanical constructs and also in software constructions of virtual biological entities. The A-Life field covers a wide range varying from the manufacture of self-replicating molecules to the evolution of self-replicating programs. The field includes computer viruses, as well as genetic algorithms and many other, not-so-familiar fields related to computer systems.

Artificial life pursuits include making animal-like robots — 'animats'. Like real insects some of these are not tightly programmed but are "let loose" after some preliminary programming to interact with the environment and learn through adaptation with it. Some animats in software format are simple, containing no more than 100 bits of information acting as genes and operating in a software world of food and simple organisms. When these programs are run over several days, the organisms increase their complexity by adding extra genetic material and hence the battery of responses to the environment — as it happens in normal biological evolution (Amato, 1990, p. 86).

An early A-Life type of program, VENUS was an open evolutionary system in which the human programmer did not restrict it by giving instructions on which directions evolution should move. The system decided for itself which of the infinite routes possible it would take. This program demonstrated important general characteristics of evolutionary systems, such as different conditions giving rise to different evolutionary paths and that small perturbations in the system and chance events could force major changes in evolution (Levy, 1993, p. 143). Illustrating the effects of evolution was a program by Richard Dawkins, the British evolutionary biologist. Working on a Macintosh, Dawkins wrote a computer program that utilized some of evolution's properties. His computer graphics program was populated by computer organisms called by him 'biomorphs'. The system, it was designed, would evolve by 'unnatural' selection, the human computer user deciding what was a desirable quality in a biomorph. Yet, the type of 'creatures' that eventually grew spontaneously out of the interaction between the program and its environment (namely the program operator) surprised Dawkins — a professional biologist — on the extent of its creativity (Levy, 1993, p. 143).

The first truly open-ended evolutionary system called Tiera was created by Thomas Ray. He initially injected the system with an organism called the 'Ancestor'. It soon displayed the general effects of evolution. Variations of the original system were evolving into better strategies for coping with the environment. It also showed the emergence of diversity. Later, having fed the system with products of earlier evolutionary runs, Ray saw the emergence of tens of thousands of genotypes. Series of definite 'eons' could also be observed in the system. This system also confirmed the emergence of punctuated equilibrium (Levy, 1993, p. 219).

Artificial life software programs have also been made that show the behavior patterns of ants, slime molds, growing animals and sea animals (Amato, 1990, p. 86). Other A-Life software mimics coevolution of parasites and host as well as the evolution of immune systems (Suran Goonatilake, 1991a, p. 32).

Danny Hills has used A-Life methods to develop programs through coevolution using a parasitic program. Such programs, he found, were very robust, unlike those written by humans. Hills also discovered that punctuated equilibrium was a feature of evolutionary processes

(Levy, 1993, pp. 189–211). Sims combined the approach of Dawkins in his biomorphs with genetic algorithms. The result was varieties of ecologies of artificial life (Levy, 1993, p. 212). Just as life emerged from the primeval soup through processes of self-organization, computer devices that are intensely interconnected would, according to A-Life theorists, generally tend to self-organize and give rise to 'life forms' hitherto unknown. Triggering mechanisms such as a hacker breaking into the system could spark off such spontaneous growth of life material (Suran Goonatilake, 1991b, p. 20).

Computer viruses are also in one sense, A-life forms. Discussions based on actual behavior of autonomous systems like computer viruses show that once such systems have emerged, they would not be subject to detailed control. In developing systems with biological characteristics one therefore creates an organism that operates according to its own requirements. These may not coincide with the interests of the designers. Such artificial biological systems would continuously discover innovative solutions. By attempting to increase evolutionary fitness, they would be guided solely by their own interest (Levy, 1993, p. 330).

Study of viruses could also lead to the evolution of entirely new designs of computers that are immune to them. In another direction, lessons learned from the release of computer viruses that become rapidly multiplying uncontrollable pests would have implications in the biological field, effecting plans for releasing new genetically engineered organisms into the environment (Thimbleby, 1991, pp. 111–114). The issues raised by "biological" problems in computer systems would benefit developments in biology (Thimbleby, 1991, pp. 111–114).

Artificial life raises issues in different disciplinary fields, such as philosophy of biology, philosophy of science, philosophy of mind and metaphysics (Bedau, 1992). As they deal with virtual life in electronic form, they illustrate, in the biology-to-computer direction the most developed form of the merging of biology and computing.

Of the three two-way mergings, genetic\cultural, cultural\artefactual and genetic\artefactual, the last is still in its infancy. But the intrusions of the biological into the artefactual and vice versa that we have documented show the potential for this merger (see Figure 8). As in other two-way mergers, biology-computer mergers occur as jostling

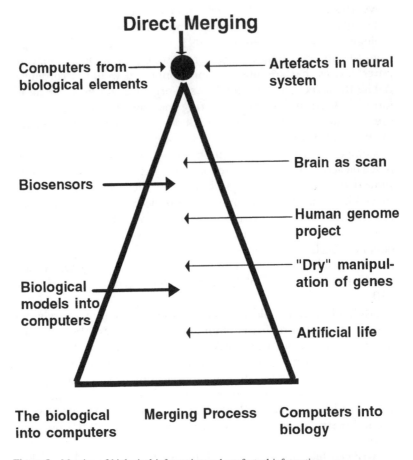

Figure 8 Merging of biological information and artefactual information

icebergs, the indirect interactions being as important as the direct mergers of the tips of the icebergs. In the coming years, when current work under way comes out of the labs, these biological-computer mergers would in many ways rival the other two merging systems.

SECTION 3

CONSEQUENCES

9: THE MACRO PROPERTIES OF MERGED EVOLUTION

Information technology and biotechnology, as they effect mergers between the three streams, will have a profound influence on both humans and nature. These influences will have both evolutionary and nonevolutionary aspects. Let us first begin with some of the nonevolutionary implications.

General Implications of Merging

Several observers have pointed out that the shift to newer technologies is accompanied by a diminution in both material and energy use (Larson et al., 1986, pp. 24–31; OECD,1989, p. 66; Junne et al., 1989, pp. 128–142). Information machines require far less energy and material than steel factories, steam engines, automobiles or other 19th and 20th century technologies. Further, information technology when incorporated within these other older technologies can make them run more efficiently with less material and energy use.

The shift to biotechnology — a shift of production to another set of information carriers, namely organisms — also means an array of new products and processes, not only in agriculture, but also in industry. The nature of agriculture could change significantly with biological means of fertilization, controlling pests and improving nutrition of plants, thus replacing current chemical means. Biological processes which use e.g., enzymes in industry including mining, would also result in far less material and energy use than do present alternatives.

At present, discussions on the stress on the global environment have been made on the relatively static picture of the predominance of 19th-century and early 20th-century technologies. The stress on the environment, because of production in agriculture and industry are very much contingent on the type of technologies used and their raw material and energy needs. Important in addition, are such associated factors as the nature of the waste products, the amount of heat dissipated and in broader terms, the entropy-generated through the production process.

The rate at which the shift to information and biotechnology takes place, and the pervasive nature of their impact have, therefore, a very strong bearing on the environmental stress on the globe, that is, on the relationships of humans to nature. The key factor for a drop in material and energy use in society will be the degree of shift in the composition of products and technological processes in the economy. When this composition shifts significantly towards chip-based and biotechnology-based products and processes, the shift will be towards less material and energy use.

Conventionally, a set of exponential growth curves in material and energy use are used to illustrate the reasons for a series of impending environmental disasters like erosion of global resources, carbon dioxide buildup, global warming, the thinning of the ozone layer, etc. But these curves assume current technologies. If one puts these exponential curves side by side with the exponential growth of the two new technologies with their reduced material and energy use, one gets a different, more dynamic picture. Two sets of exponential curves now contend for supremacy. A marked shift in the direction of the new technologies could very well tilt the material and energy stress towards less disastrous paths.

One of the perceived deleterious effects of economic activities is production of waste matter and heat. The concept of entropy has been used in discussions to describe such effects of waste products and heat that accompany human activity, and hence indirectly to describe the deleterious effects of exponential growth in conventional industrial economies. In an economy dealing with information-related products, the amount of information created is not necessarily related to a fixed amount of heat or of waste products. One can have increases of information with drops in energy and material use.

Thus, taking a biological example, a human brain which consumes less heat and material than an elephant's brain, is associated with far more complexity, organization and information content. A parallel in artefacts would be the different generations of chips. The later, more information-laden generations of chips are smaller but require the same order of magnitude of energy and material to manufacture and operate as the earlier, less information-laden generations. The implications of these two examples are that one could have increases in the information content on earth without a corresponding growth in either waste products or heat.

It should also be noted that through biotechnology, one could redesign organisms so that, for the same material input, one would have more of the products desired by humans, whether it be cereals, milk or medicines. (However, as a word of caution it should be noted that the introduction of biotechnology to agriculture could also add an increased stress on the biosphere by eroding biodiversity through the introduction of monocultures of the "most productive" plants.) Transferring these observations to the economy at large, one could state that different forms of organizing the economy and society with different mixes of technology could give rise to an ever-increasing information stock. Under this scenario, no limits seem to exist for continuous growth (except of course by erosion of biodiversity through the misuse of biotechnology). The growth will be largely in nonphysical artefacts, either biological or crystallized mind stuff in the form of information artefacts.

Nature and Volume of Information Shifts Between Lineages

If the three streams of information we have sketched are changing with respect to each other, can we have any measure either of their rates of growth or of their excision?

The rapid growth of machine information vis-à-vis the growth of cultural information that was already mentioned is also paralleled by other significant losses and gains in the other two information streams, namely the genetical and cultural.

The globalizing tendencies in the world occurring today which have been described by many writers are leading to a partial global culture. This emerging "global culture" is based largely on a hegemonic superimposition of largely Euro-American culture, legitimized and universalized across the globe.

The period prior to the modern age saw a relatively high degree of not only intraregional but also interregional discourse, for example between West Asia, South Asia and East Asia. This has now changed. These prior regional exchanges are now diminishing and the present interregional cultural exchanges are themselves partially becoming variants of exchanges within Euro-America. In addition, within the different non-European civilizational regions, (as well as within those not normally considered "civilizations"), there are fewer carriers of indigenous cultural information. These carriers include regional classical scholars and philosophers — the human repositories of millennia of serious non-European discourse. These also include the knowledge carriers of smaller groups such as hunter gatherers, pastoralists and shamans. In this generation, we are probably seeing the last of many of these latter carriers of non-Euro-American cultural information (Christopher, 1991, pp. 36–40).

This cultural information of a "civilizational" nature that is lost as well as that of the smaller groups, is not all in the realm of magic, spurious, or without practical or conceptual use. Considerable areas of physical reality have been explored within these human groupings, as exemplified by the knowledge held by e.g., shamans of medicinal and nutritional usages of plants. On the other hand, the civilizational knowledge systems possess valid areas of exploration in psychology, medicine, mathematics and ecology, to name a few areas from the Asian traditions.

The erosion of both this non-European cultural information, as well as of their human carriers is also probably occurring exponentially. Although there are incipient attempts to retrieve some of this knowledge by gathering the knowledge of forest peoples and burgeoning attempts at East-West comparative sciences, the overall thrust is towards a rapid and exponential erosion of the knowledge.

The erosion of local cultures and the parallel globalization process are occurring today amidst several ethnic revolts in the globe. These insurgencies are occurring within the globalizing tendencies at a time of the emasculation of local knowledge and culture, vis-à-vis the global system.

We can drive to a logical head these twin processes in local and global cultural information, by tracing an imaginary scenario, by imagining that in 20 years' time, most of the cultural entities now in revolt had obtained their goals. If we were then to measure the content of knowledge that would be transmitted to the children of these groups, one would notice that the largest content would very probably be that pertaining to the globalizing culture. This would include, for example mathematics and the sciences, as well as other less edifying aspects of the globalizing culture. It is this globalizing knowledge that is increasing at an exponential rate while the local knowledge at the same time is growing proportionately smaller. These two sets of local and global knowledge have their counterparts in uses in the biological sphere including in biotechnology.

Developing new biotechnology material requires access to a variety of useful genes. Plants that are unknown in developed countries have many uses which have been identified over the centuries by farmers and traditional medical practitioners across the world. Part of this knowledge is now being gathered by pharmarceutical multinationals, the plants and their properties identified, and later, the particular gene responsible for a desired property isolated to be incorporated in a new genetically engineered plant. This plant is then patented and sold as seed, possibly also to the same groups that had identified the desired trait in the first place (Juma, 1989). This is the current battleground of patent rights versus what has been termed "farmers' rights." In the process, there is a transfer of local cultural information to the global one, which also accompanies and leads to a transfer of naturally occurring biological information to a new, biotechnologically created form.

The exponential erosion of cultural information in the non-Euro-American domain is also paralleled by an erosion in the genetic sphere. This elimination, also rapid and probably exponential, is occurring largely in the areas of habitation of those very peoples whose cultural information is being eroded, namely within and around the tropics.

The possibility of transfers of information from one lineage to another, and the consequent enlargement and/or erosion of particular lineages, raises the question of the extent of possible transfers to the artefactual realm, and even the possibility of packaging in an electronic form the totality of information on earth.

Such a project in biology of transferring genetic information to artefactual information would imply, e.g., the possible reading of all the genetic sequences in all the organisms on earth and transferring this information to data bases, paralleling on a much wider scale, the current attempts in the Human Genome Project. Such a project may not sound entirely far-fetched.

Thus, there is a large degree of overlap in the genetic information of different organisms (for example, we as humans share over 99% of our genes with chimpanzees and about 40% with those of plants). We have about hundred thousand genes with three billion base pairs and it may be possible that the total genetic information on earth may be several orders bigger than this, but not an astronomically higher order of magnitude. Given the fact that the genome sequencing is increasingly seen as a highly automated, AI-driven project, it may not, therefore, be entirely fanciful to think of capturing this genetic information in electronic form.

Current silicon-based electronic devices are reaching their limits and laboratories around the world are exploring several avenues for still smaller storage devices. These include not only devices that operate at the level of atoms (nano technology) but also those that would do so at the level of an electron. These technologies would provide for the packing of enormous amounts of data in very minuscule areas. A not so fanciful question would then be, can one transfer the total genetic heritage of earth into the size of a large building? to a room? to a table drawer? to a match box? the rain-forest on a match-stick head?

Yet, a word of caution, the prevailing rather simplistic dogma asserts that DNA simply maps one-to-one to the phenotype. It does not deal with the internal dynamics of the genome, which probably is a very complex system. This idea of capturing the rainforest on a match-stick is a partial reading, a reductionist image of DNA. But, on the other hand, it may not be entirely fanciful to capture at least some of the internal dynamics of the genome in computer form.

However, another word of caution. The rainforest is not a set of iso-lated genes, not even a set of individual trees that has grown after being expressed through the dynamics of genes. It is an ecosystem, an inter-acting society of trees (and insects and animals) if you will; where one organism influences another on a day-to-day basis and the long term fate of their species is decided through processes of coevolution. And so, capturing the rainforest's information would mean capturing these dy-namics. This is an information problem of a different order, parallel to the difference, in the case of humans, between psychological models of human dynamics when only the individual is considered and sociological models where the emphasis is on the collectivity of individuals.

In the 18th century, Diderot and the Encyclopeadists had the then, far-fetched dream of capturing all existing knowledge (Dizardt, 1982). Speaking of his Encyclopedia Dennis, Diderot wished:

> to collect all the knowledge scattered over the face of the earth, to present its general outlines and structure to the men with whom we live, and to transmit this to those who will come after us, so that the work of the past centuries may be useful to the following centuries, that our children, by becoming more educated, may at the same time become more virtuous and happier, and that we may not die without having deserved well of the human race (Horton, 1983, p. 67).

Today, the technology exists even without the emerging high density storage devices for total bibliographical control and to have virtually instantaneous and total access to almost the entire formal written in-formation system. The dreams of Diderot according to information specialists may now be thus on the verge of realization as far as Western written cultural knowledge is concerned (Horton ibid). So, perhaps it may not be entirely that fanciful to imagine capturing all the formal cultural information on earth.

Current transfers of information between the different lineages have their biggest barriers in the transfer of cultural information to an autonomous artefactual information processing system, as opposed to just recording that information in artefactual format. The domain of AI is still at an infant stage. Natural language discourse and common-sensical reasoning, as opposed to formal descriptions in science and mathematics, constitute the bulk of cultural information. It is in these areas that AI is facing the greatest challenges. The time a P.C. could read a novel and engage in a discussion of it with a human, (as opposed to other acts, such as a computer interrogating data bases) seems to be in the future.

Yet, information transfers between the artefactual, the cultural, and the genetic would continue to increase, providing for dynamic information flows from one realm to the other. Some information gets translated from one stream to another giving rise to cross lineage circulation of information and of mergers. Some transferer grow exponentially, others get excised. Some can be saved by translation, some lose part of their value in translation. Some grow by processes of merging. The various outcomes of the different information shifts and mergers on earth will be seen as the result of the attendant dynamics of the information streams.

Interactions Between all the Three Streams

The previous chapters have shown how, although the three lineages have existed in isolation up to the present, they are now becoming merged. Through the new technologies, information from one stream is ferried across to another and made to merge. Information in the three streams now becomes translatable into one other, and information as an entity becomes a common currency of discourse between the three realms. These three-way interactions require further descriptions.

In the mergings between the two non-cultural streams there is initially, always a silent partner in the form of culture. So the incursions of the genetic to the artefactual for example, are at least initially, incursions from the cultural, to the genetic, then to the artefactual. It is culture, and cultural information that gives the initial template for the transfers between the other two. In that sense, what occurs in such transfers is also actually a partial merging of information from all three sources. One can give several examples of these implicit as well as more direct transfers between all three.

Thus, one can give the example of the analysis of the genome data bases which use techniques drawn from linguistics, a field of culture analysis. Generally, linguistic metaphors have been central to some of the key concepts of molecular biology. Thus geneticists speak of the *code* of the genetic system, the *expression* of genes, the *reading frames* in nucleic acids, *transcribing* of DNA to RNA, *translations* of the latter to proteins and the *editing* of RNA (Searls, 1992, pp. 579–592). At a more direct level the approaches of Chomsky, who wrought a revolution in linguistics at the same time as the molecular revolution was taking hold in the 1950s and 1960s, have been recently applied to the information structures of the DNA molecule. The use of such linguistic analysis would lead to a "knowledge of the linguistic structure of the genome." The aim is for a computer program that parses and identifies genes and other higher-level features of DNA (Searls ibid). Here, artefactual, genetic and cultural information, all three interact.

In the computer field, as we have already noted, the cultural definition of how a neuron works has been simplified and realized partly as neural networks. Hebbs' model of brain learning, a cultural construct was transferred into the design of the "Perceptron" an early connectionist device which was not a success because of the inadequacy of the hardware available then. In more recent years, computer scientists have reached the goals of the Perceptron, through neural networks. But now, the cycle having gone full circle, interconnected neural networks themselves are being used to study the brain by considering them as a model for the brain (Hinton, 1992, pp. 145–151). A process of mutual circular feedback has taken place between the biological, cultural and artefactual realms.

In genetic algorithms, a cultural description of how biological evolution works has been applied in the computer realm. Here, the principle of exchanges among chromosomes leading to new genetic configurations, which are then tested against the environment, is applied to the machine realm. Strings of programming code which take the place of chromosomes are exchanged and allowed to evolve to an acceptable solution. The "acceptability" of the solution is determined by humans on their cultural frames of reference. Another example of the intimate intermingling of all three information streams results.

But, one could extend the power of this intermingling further from the pure, artefactual genetic algorithm into the direct biological field. One could now imagine that the strings of computer program that are made to evolve to a solution, actually also code for <u>genetic</u> information and <u>genetic</u> processes, so that the software solutions now become solutions for a desired genetic outcome. One could then conceive of biological, genetic solutions being arrived at on dry runs in computer form by getting the strings of programs to actually code for genetic information so that the solution arrived at becomes, in fact, a solution in biology. Such an eventuality would result in dry runs in biology; for evolution in biology to be speeded up and then only the end result of what would have normally taken millions of years delivered after only a few hours of computer runs, to be then realized in biological form as an organism.

In this example, genetic information translated into the artefactual realm is made to evolve into a culturally acceptable biological solution much more rapidly than biological evolution by itself would. And, the resulting solution is then fed back from the computer form into a new genetic product. The genetic, the artefactual and the cultural now interact with each other intensely, directly and in very intimate ways. Histories of culture, gene and artefact now become inseparable in the process. This process can be further realized in "Artificial Life".

In "Artificial Life," life processes are mimicked at a computer, symbolic level. Various cultural definitions of life modeled after biological systems are created on the computer and allowed to develop. Some of these are entirely new "life forms" that are unknown to carbon-based life. In fact, artificial life defines itself as being not limited to a carbon-based definition of life. One can now envisage different artificial life forms being developed on the computer and their characteristics then translated into genetic characteristics, to be realized in the genetic stream. In this case too, the genetic, the artefactual and the cultural merge and interact with each other intensely.

Computers, including those with AI characteristics are being increasingly used in the genetic field to identify, store and analyze genetic information. These vary from the use of computer graphics to picture the molecular structure of genes, to the massive use in the Human Genome Project to identify, analyze, sequence and store genetic information (Favello et al., 1995, pp. 571–582). At the initial stages there would be a human intermediary in such mergings, but increasingly the mass of data and the complexity involved, as in the genome project, would involve using autonomous techniques which would increasingly make humans tangential to the process. In such a case, the identification of a phenotypal characteristic to be eliminated or enhanced would be done through automatic analysis. And in addition, the search in a data base for the required gene to be spliced-in, as well as the act of splicing-in too, could be automated.

After the major genome projects under way are completed, the identification and merging of gene sequences would be for many purposes, done by nonhuman means (Gaasterland et al., 1996, pp. 76–78). Increasingly, genetic information in computers would be scientifically manipulated in a computer form. And, "virtual" genetic products would be then created on computers before being actually expressed in biological, "wet ware" form.

One could, in fact, conceive of a nearly fully automated system occurring through developments of present day Computer Integrated Manufacture (CIM) techniques being extended to the genetic field. In CIM, the integration of the material flow in a production process with the information flow associated with it occurs through computers (Hitomi, 1990). The linking of CIM techniques into the field of life-related production activities has already been attempted in manufacturing systems for pharmaceuticals in a system that links computer-based information control and management together with computer-integrated manufacturing (CIM).

Application of a CIM system to genetic engineering would mean that through a data base, automatic means would (or to a larger extent help) do the design (in this case the genetic design), planning, as well as the actual 'manufacture' itself. It is not also far fetched to imagine the phenotypal characteristic of the product to be manufactured desired by a person or population being itself reached through artefactual information means by using a market research system that is heavily based on computer data bases.

But these market preferences across the globe also reflect broader cultural differences. An illustrative indicator of such differences would be that of gender. Gender roles are constructed historically and vary from society to society, from period to period. What are considered feminine or masculine traits also vary from society to society. They are therefore very plastic. Thus, in South Asia, the classical male roles have by contemporary Western standards many 'effeminate' characteristics that emphasize sympathy, empathy, understanding, intitutiveness and reflection. So, the plasticity of gender definition (and cultural preferences in general) match the plasticity of the computer. Market forces around the world would reflect this plasticity and give forth niches in the market to be commercially exploited. In the new technology-driven biological system, market niches — which one should remember are in fact also cultural niches — would supplement the traditional physical niches into which Darwinian evolution hitherto adapted.

The output of the market research — that is, of cultural preferences and hence the resulting cultural information — would, in the hypothetical automated manufacturing system feed into the genetic equivalents of Computer Aided Design (CAD) and Computer Aided Manufacture (CAM). The latter two could extensively use such adaptive, autonomous systems as neural networks and genetic algorithms and perform their work interacting with the massive data bases of the genome project. Computer-based, intensive market research would then feed the CIM stage, giving rise to a highly integrated, near seamless merging of cultural, artefactual and genetic information. Such a process would be the outcome of communications and profound 'conversations' between the three lineages in their interactions with their environments.

The use of suitable proteins which are naturally occurring compounds encoded by the body's DNA is a main cornerstone of biotechnology work. The discovery of suitable proteins is a time-consuming process requiring testing of a few thousand proteins a year. This protein discovery process has been speeded up through a new method called directed molecular evolutionism. Using this technique, it is possible to randomly mutate proteins millions of times in a few weeks. This process using Darwinian selection at the molecular level allows for the faster selection of suitable proteins. It is literally possible to test 10 million proteins for ten times the cost of testing just one (Molecular Evolution, July 12, 1993). This is a case of a culture-chosen and therefore culture-embedded biological molecule, evolving.

What happens now when these "molecules" are not real chemical ones, but computer generated images? The evolutionary process now takes place at a virtual level. Biological material, culture, and artefactual information now evolve merged together. Thereby, there is once again an accelerated merged evolution of genes, culture and artefact.

Although it is the culture of biotechnological science or computer science that gets directly merged in these merging processes, there are indirect mergers of other aspects of culture. One important merged cultural element is aesthetics — and through it the arts in general are brought into the process of merging.

Mention was made earlier in Chapter 2 of the intimate relationship that aesthetic factors bring to science at its creative moments. Aesthetics and the fine arts form part of humankind's cultural information continuum. They stand beside scientific information as an important part of the battery of intervention mechanisms that humans have with their environment. In an integrated, merged system the aesthetic factor affects biotechnology and information technology in their respective interventions with the environment. Thus, aesthetics helps visualize particular structures in molecules, as well as design better computer hardware and software.

Computers have been used widely in art and design (Lansdown and Earnshaw, 1989). There are even programs that help persons manipulate text to give some readable poetry. They scramble and recombine words to some degree of sophistication (Pinsky, 1995). These aesthetic approaches can come into use in those computer techniques that help design different molecules of genes and proteins. Visual aesthetic criteria would come explicitly or implicitly into such designs.

Using virtual reality systems, wearing a data glove for example, a biologist could also get the feel in his muscles of different molecules as well as the strengths of the various molecular forces that bind them together. In this type of muscle-flexing exercise, another set of aesthetic criteria, that of body movements, can help sculpt desired molecules. These could include aesthetics used in enterprises that deal with the art and science of body movements such as dance, Yoga or Chinese Qi Gong exercises.

In a merged system, aesthetics could be not only an input into the merging but also an output. Thus, efforts have been made to transfer DNA sequences into music formats through computer mediation (Weiss, 1992). This has an echo of the music of the celestial spheres of previous centuries that gave an insight for early astronomers into the workings of the solar system. Music arising from a different set of spheres, that of atoms in a genome, could well yield tunes that would give a clue to their molecular patterns, in the same manner that visual cues now yield structures of biomolecules. In picturing and modeling desired biological systems, the biotechnologist could bring a whole battery of aesthetic criteria covering a variety of senses from the visual to the tactile to the aural.

The best human/computer interface for direct transfer of information is that of virtual reality. One could eventually imagine a fully merged system where a human traverses virtual reality exploring different parts of the merged system. In the process, s/he becomes influenced by and in turn influences the biological and the artefactual, the other parts of the total system. In the ultimate, it is possible to think of a near seamlessly linked system where the different boundaries between the three streams are traversed so easily that they seem to vanish. In such a system, aesthetics becomes biology, then converts to an intelligent matrix in an artefact or vice versa. A change in one is reflected in the other stream. Let us increase the possible permutations.

Serious funds have recently been devoted by Britain's leading telecommunications company, British Telecom, that hopes to capture the entire experience of an individual as it is lived. The idea is to have a tiny implanted chip in the eye that would catch and store every experience of the individual. Extrapolating from current trends in miniaturization (increasing by a factor of one hundred every ten years), the technology would exist in a generation's time to do this cheaply. It would store a lifetime's data, which it has been calculated would fall well within emerging technology capacity. It would be possible for a person to relive other people's experiences by such means, or for that matter for the same individual too to relive the same forgotten experiences (Miller and O'neill, 1996; Gross, 1996, p. 81). So merging of past subjectivity and present experience, of human thought and computer memory, becomes another strong potential addition to the mix.

The aesthetic, in the ultimate extrapolation of this train of possibilities becomes through this intimate play of computer techniques and biology, an integral part of the whole merged system. Here, a past memory, a present thought, a poem, a dab of paint or a soft tune turns, in a sense, into a computer artefact or organism. And, extrapolating some of the incipient work that lets computers be partially controlled by brain waves, one could in an extended system (pushing the idea to an ultimate, extreme conclusion) transfer thought patterns directly into life forms.

In such an extreme system, one plays music (or for that matter, another aesthetic frame) and creates a symphony of life forms or artificial intelligences. The music (and dance) becomes through the transformation, a music (and dance) of the genes, giving rise to myriad life forms. In such a context of near cosmic creativity, one could well quote from the Bhagavat Gita as illustration of the process:

I am Life and Death;
I am the Fountain and the Seed Imperishable;
....
My celestial forms, by hundreds and thousands,
Various in kind, in color and in shape. (Shri Purohit Swami, 1977, pp. 89, 106)

Such a god-like view symbolizes the perspective from one temporary information packet marveling at what could be done from the new merged environment. This sense of omniscience is but a view from one subjectivity, from one individual, from one temporary packet of information. Similar 'senses' of wonder could be experienced from the subjectivity of packets of information in other lineages. So the 'god-like' possibilities in different perspectives exist in all the three realms.

But, could, because of the power of the technology also for deep negative human impact, the more appropriate quotation from the Bhagavat Gita be not one of exuberance but one of doom in the form of the words that went through the head of Robert Oppenheimer (Lawren, 1988, p. 215), the chief of the Manhattan Project at the dawn of another powerful technology when the first flash of the atom bomb lit up the Nevada skyline in 1945: "I am become death, the destroyer of worlds"

With the potential for a wide range of outcomes in merged evolution, a key question becomes what would ensue, celestial dance or destructive fury? With such a fluid situation, in what direction would the merged system move? Are there any parallels that can act as a guide in such situations of seeming openness, where tradition and history have seemingly broken down, and where apparently everything seemingly goes? Two other examples where this situation has also apparently occurred are in contemporary fashion and modern art.

Contemporary fashion must incessantly invent new designs for the market. Here everything is potentially possible and creativity is potentially very open. But creativity in fashion however is not random. It is constrained by the interlocking interests and pressures of markets, advertising, cultural histories and whims of designers.

Another parallel is with modern art. Over the last hundred years, almost every possible permutation and combination has been experimented with in Western art. Western art has been broken down to its perceived essentials, then reassembled several times in new formats: Impressionism, Post Impressionism, Cubism, Futurism, Expressionism, Dadaism, Surrealism, Abstract Expressionism, Pop Art, Minimalism; the list is large and constantly being added to. In the process, art has turned sometimes even to its opposite — anti-art, and to the blank canvas of no-art. Could this be the future for merged evolution, when everything is possible, when seeming randomness becomes the order.

But everything in that sense is possible not only in the realm of the cultural lineages in fashion and art. It has also been possible for at least one other lineage, namely the biological. Randomness created by mutations is the daily reality of the biological process. Chance and necessity have driven the biological machine forward through evolution. Randomness and variety have provided the wherewithal for the creation of order in biology.

The lesson is that seeming randomness does not result in an evolutionary trajectory that lacks direction. The wide range of possible outcomes in the new merged evolution will also be governed by similar considerations. Random mergers are possible here, the future remains open but would be restrained by the past. As in all evolutionary processes, there is a broad directionality for merged evolution too. The broad directionality is governed by the dynamic processes underlying the mergers themselves.

The Dynamics of Merged Evolution

The dynamics of these three lineages are driven by the interaction of their information streams with their environments. The environment, it should be noted, consists of both a physical as well as an information environment. In the case of biological systems, the latter information environment consist of information-embedded organisms such as other plants or animals with which the particular organism interacts. In the case of human culture, it is other humans. In the case of computers and AI devices, other computers.

As they flow onwards, the lineages create novel arrangements and interactions with their environments. The different arrangements constitute different windows to the external world. They bifurcate and speciate as they interact with their environments. In interacting with the environment, those flow lineages that cannot adapt to the environment are eliminated; and those that adapt well and/or are neutral to the environment, survive and continue. Speciation in lineages does not necessarily develop smoothly. Sometimes, there are disjunctures and sudden breaks at the speciating points.

The evolving three streams, it should also be noted, are governed by a deeper engine of changes in entropy. This approach to evolution ultimately rests on Prigogine's studies of thermodynamics of open systems. Each lineage seems to act as an open system, importing matter and energy and exporting entropy. They tend to self-organize through interactions with their different environments. The sudden disjunctures that they sometimes undergo are reminiscent of the dissipative structures that bifurcate at far-from- equilibrium points which Prigogine has described (Susantha Goonatilake, 1991, pp. 140–167). The general thrust of entropic arguments in evolution in the three realms have been detailed by several writers on biology (Brooks and Wiley, 1986; Jantsch, 1976), and on the economy and society (Boulding, 1976; Malaska, 1985; Allen, 1985).

There is a definite time sequence in the three lineages. The exosomatic, artefactual one comes after the cultural; and the cultural, in turn, comes after the genetic. The different lineage systems, whether they be genetic, cultural or exosomatic form a nested hierarchy. Thus, the genetic is nested within the cultural, and the latter is nested within the exosomatic. The exosomatic, therefore has nested within it, both the cultural and the genetic flow systems, the latter forming the inner core of the nest (see Figure 9) (Susantha Goonatilake, 1991, pp. 131–135).

Yet, all genetic systems do not have cultural envelopes; only a few species in the animal kingdom have cultural systems that pass learned information down the generations. And of these few, only humans have the latest outer layer of information artefacts. And of all the many human cultures that have bifurcated into a tree-like set of human subcultures, only a few have attached exosomatic systems. The subcultures with artefactual information are increasing with the explosive spread of computing artefacts. But even in the most computer-penetrated of societies, there would still be groups that would lead lives tangential to the artefactual realm.

Each lineage has been "externalized" from its inner core out of evolutionary needs. These evolutionary needs result in an outer lineage in the nest being more responsive and quicker to adapt to the environment than an inner one. The lineage of genes gave rise to an additional 'outer' lineage of culture. And, through the course of evolutionary time, so did in turn the lineage of culture give rise to an 'exosomatic' lineage of information artefacts. The evolutionary logic was the same in both the cases. The new additional information 'envelope' allowed for an increase in adaptability to the environment, a richer and faster interaction with it. The different lineages are therefore not there by accident, they are inexorably linked together.

Given sufficient evolutionary time, and suitable environmental pressure, the externalizing of the genetic to the neural lineage and from there, to the artefactual must occur. It is a phylogenetic <u>necessity</u> arising from interactions with the environment. It is a continuing process of reacting with, and adapting to the environment resulting in more flexible and quicker responses to the environment.

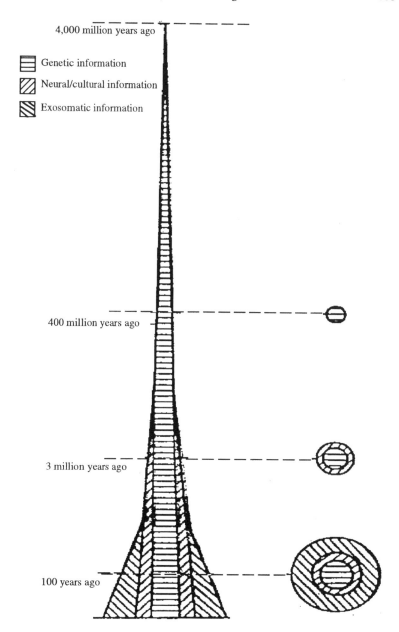

Figure 9 Some stages in the evolution of information envelopes

The three nested lineages also have different time perspectives in their interactions with the environment. The death of a genetic lineage is counted in millions of years, a very long life (Dawkins, 1976, pp. 21–26). The survivability of cultural information on the other hand is measured probably in the tens of thousands of years for central items of information and thousands or hundreds for less core information. Change in the artefactual lineage is much faster; the whole store in a computer can be wiped clean in a few micro seconds. The survival time of unchanged information is consequently longer in an inner core than in an outer core. Genetic information generally survives longer than the cultural, and cultural information, longer than the exosomatic.

The cultural system adapts to an environment much more rapidly than a genetic core; and in turn, the exosomatic nest reacts more rapidly than the cultural. Thus, an inner core works on a longer time perspective than an outer core. In reacting with the environment, an inner core changes its make-up and internal information structure more slowly than an outer core (Susantha Goonatilake, 1991, pp. 131–135). The nested lineages also vary as to their degrees of rigidity and flexibility. An inner core (e.g., the genetic) is less flexible than an outer one (e.g., the cultural).

There is also a set of cross influences within these nests. Thus genes operate on their culture through a biological system, the brain. Culture, in turn, operates and influences the artefactual. The outer container thus becomes a partial operational arena for the inner core.

Because the cultural lineage is nested within the biological, the biological setting gives some experiential limits on culture. For example, biology limits what our eyes can see in the electromagnetic spectrum. Culture, however, also allows one to spill over the limits of biology, as for example it does when it conceptualizes, without experiencing directly, the spectra beyond the visible. But still, the genetic gives some limits to cultural responses, it is, as it were the "hand-in-the-glove-puppet" of culture.

In a similar fashion to the role of genes in culture, culture in turn initially gives the preliminary form to artefactual information. Humans design the hardware and software. But the artefactual realm is becoming more autonomous with the newer technologies. Even then the human cultural imprint would still remain within the artefact, — again, like a hand in a glove.

In the evolutionary process, "scars" of earlier encounters with the environment encoded in the information stream remain as past cognitive structures, as historically constructed world views and these limit the flexibility that is possible. The later, more flexible lineages carry the imprint of the inner core which partially guides the outer lineage. Thus, in the latest envelope, the computer system, 'ghosts' of past genetic and cultural experience haunt and steer it. Four billion years of genetic life, and ten thousand years of cultural life stand as a back-drop to the information content of the latest chip and its software. An inner core limits the nature of responses of an outer core to changes in the environment (Susantha Goonatilake, 1991, pp. 131–135).

Summing up, what has been said in earlier chapters all three lineages have, the properties of conservation and novelty creation, speciation and integration; "egocentricity," nestedness of the different lineages, differing flexibilities in the nested lineages, varying reaction times of the different lineages to changes in the environment, differing survival times of the information lineage, co-evolution and, above all, a general time directionality. The lineages, in a process of self-organizing, also undergo what has been called 'autopeosis'.

Many of these characteristics of the individual lineages are deeply changed by the new interactions between them wrought by the two new technologies (see Figure 10).

Changes Through the Mergers

In all the three individual streams there was conservation of information from each lineage's past heritage. Information structures accumulated earlier, connected present information structures with the past (Susantha Goonatilake, 1991, pp. 121–123).

When the three lineages intermingle, this continuity with a past information structure is disturbed. Thus in biology, a species defined the integrity of a particular sublineage. Information could not cross the species boundary, and there was no interbreeding between species. When transgenic information transfers are made through biotechnology, this species integrity is broken. Conservativeness of past information still exists, but presents itself outside a [sub] lineage. Further, the transgenic mixing is done — at least initially — through another lineage — culture, cultural information providing the initial template for the mixture.

The merging through the new technologies also changes the hierarchy of reaction times between the three nested lineages; and the associated survivability of information gets disturbed. The later lineage whether it be culture or artefact was faster than the earlier one, whether

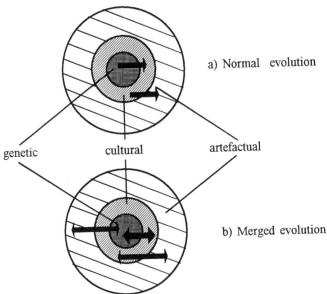

a) Normal evolution

genetic   cultural   artefactual

b) Merged evolution

Note : Arrows show direction of flows

Figure 10   Cross-envelope information flows

it be gene or culture. With the merging, this sequence of reaction times is disturbed. Because of influences from the outer elements (respectively genetic and cultural), evolution in the individual lineages becomes faster. Genetic information changes faster now with cultural and artefactual information incursions, and cultural information changes faster with artefactual information incursions.

Also, as a consequence, the information from the outer layer which had a relatively shorter life time, now lives longer in the inner one. So, artefactual information lives longer when embedded in cultural information, cultural information lives longer when embedded in genetic information and artefactual information lives longer than cultural information when embedded in genetic artefacts.

In becoming a single evolving whole, the historical sequence of biology giving rise to culture, giving rise to artefact and each inner core lineage acting as it were a 'hand-in-a-glove' becomes changed. Being its inner core, genes constitute the partial "hand-in-the-glove" of cultural information. In the same way, culture is partially the hand in the "glove-puppet" of artefactual information. This means that when the mixing of genes into new combinations is done through artefactual information, it is indirectly done through culture, which in turn is influenced by genes. The artefact now reaches back and changes culture or gene, culture reaches back and changes the gene, the glove turns back and changes the hand.

Instead of a unilinear sequence of cores and envelopes, recursive loops between them are established. Genes now reach back indirectly through the chain of culture and artefact and through them partly redirect their own mixing. Similar recursive loops occur for example from culture to artefact alone, when say a CAD system's output helps a human to change the CAD system's design. These recursive loops help bind the three streams together. They also now become determinants of evolution in all three lineages.

Particular means of dealing with the environment have been ingrained in the lineages through their particular histories. These characteristics are conserved and passed onwards into the future. On the other hand, with changing circumstances, novelty is also created within the flow system giving rise, for example, in biology to mutants. However, in the new lineages' admixture, novelty is also created from novel combinations of lineages. Novelty here is achieved primarily by reshuffling past information across the three lineages.

Phylogenesis of the different lineages is also effected. Earlier, as in biology systems, a phylogenetic tendency for greater diversity and greater and greater information existed (Holzmuller, 1984). This phylogenetic tendency is now increased, as a greater shuffling of information is now possible, leaving room for more combinations. This would be like the introduction of sexual reproduction in evolution which brought in a greater shuffling of genetic material. The rate of evolution would be speeded up analogous to the speeding up of evolution which was brought about by the introduction of sexual reproduction in the biological field. The information contents of the three lineages are now to be viewed as a single reservoir of information whose shuffling yields entirely new patterns.

Evolving Epistemologies

The different lineages in interactions with their environments have particularly structured windows to the outside world. Their characteristics are best described through the emerging perspectives of "evolutionary epistemology."

Evolutionary epistemology has a central tenet which states that not only does evolution produce cognitive phenomena, but that evolution itself can be described as a process of acquiring cognition (Wuketits, 1990, p. 53). Bio-epistemology describes the coming of cognitive structures in the biological field, from the most primitive of organisms to the most sophisticated (Wuketits, 1990, p. 53).

The biologist Konrad Lorenz pointed out that structural features that characterized the living world encoded the world, that is encoded the environment within which the organism lived. For instance, the shape of the fish encompasses the nature of the fluid environment in which it lives, as does the structure of its eyes. So, the fin and eye of a fish are adapted to living in water as are the wing and eye of a bird to flight (Hahlweg and Hooker, 1989, pp. 25–30).

This mapping of the environment in the organism can be demonstrated by the manner in which photosynthesis and vision coevolved together. The world is visually sampled by creatures using only a small and a particular part of the electromagnetic spectrum. Wachtershauser has shown how at the beginning of life on earth the process of photosynthesis itself sampled and was locked into this spectrum and correlating it with food. Generally, complex molecules are broken down by the electromagnetic spectrum, so emerging life forms had to find and stay within a spot of optimum radiation. The early photosynthesizers, therefore, survived within a very narrow niche of the electromagnetic spectrum. Wachtershauser traces the evolution of vision to sample this particular part of the spectrum, and observes that vision is but a coninuation of this early tracking (Wachtershauser, 1987, pp. 121–137).

Generally, the experience of all animals is colored by the historical spectacles that are built into them, which have grown up through evolution. These congeal the experiences of a species, and of the legacy of earlier species which had gone before it (Hahlweg and Hooker, 1989, pp. 25–30). Thus humans' biological spectacles are governed by the 1% of genes that are unique to them, as well as the 99% of genes that they have in common with chimpanzees or the 40% they have in common with plants. These spectacles constitute past knowledge, congealed history.

Biological organisms have in that sense, "world views," a mode of perceiving the environment (Greene, 1985; Morin, 1981). Different sublineages with different genomes, with different means of cognizing the world, hence have different cognitive maps and different world views. Different species thus become different evolving epistemologies on the external world. When the genome is long, and complex with a large battery of responses to the world, its "world view," and its range of cognition is larger.

As Lorenz put it:

> Kant's statement that the laws of pure reason have absolute validity, nay that every imaginable rational being, even if it were an angel, must obey the same laws of thought appears as an anthropocentric presumption. Surely the "keyboard" provided by the forms of intuition and categories — Kant himself calls it that — is something definitely located on the physico-structural side of the psychophysical unity of the ... organism (Lorenz, 1989).

The genome's structure and content generally becomes bioepistemologically a window from the lineage to the external world. Organisms, therefore, have "innate hypotheses" on their worlds. They expect some regularity in their world, but not perfect knowledge or perfect certainty. They have, for example, developed particular sense organs or nervous systems that can process information relating to only particular structures of reality (Wuketits, 1990, p. 88).

An animal's apparatus for perceiving the environment gives rise to certain "models" of reality. It constructs models of particular parts of the world. These information processing activities can be labeled acts of cognition. They are not cognition in the sense that the animal necessarily reflects on the reality presented to it in the manner a human would. Evolutionary epistemologists use cognition and knowledge in a more enlarged sense than that used by philosophers. They imply that there are epistemic (cognitive) activities in all animals (Wuketits, 1990, p. 54).

In the neural system too, different subjectivities and different world views are constructed in different animals by the evolutionary process (Jerison, 1985). In some animals, olfaction is more important than sight, in others 'sight' extends to sections of the electromagnetic spectrum beyond human perception. Mammals have a "world view" different from birds, and the primates, a still different one from other mammals (Nagel, 1974).

The above reference is only to the broad backdrop to the subjective world, the hardware of brains. But some brains transmit information down the generations through a cultural lineage. This is subjectively perceived and processed information. The mind is a symbolic system, a particular internal representation of the external world (Johnson-Laird, 1988, pp. 34–35). "The world everyone sees is not *the* world but a world which we bring forth with others" (Maturana and Varela, 1986, p. 245). The mind's information constitutes a social point of view, social "world views." The "world views" associated with cultural lines have been the subject of extensive study of social scientists in their studies on ideologies, forms of social cognition, social constructions of reality, and the work on the evolutionary epistemology of science.

The broad characteristics of these cultural windows to the external world also hold true generally of the historical evolution of broad symbolic systems such as scripts, languages, arts or sciences. All of these are cognitive systems and cognitive maps that interact with their environments and evolve (Artigiani, 1988, pp. 237–61).

The cultural world views are not only associated with broad cultures as a whole, such as a religion or a nation, but also with social classes that arise from the major cleavages in society. An upper class uses a different set of cultural symbols than, e.g., the working class. The class-wide social constructs of reality and their evolution have been studied in detail, for example, by Lukacs (1923) in his work on history and class consciousness. Narrower cultural windows than class are those associated with professions, which bring along their own world views. These professional windows have been studied in detail in industrial sociology and the sociology of professions. The world view associated with a social grouping also constitutes an evolving social epistemology that changes with the environment. And corresponding to the differing flow lines, there are many differing cognitive systems, different social epistemologies.

In the exosomatic line too, different "world views" occur. First, the information that is mapped is selectively drawn from the external environment either through the human hands that feed it, or through the different sensors with which it interacts with the environment, or through the pre-filtering that is done through its programming languages and similar higher level information operations. The information that is thereby selectively mapped internally gives a set of particular windows to the external world. With higher level information processing using Artificial Intelligence, the exosomatic flow will acquire characteristics similar to the cultural line. Increasingly, AI devices would construct more sophisticated internal representations of the external world (Johnson-Laird, 1988).

The artefactual lineage's snapshots on the world would thus continuously change and evolve. Such artefacts will create new world views in the future as the quality and quantity of artefactual information increases, giving rise to novel solutions brought about, say, by the newer relatively autonomous AI techniques. The different artefactual sublineages would therefore have also several different "world views" as their relationships with their environment change in their interactions with it.

Each lineage, genetic, cultural or artefactual thus operates by selecting meaningful data while rejecting others, at the same time creating structural windows of meaning to the world outside. This process gives each lineage its own particular cognitive identity, its own "egocentricity" (to use the word derived from Morin). Such an egocentricity gradually builds up historically in a given lineage.

These world views arising from the evolutionary epistemology in the three lineages incorporate also tendencies and biases in interactions with the environment. They constitute human values embedded in the cultural lineage and their equivalents in the case of the other two egocentricities. These world views could, therefore, provide for a common factor through which to enter into the realm of "values" in each stream. This could be a window into an objective examination of the "subjectivities" of each lineage and hence provide for a common general perspective and a valid framework of the "ethics" of each lineage vis-à-vis its environment. It could thus become a framework for a truly universal "eco-ethics" in the largest sense of the term.

The acts of cognition in all these three realms, it should be also noted, are an act of becoming, not a fixed representation and a consequent reaction to the world outside. Cognition in the flow lines constantly creates meaning (Morin, 1981, p. 133; Morin, 1985, p. 135); it is a continued history of unfolding, of meaning, of becoming (Maturana and Varela, 1986, p. 113).

The lineages, as they traverse down history, tunnel as it were through time. The evolutionary epistemology associated with the tunneling means that the cognitive windows associated with a lineage constantly change. One can describe this as a buffeting by environmental forces of the cognitive windows to the outside world.

If one were a "passenger" through time accompanying the flow of information in a lineage, one would have a ride through time somewhat like in a roller coaster. The roller coaster would swing to and fro corresponding to twists and turns in the evolutionary tree, gathering and shedding information as say, moss. The evolutionary tree is not just one lineage but is a multiplicity of sublineages, of species. These sublineages themselves shift as they are buffeted in the time travel through the environment.

One can thus traverse down any evolutionary system through its branches and 'see' the outside world unfolding and changing, becoming more varied, and different apertures emerging as cognition and gestalts change. In the process, world views enlarge and occasionally contract (see Figure 11). This could best be pictured like a ride down the roller coaster with a video screen in front. The screen itself contracts and enlarges. The screen's images change. Color is added. Sound is added. Its acoustic spectrum changes, smells are added and are changed. There are also turning points in the roller coaster which result in different pictures on the screen, new cognitive maps are projected as say new species, or new subcultures come into being. The roller coaster goes up and down, turns and bifurcates corresponding to environmental changes and the lineage's internal self-organizing dynamics.

What will the future of these windows be in the era of merged evolution? Merging means that there are cognitive windows being added on to the existing cognition system of a single lineage or a sublineage (see Figure 12). The ferrying-in of information from lineage to

WORLD VIEWS BECOME RICHER

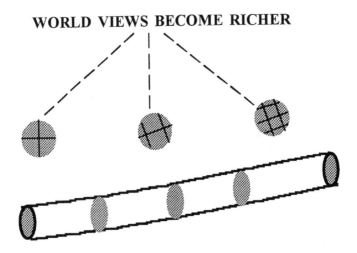

Figure 11   Isolated lineage "tunnels" through time giving rise to changing world views, which gradually become richer

lineage, alters the structure and content of information in a lineage, resulting in the lineage's cognition of the changing world. In the process of merging, the lineages' cognition gets enlarged or diminished, new features are added on, others get excised. The picture in front of the roller coaster now changes more rapidly, as does the buffeting of the roller coaster itself. Generally, the cognition becomes richer and more varied. The battery of possible interactions and hence the richness of the cognition with the environment increases with the phylogenetic ascendancy of the lineages which is brought about by the increased introduction of new information to the lineage.

In addition, the three lineages in the process of merging have to be considered also as one evolving whole. This macro lineage of the three together has also, therefore, its own cognition on the world. The macro single lineage is built up through the mergings of the three. So, at another level, the three has to be seen as a single system which has its own single composite window to the world.

This composite window cannot be described in terms of the cognition perspectives of any one lineage. This would be similar to a human not being capable of adequately describing the cognition to the external world in terms of one information interface only, such as sight, sound, touch, smell or taste. A human's cognition is a composite of all the

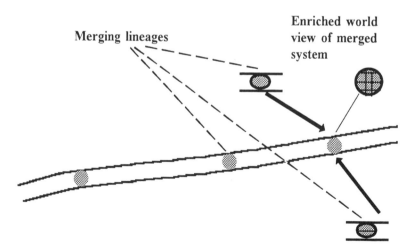

Figure 12   Three lineages merge giving rise to changed world views. View suddenly becomes richer. Histories accelerate.

information inputs into it. So the cognition of the information sublineage associated with the human species is a lineage built up from these sensory inputs and which changes historically as the human species tunnels through time. Further, the lineage of humans is different from, say, that of bats, because the two sample different segments of reality through their sensory organs. In a parallel manner, the three merged lineages now present an evolving single set of windows with changing cognitions to the external world (see Figure 13).

The broad characteristics of merging sketched above imply that the evolutionary implications of the new technologies are many. They change key characteristics of each lineage such as speciation, memory retention, flexibility and speed of reaction to the environment, hierarchies in nestedness, rates of evolution and 'world views' as well as developing into one single macro lineage.

Conclusion: The Real "End of History"

The interactions between the cultural aspects of the social world and the new technologies can therefore be described as interactions between

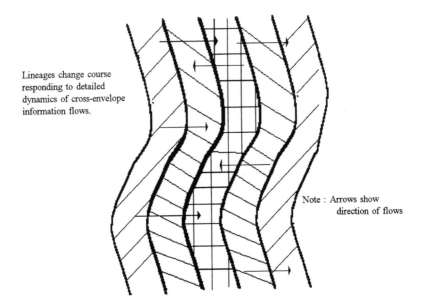

Lineages change course responding to detailed dynamics of cross-envelope information flows.

Note : Arrows show direction of flows

Figure 13   Merged Evolution

the three lineages. One could now say that the two new technologies allow for the intense merging of the three information streams, so that for all purposes in the future, biology, culture and computer have to be seen as one evolving whole. Some of these deeper interactions are of the most fundamental kind and deal with, for example, what it is to be truly human, both culturally and biologically. These core issues did not exist for the earlier industrial technologies or even perhaps for the paleolithic and the neolithic transitions.

The two new technologies encroach directly on the 4 billion-year history of biology and, say, the 10 thousand-year history of human culture. In mixing together the constituents of these two histories with a newer one into one whole, history as we know it, changes dramatically. Biology, history and artefacts now become one entity.

Current approaches used for discussing human interactions of other technologies do not capture these particular deep changes. The dynamics we have described of the different information lineages provide for a new and different view of the world. These dynamics would give the framework for a powerful conceptual "engine" that drives both natural and social history of the emerging future.

Some of the questions raised by the two new technologies go down to the core religious and philosophical assumptions on which human society rests. While being in many ways technologies of social liberation, the new technologies are thus not ultimately comfortable ones. There are disturbing elements in their core. The new technologies question some of the most cherished self-perceptions of humans and of what it is to be uniquely human in a cultural and biological sense. But the logic of the intertwined social and technological systems now drives the technologies almost inexorably forward.

This is, in many ways, not only the end of biology as we know it, but also the end of human history and of artefacts as we have hitherto known them. The 'end of human history' has been a recurring theme from Hegel to Marx to lesser recent commentators. But the end of history that is now emerging is not just a speculative construct of the future. It is more real and down-to-earth than the earlier formulations.

The result is a common history of biology, human history and artefacts, a history that accelerates faster than any of the earlier lineages, taken together. And, to understand each of the individual lineages, a knowledge of all three as a whole now becomes essential. One form of history is at an end, another entirely new history now begins.

10: AN EXTENDED SOCIOLOGY: THE STRUCTURE OF NEW "COMMUNITIES"

One of the areas that will be redefined dramatically through the new dispensation of merged evolution is the concept of what constitutes "social" and what constitutes "community." The result will be a new way of looking at "communities," their constituents and their dynamics.

A community's members communicate with their "significant others" and change their internal information states (and their internal and external behaviors). What is meant by significant others will, however, soon spill over because of merging, from our normal usage of the term for human interactions to other forms and so change the future of communication. The future will thus result in intense communications not only between machines and humans, but also with genetic systems so that information in the three realms of genes, culture and machines will result in one interacting whole. The three for all purposes would be interacting as one communicating system.

This meta communicating system will make the present communication modes and patterns appear trivial. These new merging effects will be played out and realized though dramatic changes in the communications matrices of the world. Communities are but the collectivities within which this communication occurs and ensuing actions result. What constitutes interacting communities and communication patterns would be changed and new amalgams would result. Let us examine some of these new 'communities.' We will first consider such communities of unmerged information systems ('uni-nets') and then the merged ones (hybrid nets).

'Uni-Nets'

We have already mentioned that certain theorists hold that many, if not all, information entities operate not in isolation but in collectivities, in 'societies' (Marijuan, 1996, pp. 87–96). So, if we have to fully appreciate the properties of information entities, we have also to see them as interacting societies. Let us first sketch these 'societies,' by taking the biological example first, where the DNA itself is organized in collectivities as chromosomes and as part of a gene population.

The genetic material, DNA chains in the cell nucleus, constitute chromosomes. The mutual exchange of different segments of chromosomes — which contain hundreds or thousands of nucleotide bases — results in the reorganization of the hereditary material. The possible genetic variation is thereby increased to a very high degree.

At any given point in the DNA chain, a gene may have several forms termed 'alleles.' In a large population of genes, there could be several alleles in a given locus. The presence, in a given population, of these multiple alleles provides the 'genetic pool' for evolutionary selection. Therefore, in a given reproductive community, there is a large pool of genes. Any individual organism at a given time holds only a small part of the total contents of the genetic pool; evolution occurs through selection from this genetic pool and not by selection via the individual. The pool constitutes the macro 'society' of genes within whose dynamics evolution takes place. There is also evidence that selection, evolutionary change, takes place not only at the level of the organism, but also at the level of the community and ecosystem (Brandon, 1990, p. 93).

The gene population is the fundamental unit of evolution. Within it, individual genes or particular combinations of genes, may be rejected or rewarded in the encounter with the environment. This pool has within it genetic material that can cope with a relatively large number of unforeseen changes. Selective pressures from the environment would then pull out these genes suitable for survival. Experimental work has also shown that when there is a large amount of variation in the genetic pool of a given population, the rate of evolution is faster than in one with a smaller amount of variation.

The concept of biological collectivities, societies, is also found in the idea of Gaia. Here the whole biological world is considered by Lovelock (1986) to be one interacting whole, one large macro society in which all biological entities are embedded. A recent theorist of general evolution, Hoffmeyer (forthcoming) has also extended this view of biological societies, taking into consideration some current theoretical work and has put forward the suggestion that the interconnected whole of species is a global web, a global semiosphere. Another theorist, Kampis (forthcoming), again points out that evolution takes place within an interconnected web of species. Natural selection is a result of the evolution of this web, and not vice versa.

In addition to these 'societal' interactions among genes are of course the societal interactions among cultural entities, namely humans.

Humans exist in various discernible groups such as classes, ethnic and religious groups and nations. Sociologists and social psychologists study these entities in great detail. In fact the work of these professional groups is devoted exclusively to the study of these collectivities and has helped us understand human interactions. The literature on these societies is very large and gives very detailed descriptions.

The 'societies' among computers are brought about by the telecommunication links between computers. The telecommunication industry may be growing as fast as the computer industry. Many of the telecommunication links have in the past only been between humans. But increasingly the interconnections are with other information devices — between computers. The growth of the machine-to-machine traffic is much faster than between humans. We have also documented the various communication networks that are girdling the globe today connecting computers and allowing for today's commerce and other essential activities to be done. The transfer of two trillion dollars around the world daily is essentially brought about by these links between computers. The fastest growing of such computer-to-computer societal links is, of course, the Internet.

The Internet, which grew out of defense research, is today perhaps the most widely discussed phenomenon in the information technology field. The Internet connects groups of computers around the world, exchanging and processing information between both machines and humans. It is essentially a network of networks, a vast and rapidly growing collection of 'societies' of machines. The number of computers connected to the Internet in mid-1996 stood at 50 million and was growing at a rate that doubles every 12 months. Soon most computers will dwell within it. President Clinton announced a plan in late 1996 for every U.S. house to be wired into the Internet by the year 2000.

This rapidly expanding Internet is a society of groups of computers, interacting with, and changing their internal information states. These machine societies are arranged and grouped together partly according to their common characteristics. With growing sophistication and increases of links between computing devices, such as the uses of wireless telephony and fibre optics, the sophistication and importance of this society increases.

This global interconnected artefactual information system is not one uniform system. It consists of islands of information, different virtual communities, that correspond partly and initially to human subcultures. These virtual human social islands which exchange cultural information on the computer-based 'electronic commons' could for example, be classes, or ethnic groups or companies. The islands of artefactual information are initially direct mappings of the information of these human social islands. As the artefactual information grows in quantity and is further processed, the initial human stamp on the computer subcultures would be lost. They would increasingly become distanced from the initial human stamp on their collectivities. Within this autonomous state, some new information dynamics will develop within the society of computers. Such interconnected computer networks allow for very interesting evolutionary dynamics reminiscent of biological and societal ecologies. New electronic communities would emerge. Let me give two examples describing the richness that is in store in these computer societies.

Tom Ray a computer specialist has initiated an open-ended experiment called by him a "digital biodiversity reserve". Here, a small self-reproducing program would be released into a collection of interconnected computers called the "virtual Internet." The idea is that soon the system will be populated by artificial organisms which begin to evolve. He had already built in 1992 an electronic universe of small organisms that evolved with surprising diversity. This system autonomously came up through its evolutionary run with a set of biological actors like parasites, immune systems and elementary social interactions. Although the creatures let loose on the virtual Internet would be relatively benign, there is no guarantee that they would not evolve characteristics detrimental to the virtual Internet. If released on the real Internet, the results could bring in many pleasant and unpleasant surprises (Flower, 1996, 33–35; Dibbell, 1996, pp. 49–50). The lesson seems to be that digital ecologies and digital jungles are autonomously created after an initial prompt. It seems to be a systemic characteristic of information collectivities having some intelligence.

'Agents' are new programs that do the bidding of their human mentors in digital collectivities. They can be made also to work as groups. Artificial evolution can be brought in to filter desired characteristics of such groups of agents, leaving behind a collection of the best agents, Such artificially evolving systems have already being bred for example, to search a data base and retrieve articles for the user (Maes, 1995, pp. 84–86). This [artificial] evolutionary approach would result in the coming years, in entire electronic sub ecosystems living in electronic networks such as the Internet. Useful agents will survive and reproduce, less useful ones will get excised out. These digital life forms will fit into particular ecological niches in the electronic web. Phenomena familiar to carbon-based life, like parasitism and symbiosis will appear in digital format (Maes, 1995, pp; 84–86). Through such interactions both the human and computer communities will be transformed.

Hybrid Nets

The three types of societies described above — three types of intra-connected nets — are the genetic, the cultural and the digital ones existing as individual societies on their own. However, we have discussed earlier how their constituent information entities are getting merged, forming hybrid entities. Such hybridization extends also to the societies and nets. Let us explore some of these hybrid nets, using a selection of biological, artefactual, and cultural hybrid networks.

We have earlier mentioned how dry runs can be made on biology in computer systems. When this occurs in a network, a biological-digital-cultural hybrid net results. There are many such emerging hybrid nets. Here is one example.

The entire sequence of the yeast genome was deciphered recently. Scientific groups are now doing vital experiments as a followup to this important achievement. The experiments however are done 'dry', not on the yeast but on its sequence in the computer data base. The manipulation is also done remotely using the Internet. This computer analysis lets geneticists study for the first time issues of the organization of genes (Inside the gene machine *New Scientist*, April 27, 1996, pp. 26–29). Here is an example of a hybridized net of biology, artefact and culture. There are three nets, one the actual set of genes, one electronic on the Internet's computer data bases, and the other, the human groups of researchers interacting culturally with each other (Halpert, 1993).

Because of globalization, a set of transborder human and computer communities are emerging, linked daily by the global chains of electronic media. Many multinational corporations are turning their worldwide operations into virtual communities, where the decision making is spread throughout the global system through networks of computers and networks of employees spread across the world. For example, Ford has brought her designs under a single 'electronic roof.' The interconnected network allows branch offices to exchange designs in an instant electronically. Data files are sent across the world and colleagues in different parts of the globe work on the same design aided by interconnected computers. Later, a design mutually agreed upon is sent to a computerized milling machine to turn out in a few hours a clay model. This is a hybrid net of human culture and artefact where a network of computers interfaces with a network of humans.

Generally, electronic communities now emerging around the world constitute what have been termed "virtual communities." They also include "virtual offices" interconnected by computers and telecommunication links. The "virtual corporation," a network of independent companies similarly interconnected is one other category of virtual community (Nagel, 1993, p. 64). But as the human groups within them not only exchange information among themselves but also interact as groups with computer collectivities, such virtual communities often turn at least partially into hybrid nets.

Humans in groups interacting with computers across existing networks for, e.g., currency trading, or on the Internet, are also engaged in hybrid networking acts. When a currency trader interacts with another, mediated through a computer network, a hybrid net results. When a set of computers as part of a network triggers a 'sell' program for disposing of stocks and a set of humans react to it, a hybrid situation results. When the Internet connects only with, and exchanges information only among its computers, no hybridization occurs. Neither would it occur when humans use the telephone as part of the Internet and communicate with each other orally. But as soon as, humans connected with each other interact on the network with interconnected computers, then a hybrid cultural-artefactual net results. The societies of culture and artefact touch base and form a common communicating matrix.

There are other cultural-computer hybrid nets. Thus, mass customization today uses information technology to target smaller and smaller groups, down to the individual shopper. This is done by extensive use of computers, flexible manufacturing systems and targeted marketing techniques. Several electronic products like some brands of computers have been mass customized for several years. Other products include large trucks and luxury hotels. The individual customers specify the features required and components to be used (Holusha, 1996, pp. D1, D7). Apart from these high cost items, customization has also come to more street level consumer items. Some clothing manufacturers have been selling custom fit jeans and others have embarked on selling custom fit shoes (Holusha, 1996). The result is a new hybrid terrain of market and production niches — which are social and cultural niches — interacting with computer networks.

Apart from these more obvious culture/artefact hybrids there are some other very fascinating examples. One example is made at the Media Lab at MIT and results in an electronically generated participatory musical experience called "The Brain Opera." It is a precursor of merged hybrids to come. The music is generated out of a collective hybrid of cultural and artefactual interactions. The interconnected system of instruments, computers and humans — some operating on the Internet — give rise to humans having a particular participatory aesthetic experience (Rothstein, 1996, p. 31). And to the participatory network of computers, one could add, this particular hybrid also gives rise to the 'particular experience' of their information stores being changed through collective interactions with humans.

The on-line subcultures in the Internet, comprise an ecology of subcultures, an ecosystem. Some are frivolous, some are smutty and some contain the most current science-in-the-making, as scientists publish preprinted reports electronically. This virtual community can be used for a variety of human functions resulting in as many communities as that exist in the communities of face to face interactions. Often people meet in cyberspace years or months before they meet in person, if ever. Rheingold has observed that as the system spreads, it creates micro communities in the same way that organisms create colonies (Rheingold, 1993, pp. 3–6). But at least part of the time, the human groups within the Internet interact with interconnected computers which process their information, not just channel it to other humans. The spread of virtual micro cultures will inevitably be accompanied by the spread partially of hybrid communities.

Within these hybrids, the two nets, cultural and artefactual, have 'conversations' when they touch base and exchange information. Entirely new meanings and constructions of reality will arise at such networked sites of the Internet. Here multimedia will interact with activities in the network, will react with software, and yield new discourses and new meanings (Luke, 1996, pp. 12).

But as in other ecologies, these conversations can be interrupted. A cold virus can lay low a whole set of human communicators and temporarily silence them. A computer virus can temporarily disrupt the work of a computer network. At a still more disruptive level, war on the information web could erupt to disable the threads of communications and webs of commerce. Such cyber wars using viruses and cyber bombs would be weapons of choice in the future (Cyber Wars, January 13, 1996, pp. 89–90), targeted on the collectivities of computers, just as biological weapons and other arsenals would aim at disrupting the human end of the hybrid. The hybrid net of culture and artefact information would then be a battleground. The result would be aggressive "conversations" with lethal intent.

Hybrid-Net 'Travellers'

These merged hybrid nets can be traversed by information entities to collect and process information. Some of these travelers are themselves hybrid, some only single information entities. To illustrate how they would operate in the future let us now give two examples of these travelers.

The globalization trend in the world is leading to the emergence of a new type of global worker, an "electronic immigrant"(Pelton, 1989 pp. 12). The precursors of these electronics migrants have already been seen in the relatively unskilled activity of data entry workers in developing countries who keyed in data for firms in developed countries (Clerical jobs Wall Street Journal, February 26 1985). In the same vein, telemarketing in the United States has occurred from Jamaican soil, and insurance claims for America have been processed in Ireland (Burgess, 1991). The new type of professional worker, "telecommuting" over thousands of miles would span a spectrum of similar skills. Some of this network already exists when traders of currency and stocks buy and sell currencies world wide. Other examples include software exports from developing countries such as India which have been growing rapidly over the last few years ("No looking back" *Indian Express* Jan 9, 1997). These human travelers traverse electronically both computer and human networks.

There are also cultural/artefactual hybrids that are designed to roam the electronic ecology. Thus, Avatars are electronic representatives of individuals in virtual worlds. Put into a home shopping virtual world, a video image of the user can be sent searching through virtual shopping malls (Flynn, 1996, pp. D3).

Agents, the autonomous programs that act on the [cultural] requirements of their owners are an emerging technology that will ease computer usage. They are direct hybrid products of culture and artefact that scour the hybrid nets of their users and computers. These agents would know the user's interests and do data searches and other related activities on their behalf. In such events both humans or their agents can initiate actions or communications, monitor events and see that other tasks tailor-made to the user are completed. The user could have several such alter egos, one for each type of task, operating in different locales. Some of these agents will search for information or monitor events, others would have the authority to represent the user in his absence or perform transactions on his behalf, like buying on line. Agents will take the place of personal secretaries. Instead of interacting with their agents through a keyboard or mouse, users could speak to them or gesture. In return the agents would manifest themselves as life-like entities on the screen. They could express themselves with, e.g., say body expressions, animated facial expressions or by voice output (Maes, 1995, pp. 84–86).

Agents are being built that organize themselves on AI principles. They program themselves. Such agents would change their behavior corresponding to their experience including interactions with other agents. These agents continuously watch the user's actions and automate any regular patterns that they detect. Agents would learn from other agents to do similar tasks. This collaborative actions of agents would lead them in a swarm to act in intelligent, sophisticated ways although the individual agent itself will be by itself relatively unintelligent (Maes, 1995, pp. 84-86).

Agents are middle-ground hybrids between culture and artefact. Scouring the matrix they will transform the electronic ecosystem, evolving into niches, and by changing the habits of their human mentors will change also the latter's social ecology.

Agents, partially represent us, they are our constructed virtual selves. But, in a general sense, we are to others all constructed, virtual selves. We exist in another observer as an 'other,' a figment of perception. This perceived self could in an information society today, dwell also in the recesses of a computer. Thus data banks, credit card records and the like are not just files but also our virtual selves. One's selves are located elsewhere, electronically matching more or less one's real self. It is analogous to one's past selves in one's memory bank, such as that of a child, schoolboy, student, etc., with which, in his/her own head, a person has a referential interaction. But these selves out there in data banks are interrogated and integrated by other users of the system. To them the virtual self is the real self, 'I' do not exist, they have not seen me or spoken to me.

Yet these virtual selves are historical selves, constructed and congealed from historical developments and struggles. It is now virtualized as data and thrown into an arena of general discourse. The virtual object of data here is not just a passive one which is pushed around by the different operators of the object. If it has internal rules derived from our past history, say of credit or medical record, it will also change according to some knowable means. But if this virtual self, existing as a packet of computer data has associated with it data manipulation possibilities such as the ability for randomizing or of operating on it with AI techniques such as genetic algorithms and neural networks, then a different situation arises. It takes a new self-constructing role.

Such a virtual self, say an agent, is no longer just a construct of the past but now has an internal life of its own. It changes itself like an elf or *pretha* moving around, having two-way interactions with one's real self. One's ghost has come to virtual life. The mirror image interacts with the real object, or in a different sense, the mirror manipulates its own image. If this AI-possessed data package is also modelled and projected on a virtual reality cyberspace, then the interaction with one's other becomes much more varied, less predictable, in a literal sense 'fantastic.'

Identity Politics in Hybrid Space

The hybridization of the lineages creates two sets of value and ethical questions. One of these questions relates to the identity created by the new interventions. The other relates to what 'value orientation' or 'subjectivity' each of these lineages has. Let us first take the identity question.

One of the necessary outcomes of the merging is that conventional views of human and other identities will vanish. With incursions of genes from not just two natural parents, but in the future from a variety of donors for different genes, conventional definitions of biological identity become problematized. 'I' then comes with a question mark.

There is also another intrusion to human identity occurring through information technology. The senses and so parts of the "mind" are, through electronic means, now being extended beyond one's person. By pressing a lever, clicking on an icon or speaking to a device I can effect an event remotely and that effect can also be fed back to me so that I internalize this feedback experience. This, and the extensive cloning of human capacities through a computer, tend to spread an individual human's identity widely over artefacts. When, through electronic prostheses and communication devices, 'my' identity is thus spread far and wide, beyond my biologically given reach of my hands and voice, 'I' again has a problem.

In a similar fashion, through hybrids, identity also become a problem in the other information realms. Culture is no longer just processed by human biological systems, it is processed through genetic and artefactual means. And, artefacts now have genetic and cultural incursions. In all three realms a presumed single unchanging identity is no longer tenable, a conclusion also arrived at by empirical studies of hybrids.

Thus, Turkle has documented ethnographically how identity and the idea of self is blurred in cyberspace (Turkle, 1995). In cyberspace identity vanishes. Persons can, and do take alternate identities. One can take one's own identity, somebody else's or even multiple ones. The self is technologically deconstructed here (Rheingold, 1993). Cyborgs — biological/artefactual hybrids — in Donna Haraway's articulation, breach boundaries of what constitutes distinct categories. Cyborgs do not stand still, they constantly change and mutate (Haraway, 1995). And, this breaking down of an individual identity through the processes of localization and globalization, whereby identity is spread over several areas has been considered by emerging theorists of cyborgs as essential characteristics of "cyborg politics" (Gray and Mentor 1995: 453–469). There have also been calls for a cyborg 'anthropology' to deal with some of the more obvious symptoms of merging (Downey, Dumit and Williams 1995: 341–347).

This boundary breaching requires a perspective on these changes that takes into account problems raised by the 'I' being questioned. Identity in these instances is ever changing, evanescent, fleeting. With further advances in biotechnology and information technology these questions of identity, and of associated philosophical, social and ethical modes become more complicated. An added important question to be examined also arises. What is the subjective framework from which to view the environment from one of these hybrid lineages, say from hybrids of the cultural-artefact, artefact-genetic or the genetic-cultural streams?

One can have an entry point into exploring both these key questions of identity and subjectivity by examining the human identity and subjectivity that we are all familiar with.

The Evolutionary View from Within

We have already mentioned earlier how lineages' world views change and gave as illustration the metaphor of a traveler going down a roller coaster, which helps to describe the view from within an evolutionary lineage. This is a view from the lineage's 'subjectivity,' from its semeiotics, internal signposts.

Specialists in all three lineages, including biologists, have spoken of such subjectivities of lineages. But this has been in an impersonal sense, from an outsider's point of view. Would then a view from the inside of a genetic lineage or an artefactual one, have the same 'subjective feel' as say the view from within culture that passes through our heads? What then, is the subjective view from such a nonhuman lineage? What is it like to be within such a lineage and view the environment outside? Philosophers have asked the question of how it is to be like a bat and have described in detail how a bat perceives the world (Nagel, 1974). Can we do the same thing for our non cultural lineage? Let us explore further.

A view from a lineage is not just a snapshot of the environment, it is more like a movie. We see from the lineage's vantage point events unfolding as it traverses from the past through the present, onward to the future. It is very much like the subjective flow of streams of thought going through our heads, which is not just one fleeting thought-entity but a view of a thought process, a stream.

In recent philosophy of evolution these issues of process, identity and subjectivity have all been raised by several writers in the field.

Thus, Salthe has suggested that evolution is semiotic rather than material. He proposes that such a perspective is necessary because the systems in which we are interested in evolution, envelop us within them. This internalist viewpoint he says must take into account the observer, that is, say, of ourselves. Following the 19th-century American philosopher Peirce, such a perspective would mean that semeiotics becomes a kind of scientific epistemology (Salthe, forthcoming). Jesper Hoffmeyer (forthcomming) also taking a Peircian point of view, has shown how species form interactions with other species whereby the 'habits' (again using a Peircian term) learned by one become a sign to be interpreted by another. And Kampis finds that to picture evolution, process philosophies such as those of Whitehead which reject a notion of permanent identity are very useful. The units that undergo change in evolution are seen as subject to temporary organization with only a transitory identity. Kampis finds that these notions are necessary for coevolutionary scenarios (Kampis, forthcoming). Apart from Whitehead and Peirce other philosophers being evoked in these discussions on evolution are David Hume, Huxley, and Ernst Mach. All these writers have dealt with one or other of the problems of identity, continuity and process; issues all central to the evolutionary perspective.

One person who has made a very significant attempt to tackle the subjective properties of these hybrids in the field of cultural information is Derek Parfit (1984) in a book *Reasons and Persons* (Parfit, 1984). This book aroused considerable interest, the *Times Literary Supplement* reviewer considering it "by any standard the most notable contribution to moral philosophy in the last hundred years" (Scheffler, 1984). Western civilization's adoption of science had required the gradual exorcising out of several collective devils. These included the relations between humans and the cosmos which was broken by Copernicus, between humans and other forms of life, which was broken by Darwin and between humans and their unconscious broken by Freud. The current emerging breach is between humans and machines (Gray, Mentor and Figueroa–Sarriera, 1995: 1–17) and it is this problem that Parfit has addressed. Among the issues raised by the book is the nature of the person. Parfit reaches here 'reductionist' conclusions on persons and their continuity. This position Parfit extends to a discussion on the nature of rationality and morality. In this latter discussion, he denies the importance of self-interested reasoning and of prudence. From the time of Aristotle, it had been a central tenet of Western philosophy that assessing prudentially was where one's best interest lay. This was not a crude argument for selfishness and greed. The position is best understood by posing it in another direction, namely, what is more irrational than consciously to act in a way that frustrates the interests of both oneself and those one loves. An extension of this argument is that morality coincides with self interest.

Parfit uses many arguments against this self-interest theory, the most important being his description of personal identity and continuity. He argues what would happen in three hypothetical instances of changes in the internal makeup of individuals: first in an 'Enterprise' type scan (of the TV film series Star Trek) and recreation of a human at a remote end; second, of hypothetical surgical interventions in the brain with implantation of memories, and third, of brain transplants. All these raise deep questions regarding personal identity. But what can be believed with reason in all these cases is only the physical and psychological connectedness from one instant to another of a person. That is Parfit points out, all that one can truly assert.

But, in both connectedness and continuity, there are differences personal identity can have. In the extreme, the answer to a question such as 'do I die'? does not have a definite answer. Parfit brings forth his discourse on morality and ethics through the notion of past and future selves being considered comparable to our present ones.

But some of these positions coincide with Buddhist ones, as Parfit readily admits. These include the lack of identity, of 'self,' where in Buddhism there is only a changing stream of impersonal body and mind elements and where sameness and difference exists within the stream. The Buddhists would say that in the examples of the brain transplants and other examples of changes in identity that Parfit gives, they are 'neither the same nor different' (*na ca so na ca anno* in Pali).

Parfit, however, admits that persons are subjected to experiences and act on the world. But to him, this is largely a conventional use of language. Parfit says "though persons exist, we could give a complete description of reality without claiming that persons exist"(Parfit, 1984, p. 212). Recognizing that these views may be difficult to feel subjectively although they can be argued out theoretically, he says that "Buddha claimed that, though this is very hard, it is possible. I find Buddha's claim to be true" (Parfit, 1984, p. 280). One should note here that for Buddhists too, internally grasping the theoretical insight is difficult. In fact one of the important meditation devices in Buddhism is precisely to acquire internally this view of the changing self by observing one's self as one changes.

Parfit's argument is from the point of view of a 'person' whose interiority had become changed either through biotechnology or information technology and becomes a hybrid. He does not spread this hybridization problem more generally to that of hybrids in the other two lineages, or hybrids of all three lineages taken together. Especially the question of morality and ethics, of looking at the world from one subjective framework of another lineage or combinations thereof, is not examined.

If Parfit has direct echoes with Buddhist analysis, so have some of the classical writers referred to by the evolutionists working on the philosophy, process and semiotics of evolution. Thus many of the classical writers like Hume, Huxley, Mach, Peirce and Whitehead that have been evoked by Salthe, Hoffmeyer and Kampis and others have also been directly or indirectly compared with, or have drawn sustenance from Buddhism. And the issues raised by Salthe, Hoffmeyer, Kampis and several others find deep cords of resonance in Buddhist literature, just like the earlier related work of Derek Parfit. The following section summarizes these resonances with some of the key philosophers being evoked in evolutionary theory.

There has been a large set of writings on the surprising parallels between Buddhism and Hume, (Jacobson, 1969; Jacobson, 1988, p.

119); between Huxley and Buddhism (Rajapakse, 1985) and between Mach and Buddhism (Blackmore, 1972). But the philosophers that are more quoted in current philosophical discussions of evolution are Whitehead and Peirce. Till Whitehead and Peirce arrived, Jacobson notes, Buddhism was virtually the only serious process philosophy around (Jacobson, 1988, p. 67). Let us briefly mention some of these parallels between Buddhist philosophy and process philosophy.

Thus, Peirce "related his convictions more specifically to Buddhism than anyone had previously done" (Inada and Jacobson, 1984, p. xii). To both Peirce and Buddhism, the immediacy of experience is most important and there is no notion of a self. In Peirce's words "One is immediately conscious of his or her feelings but not that they are feelings of an ego — the self is only inferred; there is no time in the present for any inference at all" (quoted in Jacobson, 1988:71). Peirce's law of love, "agapism," also had similarities with Buddhist categories. And he, like Buddhism, equated truth with righteousness (Bishop, 1982, pp. 265–271). A Buddhist text on logic of circa 600 A D Nyayapravesa ("Introduction to Logical Methods"), also has basic syllogisms found in Peirce (Factor, 1983).

Whitehead and Buddhism both accept the instant flow of phenomena and the interconnectedness of all phenomena (Inada and Jacobson, 1984, p. 133). And, the idea of the nonself in Buddhism, Kenneth Inada points out, is consistent with the Whiteheadian ideas of process philosophy (Inada, 1979). Whitehead's work became the first fully developed Western philosophical system in which Buddhism found general sympathy.

The contemporary process philosopher Charles Hartshorne also finds other commonalities between Whitehead and Pierce with Buddhism (Jacobson, 1988, p. 23). Ames also shows that Whitehead and Peirce and Buddhism have several other common themes. These include the immediacy of the present experience, a naturalistic framework, testing of ideas on the basis of their results, the rejection of dualisms, and the idea of individual freedom (Ames, 1962). Having overviewed some of these similarities, Robert Neville (1984) suggests that Buddhism as the process philosophy with the longest unbroken tradition in the world has much to offer modern process philosophers.

A Heuristic Approach

In the absence of other developed systems that tackle together, issues of process, identity and subjectivity brought by the new hybridization and merging, we are therefore perhaps left only with Buddhist philosophy. There appears to be only this philosophical system that has taken the aspects of subjectivity, a questioned 'I', and process seriously and developed an extensive philosophical and observational literature.

Since it is the only scheme around, I will use it heuristically here to see whether it can throw light on some of our questions. Before doing so in a book written from a Western scientific perspective, I will have to justify the legitimacy of using this literature, even as a heuristic. (I should also add that although born a Buddhist, I remain the only person in my country of origin — Sri Lanka — to have been persecuted for sacrilege, for which incidentally there is no Buddhist position).

Buddhist philosophy has concepts that bring together in a process philosophy the internal world of flow phenomena, the external environment in which the phenomena operate, as well as the interconnectedness of phenomena. These are also elements common to evolutionary theory specially to the problems that we have posed of identity, process and subjectivity. It would therefore appear that Buddhist observations already made on the behavior of our subjectivity could be a useful entry point to discuss the internal views of our lineages. Parfit's view of cyborgs has already attempted a 'Buddhist' position on the new dispensation.

Let me add a few others. Thus several recent theorists on virtual reality have suggested using Buddhist approaches for discussing some of the contentious epistemological issues that are emerging in VR technology. These include the inventor of the data glove as well as a prominent writer on VR, Rheingold (Cochran, 1992, p. 79). And Varela, who introduced the concept of autopeosis to evolutionary theory, has used Buddhist perspectives.

Varela, has pointed out that the Buddhist experiences of observing the mind are in the tradition of scientific observation (Varela et al., 1993, p. 23). The validity of <u>some</u> of the Buddhist observations on mental processes, including those of the many practitioners who came after the Buddha have been increasingly corroborated by research within the last twenty years as Western psychologists and physicians have taken these observations seriously and attempted to validate them (representative of this literature are: Kabat-Zinn et al., 1992; Walsh 1988; Sweet and Johnson, 1990; De Silva, 1984; Goleman, 1981; Bograt, 1991; Donaldson, 1992).

Varela and others have written a book *The Embodied Mind* with applications in the evolution field itself that basically transfers Buddhist observational practice and theory to the realms of evolutionary theory and cognitive science (Varela et al., 1993, p. xviii). In this book the authors discuss aspects of what I have considered flows in the three lineages, namely the internal flow of our thoughts (that is, of culture within our minds); the flow of genes (that is, of evolutionary biology); and the flow of "artificial thoughts" (that is, of artificial intelligence) (Varela et al., 1993, p. xiv).

This Buddhist practice and theory have a large collection of technical matter based on detailed observation that could be useful to our own project. The observation and analysis there, in many ways parallel — albeit perhaps notably only in narrow realms such as this — some of the rigor that one observes in modern science. I will explore part of these Buddhist observational and theoretical approaches through one of our lineages, namely the flow of culture, where, in the minds of humans, culture acts out its role, taking the form of mental activity, and a stream of thoughts.

"Information" in Thought Streams

Thoughts as they arise internally in our minds and flow have been subject to careful observation and analysis in Buddhism. Some of the psychological aspects of this observation have been recently validated by the clinical studies in the West already noted. In this Buddhist literature, a class of questions is raised that directly parallel in many ways, some of the questions that occur today in the era of the cyborg and the gene-transplanted hybrid. This literature will be recalled by citing classical texts and the work of Western philosophers on these texts.

In Buddhism, there is nothing durable or of static being. Physical elements change, as do mental phenomena; all are in a state of perpetual becoming. In the Buddhist analysis of identity, there is no individual, only a stream unraveling within the mind, fleeting strings and chains of events ("Anatta" *Encyclopedia of Buddhism*, 1961, Vol.1, p. 567). This analysis is partly arrived at from directly observing the innermost subjectively felt inside of a person. In fact, one of the objectives of Buddhist mental exercises, 'meditation,' is to observe, experience and describe for oneself this lack of self and of permanence from within one's own streams of thoughts and mental phenomena. From within our own innermost subjectivity, the problem of identity and of an abiding "I" is shown to be a false one.

If this be the real state of "I" from both an external material point of view, and internally from a subjective point of view, then what does this entail for our own streams of information, the lineages? All three lineages have fleeting characteristics. They are all ever-changing, hybridizing streams, whose identity is not in a snapshot existence of being, but in a process of becoming, an unraveling.

From such a perspective then, the questions on identity raised by the two technologies are seen differently. From that perspective, the existential angst of being a hybrid, of having genes of plants and animals inside one is seen differently. The problem of one's 'self' being spread over several artefacts now loses its potential terror. The threat of being a cyborg, of Frankenstein's creature, the concern of Jeremy Rifkin, the fundamentalist critic of biotechnology is seen differently.

Jeremy Rifkin complains that under the new dispensation living things are not considered as plants and animals, as carrots and hens, but only as collectivities of information. This drains all living things of their aliveness. They become instead abstract messages. Life now is only a code waiting to be deciphered. The mystery and sacredness or inviolability of life are removed, complains Rifkin. No longer, under the new knowledge and its applications, are there any recognizable boundaries that should be respected. Rifkin further worries that as biotechnology develops and spreads, it transforms and creates life forms. It strips living things of their identity. It then replaces the "original creations" with replicas made through the technology; "the world gradually becomes a lonelier place" (Rifkin, 1987, p. 29). Buddhist analysis stripped this seeming sacredness and identity more than two and some half millennia ago.

A gene therefore does not make a sentient being. Only the stream of a being's existence, of an onwards flowing history constitutes the human or the cyborg. A person does not exist as a unique individual but as a constructed ever changing flow, an onwardly moving lineage. If to this lineage are added new elements, new parts, it is but in the very 'normal' nature of such constructed streams. The artificial introduction of elements to the cultural flow from genes or artefacts is but another manifestation of the 'normal' construction of such flows. From a realist's perspective, there is no difference.

But experiencing in an internal sense, the intrusion of the new technologies that remake us biologically and culturally, is disturbing. It challenges our sense of self. "This idea that I may not be, I may not have, is frightening to the uninstructed" as classical Buddhist texts put it. And, as the belief in an abiding self is deep-rooted in humans, this position is 'against the current' as the texts say on one other occasion

(Rahula, 1978, p. 56). In such circumstances one may desperately try to cling to the idea of at least the mind through which we experience the world as unchanging. But in such instances, the texts are again very firm, rejecting the views of persons who take the thing called the 'mind' or 'consciousness' to be an unchanging substance. In that case it would be better, the texts argue, for a person to take the physical body as an unchanging 'self,' rather than thought, mind or consciousness, because the body at least appears more solid than the mind (Rahula, 1978, p. 65). Interiority and consciousness are demystified into very mundane components. As the 5th Century Sri Lankan classic of higher Buddhist psychological observation *Visuddhi Magga* (Gunaratne, 1982, p. 12) put it: "There is no doer but the deed. There is no experiencer but the experience. Constituent parts roll on, this is the true and correct view."

When it is inevitable that we are constructed and reconstructed, from biology, culture and artefact, this could be our epistemological, philosophical, ethical and subjectively felt guiding principle. This could be the necessary view on the interiority of robots and of constructed hybrids, as they navigate reality, and tunnel through time in our lineages. This would be the view to be internalized in the inevitable day of the cyborg.

This Buddhist process philosophy therefore challenges some of the basic assumptions of the self as an ethical agent. Its doctrines of no-self, momentariness and conditioned origination raise, Peerenboom notes, questions on 'who' is the moral agent. Buddhism requires that the agent is not an assumed atomistic individual but a person within both a social and natural context. Ethical responsibility is now spread over the whole community. 'My' ethical responsibility as I intrude genes into my interiority and extrude myself on to the Internet is spread over a wide catchment area. This perspective goes against reading an either-or, dualistic reading of freedom and determinism (Peerenboom, 1989).

From this perspective, one analyzes oneself, knows oneself, only to realize that there is no self in the first place. This is not an intellectual knowledge but an internally observed, felt, subjective knowledge. When the realization dawns that I am not a thing but a process, to know oneself becomes to make oneself, to guide the self that is not there (Kolm, 1986; Loy, 1992). This perspective, based on observation has given rise to a guide to the subjective orientation to the external world. This orientation rests on the observation that there is nothing mysterious or permanent in the internal subjectivity. Interiority and subjectivity is a constructed system having particular properties. It is not entirely far fetched to think that this perspective could provide pointers in the case of our merged streams.

Buddhist subjectivity also does not make recourse to the dichotomy of mind and body brought about by Descartes at the beginning of the Scientific Revolution. In Buddhism, mind and body are connected together. The Cartesian dichotomy is today breaking down and yielding in several disciplines, a different view of the subject-object, mind-body relationship.

Descartes' division of mind and matter was also accompanied by a mechanical view of the animal body. He said:

> If there was a machine that had organs and the external features of a monkey, or some other animal, we would have no way at all of knowing that it was not, in every aspect, of the very same nature as those of animals. (Descartes, 1973, p. 242)

Descartes, however, did not fully include humans in this category because, he thought only humans had the power to communicate and comprehend complex thoughts.

But the machine metaphor itself has been used in the Buddhist tradition. As illustration here are two selections from the writings of the authoritative 5th-century commentator of the Sinhala tradition, Buddhaghosa:

> The mental and material, both are here in fact,
> A human substance though cannot be found,
> Void it is, set up like a machine,
> A mass of conflict, like a bundle of grass and sticks.
> (*Buddhist Encyclopedia*, 1984, Vol 1, p. 186)

Buddhaghosa continues describing this "self"-less human machine further:

> As a puppet walks and stands through a combination of wood and strings, although it is empty, without life, without impulse, so this contraption of mental and material factors, void, without soul, without free will can walk and stand, as if it had will and work of its own. (*Buddhist Encyclopedia*, 1961, Vol. 1, p. 186)

This is very much a description of the internal life that many a robot specialist would find congenial.

Given the above perspectives we can now see whether some of the concerns expressed by recent writers on evolution referred to earlier have been met from this Buddhist theoretical and observational heuristic. There are many resonant echoes.

Approaching evolution through the process philosophy of a Whitehead, Kempis reiterated the call for an 'endophysics,' an internal physics, as suggested by O.E. Rossler, a science that takes into account observations from within (Kampis, forthcoming). Such an endophysics of processes from within is seen in the flow of thoughts in a person, which has been described and analyzed in great detail in Buddhism. Salthe states that the correct perspective for us to take for the internalist point of view would be to become disinterested observers at one time, and at another time, interested actors (Salthe, forthcoming). To use a Buddhist expression, the observer in a thought stream should be like the lotus flower, both within the waters (of subjectivity) and above it (in the realm of objectivity), the metaphor used to describe the ideal observational platform in Buddhism. Eric Minch on the other hand, evoked the idea of a morphogenetic movie in evolution, a succession of structural snapshots (Minch, forthcoming). This parallels directly a Buddhist metaphor used to describe the 'endophysics' of the thought process, the illusion of a moving line created by a rapidly spinning fireball. The interdependent web of Hoffmeyer, the global semiosphere, has also its parallel in the Buddhist interrelated web of dependent origination. And, Peirce's 'habits' have their parallels in the Buddhist descriptions of 'the ruts and grooves of the mind' formed by the flow (Hoffmeyer, forthcoming).

It appears that an interaction between the semiotics and processes of evolution and of Buddhist observations and theoretical orientations could indeed be fruitful. If one wants to explore evolution and processes as an internal process then there seems to be much in the storehouse of Buddhist technical literature that could be used heuristically.

Having therefore being forced, in the absence of any other useful and relevant literature, to use Buddhist observation to explore the subjective feel of the different streams, we find that indeed there are commonalities between their constructed nature and our own constructed subjectivities. Viewed from detailed observation of one's internal life, this subjectivity is demystified into everyday mundaneness. And, this phenomenology of the flow of human thoughts, could be extrapolated to schemes in the other hybridized spheres. The Buddhist observations could give some pointers to a subjective compass of the inevitable mergings of the three streams.

From such a perspective how would the world appear as one whizzes down a lineage? Experiences fly through as in a tunnel. In one's physical-mental evolution and becoming ("one" meaning a biological entity, a cultural being, or a computer with intelligent characteristics), different historical lenses, different evolving realities present themselves as an unreeling film. These snapshots come from the future, but one exists only in the present. Analyzing them into different components, one does not find anything 'there.'

We can now summarize how our merged hybrid communities will behave.

Communities Transformed

In the merged system information is ferried from one lineage to another, in the process being translated from the language of one lineage to another. There are other interesting characteristics of these properties of hybrid-net 'conversations.'

The different information communities (genetic, cultural, artefactual or hybrids) are social webs, collectivities of information carriers. That is, these carriers communicate with others and change their internal states and hence the internal and external behavior of their constituent members. What is the general image that now emerges of interactions within communities and between communities, within units and between them, in hybrids of the new dispensation?

The interactions between these communities of lineages take place at two levels. There is the direct encounter and an indirect encounter as the two merge, like two icebergs interacting giving rise to a merged system at points they touch. These indirect and direct processes we have discussed in detail in earlier chapters. Deep subterranean forces may spring within a [human] social structure and give rise to a cultural entity. This gets expressed as a biological or artefactual entity. In turn, artefactual information or biological information rising from their collectivities' innards generates fresh traveling information hybrids that traverse down the deep icebergs and reshape their social structures. A traveling hybrid entity sometimes 'dive bombs' into this mixed ocean current and carves a new subjective pathway. These pathways interconnect and subtly change the communities.

These dive-bombing entities are information hybrids. They could be at times machine-biological hybrids, cyborgs, or different other combinations, two by two or all the three information realms together. It may not be inappropriate to give a common name to these hybrids that thus traverse fields of information. Cyborg is clearly an indicator of such a term for one combination but is not wide enough as it does not cover all possible combinations.

Words like *avatar* and *pretha* from Sanskrit have entered the multimedia and virtual reality vocabulary to denote information entities that are represented in virtual space. These terms have connotations from the Sanskrit of fleeting life-like forms. But still they are not wide enough, they do not cover all the hybrids. Drawing again from the Sanskrit, we could perhaps coin a neologism that captures both the evanescence as well as covering combinations of all the three realms. We will call such a mixed information entity a *Bahutar*, 'Bahu' in Sanskrit implies multiple or plural and 'tar,' movement.

The image that emerges is of an ocean of communities, existing at different levels, the genetic, the cultural and the artefactual. They interact with, and in, different environments — the genetic, the cultural and the artefactual — and change their states. Currents and bubbles of information, *Bahutars* rise, fall and circulate, from both internal dynamics of each community as well as those from interlineage dynamics. There are processes of localization and globalization in and across all the three realms. There are continuous processes of organization of communities within the system, sideways, upward and downward. A truly witch's brew — or if you wish, a wizard's brew — of communication possibilities, of shifting dynamic communities results.

These dynamics lead to changes in the evolutionary characteristics of each lineage and sublineage, including the internal perceptions from within a lineage, namely in the language of evolutionary epistemology, its "meanings" and "hypotheses" on the world. Sets of webs of meanings result. The webs have views from each information tunnel (gene, culture, artefact or hybrid). At points of permanent or temporary contact of the different webs a sort of wormhole between nets results. Through these channels that connect them, crisscrossing is now possible across the combined structures, across the uni-nets and hybrids. Traversing these crisscrossing pathways is like traversing through a changing ocean of genes, culture and artefacts. Thermodynamically this is also an open system with a constant increase of organization within the system, accompanied necessarily by changes in inflows and out-flows to and from the system. The study of social phenomena in the new millennium should necessarily take into account all these varied factors. A future sociology must incorporate the dynamics of all three realms. The world of communities would never be the same.

REFERENCES

A window on the mind: Researchers manage to grow brain cells in the laboratory, (1990, May 14) *Time*.

Abu-Mostafa, Yaser & Psaltis, Demetri 1987 Optical neural computers, *Scientific American*, **256** (3), 66–73.

Ahamed, Ifthikhar 1989 Advanced agricultural biotechnologies: Some empirical findings on their social impact, *International Labor Review*, **128** (5), 553–569.

Albery, John 1986 You know it makes sensors, *New Scientist*, **109** (1495), 38–41.

Alexander, Tom (1982, May 17) Teaching computers the art of reason, *Fortune*, **117** (11), 125–127.

Allen, Peter, M. 1985 Towards a new science of complex systems. In S. Aida (Ed.), *The science and praxis of complexity*, pp. 2–12, Tokyo: United Nations University.

Altman, Lawrence, K. 1996 Studying rare disorder: Scientists find gene affecting aging, *The New York Times*, April 12, 1996, p. A 27.

Amato, Ivan 1990 Artificial life: Stepping closer to reality, *Science News*, **137** (6), 86.

Anderson, Arthur 1986 Trends in information processing technology, *New Information Technologies and Development*: ATAS Bulletin, Issue 3, New York: UN Center for Science and Technology.

Anderson, Ian 1991 Simple test screens genetic diseases, *New Scientist*, **132** (1792), 25.

Anderson, Ian 1986 Will the computer tell the President? *New Scientist*, **110** (1512), 20.

Anderson, Christopher 1990 Genome Project to tackle mass screening, *Nature*, **348** (6302), 569.

Anderson, Ian 1989 Brain Waves give a voice to Disabled People, *New Scientist*, **121** (1651), 38.

Anderson, W. French 1995 Gene therapy, *Scientific American*, **273** (3), 124–128.

Andima, Haron, S. & Shem Arungu-Olende (1987, February) The use of microcomputers for financial modeling of a public utility in a developing country, *Microprocessing and Microprogramming*, **19** (2), 79–82.

221

Angier, Natalie (1992, September 29) Many Americans say genetic information is public property, *New York Times*, p. C 2.

Angier, Natalie (1993, March 4) Scientists find long-sought gene that causes Lou Gehrig's disease, *New York Times*, p. A 1.

Angier, Natalie (1993, March 12) Study suggests genes sway lesbians's sexual orientation, *New York Times*, p. A 11.

Angier, Natalie (1994, February 11) U.S. dropping its efforts to patent thousands of genetic fragments, *The New York Times*, Feb 11, 1994, p. A 16.

Angier, Natalie (1996, Nov 29) People haunted by anxiety appear to be short on a gene, *New York Times*, p. A 1.

Annas, George, J. (1990, November/December 6) Outrageous fortune: Selling other peoples cells, *Hastings Center Report*, **20** (6), 36–39.

Arndt, Stephen, Clevenger, James & Meiskey, Lori (1985, July-December) Students' attitudes towards computers, *Computers and Social Sciences*, 1 (3–4), 181–190.

Arriaga, Patricia 1986 Distinguishing between the myth and reality of the information society, *New information technologies and development: ATAS Bulletin*, Issue 3, New York: UN Center for Science And Technology.

Artigiani Robert, 1986 Language logic and energy: A thermodynamic sketch of Greek development, *Mondes en Developpment*, 15 (3), 54–5.

Artigiani, Robert 1987 Revolution and evolution: Applying Prigogine's dissipative structures model, *Journal of Social and Biological Evolution*, 10, 249–64.

Artigiani, Robert 1988 Scientific revolution and the evolution of consciousness, *World Futures*, 25, 237–61.

ATAS Bulletin No 3: New Information Technologies and Development No 3. June 1986, Center for Science and Technology, United Nations, New York, p. 5.

Attwood, Brett 1996 Computer Programs use brain power, *Billboard*, 108 (40), 80.

Ayala, Francisco, J. 1978 The mechanisms of evolution, *Scientific American*, 16, 56–69.

Ayala, Francisco, J. 1985 Reduction in biology: A recent challenge. In David J. Depew and Bruce H. Weber (Eds.), *Evolution at crossroads: The new biology and the new philosophy of science*, Cambridge: MIT Press.

Ayres, Robert 1987 *Self organization in biology and economics*, Research report, Luxenburg: International Institute of Applied Systems.

Ayres, Robert & Miller, Steve (1982, May/June) Industrial robots on the line, *Technology Review*, p. 18.

Baark, Erik & Jamison, Andrew 1990 Biotechnology and culture: The impact of public debates on Government regulation in the United States and Denmark, *Technology in Society*, 12, 27–44.

Bagchi, Amiya K. 1987 *The Differential impact of new technologies: A framework for analysis*, Geneva: ILO Working Papers 12.

Bains, Sunny 1990 Many holograms multiply data storage, *New Scientist*, 128 (1742), 28.

Bajaj, Y.P. (Ed.). 1988 *Biotechnology in agriculture and forestry*, 4. Medicinal and Aromatic Plants, New York: Springer-Verlag.

Balsamo, Anne (1993 Spring) The Virtual body in cyberspace, *Journal of Research in Technology and Philosophy*, 28–35.

Bankowski, Zbigniew (1989, April) Ethics and health, *World Health*, pp. 25–26.

Baringa, Marcia 1990 A muted victory for the biotech industry, *Science*, 249 (4966), 239.

Barnes, Barry 1982 *T. S. Kuhn and Social Science*, London and Basingstoke: p. 90. The Macmillan Press Ltd.

Beardsley, Tim 1996 Vital data, *Scientific American*, 274 (3),76–81.

Bedau, M.A. 1992 Philosophical aspects of artificial life. In F.J. Varela, & P. Bourgine (Eds.), *Towards a practice of autonomous systems. Proceedings of the first European conference on artificial life*, 101–108, Cambridge: MIT Press.

Bell, Daniel 1973 *The Coming of Post Industrial Society*, New York Basic books.

Bendix, Reinhard 1963 *Work and authority in industry*, New York: Harper Torch Books.

Berer, Marge 1990 The perfection of offspring, *New Scientist*, 126 (1725),58–59.

Berman, B. J. 1992 Artificial Intelligence and the ideology of capitalist reconstruction, *AI and Society*, 6 (2), 103–115.

Birnbaum, N. 1980 The State in contemporary France. In R. Scase (Ed.), *The State in Western Europe*, pp. 67–80, London: Croom Helm.

Birnbaum, Joel S. 1985 Towards the domestication of computers. In Joseph F. Traub (Ed.), *Cohabiting with computers*, pp. 45–51. Los Altos, California: William Kaufmann Inc..

Bishop, Donald H. 1982 Peirce & Eastern Thought in Ketner, Kenneth L., Ransdell, Joseph M.,; Eisele, Carolyn; Fisch, Max H.; and Hardwick, Charles S. (Eds.),

Proceedings of the C.S. Peirce Bicentennial International Congress, Graduate Studies Texas Tech University 1982, p. 265–271.

Bishop, Jerry E. (1993, Jan 14) Gene-activating therapy gets boost from study on treating blood disorders, *The Wall Street Journal*, p. B 6.

Blackmore, John T. 1972 Mach and Buddhism in Blackmore, John T. *Ernst Mach, His Work, Life and Influence*, University of California Press, 1972, pp. 286–355.

Blakeslee, Sandra (1996, June 23) Researchers track down a gene that may govern spatial abilities, *The New York Times*, p. C 3.

Blank, Robert H. 1982 Public policy implications of human genetic technology: Genetic screening, *The Journal of Medicine and Philosophy*, 7 (4), 355–374.

Bledsoe, W. W. & Loveland, D. W. 1984 Automated theorem proving: After 25 years, *Contemporary Mathematics*, 29 (5), 12–21.

Bloch, Marc 1961 *Feudal society*, Chicago: University of Chicago Press.

Bloom, Barry R. 1989 Vaccines for the Third World, *Nature*, (Nov. 9' 89) 342, 115–120.

Board on Science & Technology for Development Office of International Affairs 1982, *Priorities in biotechnological research for International development*, Proceedings of a workshop, National Research Council, p. 30, Washington, D.C.

Boden, M. 1980 Artificial Intelligence and biological reductionism. In Mae-Wan Ho and Peter T. Saunders (Eds.), *Beyond Neo Darwinism*, pp. 317–330, London: Academic Press Inc.

Boden, Margaret 1988 *Computer models of mind: Computational approaches in theoretical psychology*, Cambridge: Cambridge University Press.

Bograt, Greg 1991 The Use of Meditation in Psychotherapy: A Review of the Literature, *American Journal of Psychotherapy*, July 1991 **XLV** (3), 383–412.

Boden, Margaret 1990 *The creative mind: Myths and mechanisms*, London: Weidenfeld & Nicolson.

Bonte, P. 1981 Marxist theory and anthropological analysis: The study of nomadic pastoral societies. In J.S. Kahn, & Josep R. Llobera (Eds.), *The anthropology of precapitalist societies*, pp. 22–57, London: MacMillan.

Boulding, K. E. 1978 *Ecodynamics: A new theory of societal evolution*, London: Sage.

Borman, Stu 1989 New instrumentation to speed DNA sequencing, *Chemical and Engineering News*, 67 (48), 6, (Nov 13 '89).

Bourdieu, Pierre 1991 The peculiar history of scientific reason, *Sociological Forum*, 6, 3–26.

Boulding, Kenneth 1976 The great laws of change. In M. A. Tang, F. M. Westerfield, and J. S. Worley (Eds.), *Evolution, welfare and time in economics*, pp. 37–44. Toronto: Lexington Books.

Bower, B. 1990 Computers get a boost as psychotherapists, *New Scientist*, 126 (1700), 37.

Bowers C. A. 1988 *The cultural dimensions of educational computing*, New York: Teachers College Press.

Boyer, R. S. & Moore, J. S. 1979 *A computational logic*, New York: Academic Press.

Brain cell transplants may treat retardation (1995, March 23) *New York Times*, p. A 20.

Brandon, Robert N. 1990 *Adaptation and environment*, New Jersey: Princeton University Press.

Braverman, Avishay & Hammer, Jeffrey S. 1988 Computer models for agricultural policy analysis, *Finance and Development*, 25 (2), 42–44.

Brodner, Peter 1990 Towards the anthropocentric factory, *Tokyo international workshop on industrial culture and human centered systems*, Tokyo: Kezai University.

Brody, Herb (1990, August/September). The neural computer, *Technology Review*, p. 32.

Bromley, Allan 1983 Inside the world's first computers, *New Scientist*, 99 (1315), 81–84.

Brooks, Daniel R. & Wiley, E.O. 1986 *Evolution as entropy: Toward a unified theory of biology*, Chicago & London: The University of Chicago Press.

Brown, William "The Needle Point with 3D View of Life," *New Scientist*, 127 (1736), 30.

Brown F. 1984 *Scientific rationality: The sociological turn*, Dordrecht & Boston: Reidel.

Broyles, William Jr. (1984, November). Why men love war, *Esquire*, p. 58.

Brzezinski, Zbigniew 1970 *Between two ages: America's role in the technetronic era*, New York: Viking Press.

Buchanan, B.G. & Mitchell, T.M. 1978 Model-directed learning of production rules. In D.A. Waterman, & F. Hayes-Roth (Eds.), *Pattern directed inference systems*, pp. 297–312, New York: Academic Press.

Encyclopedia of Buddhism 1961 G.P. Malasekera (Ed.). (Vol. 1, p.186). Colombo: Govt. Press.

Buddhist Encyclopaedia, G.P. Malalasekera (Ed.), Government of Sri Lanka, Colombo, 1984.

Bugliarello, George (1989, December). Merging the artefact and its maker, *Mechanical engineering*, pp. 46–48.

Burgess, John (1991, Oct 7). White collar jobs go offshore, *New York Herald Tribune*, pp. 5.

Bylinsky, Gene (1991, June 3). The marvels of virtual reality, *Fortune*, 126 (12), 138–143.

Bylinsky, Gene (1994, May 30). Genetics: the money rush is on, *Fortune*, 129 (11), 94–108.

Bylinsky, Gene & Moore A.H. (1983, February 21). Flexible manufacturing systems, *Fortune*, 118 (4), 88–92.

Cabling of the Brain, *Economist*, 15 June 1985, p. 84.

Calem, Robert E. (1994, January 2). In far more gadgets, a hidden chip, *The New York Times*, Section 3, p. 9.

Callahan, Daniel (1990, July/August). Religion and the secularization of bioethics, *Hastings Center Report*, 20 (4), 2–4.

Campbell, Courtney S. (1990, July/August). Religion and moral meaning in bioethics, *Hastings Center Report*,20 (4), 4–10.

Carpenter, Betsy (1989, May 8). The body's master controls, *U.S. News & World Report*, 57–59.

Chan, Vincent W. S. 1995 All optical networks, *Scientific American*, 273 (3), 56–61.

Chithelen, Ignatius 1989 AI: New technology learns Wall Street's mind set, *Wall Street Computer Review*, 2 (9), 3.

Christopher, Joyce 1991 Prospectors of tropical medicines, *New Scientist*, 132 (1791), 36–40.

Churchland, Paul M. 1995 *The engine of reason, the seat of the soul: A philosophical journey into the brain*, London, Bradford.

Clark, Andy 1987 Cognitive science meets the biological mind, *New Scientist*, 116 (1581), 26–27.

Clay, Carr (1989, April). Personnel computing: Expert support environments, *Personnel Journal*, 68 (4), 117–126.

Clerical jobs are moving to countries with cheap labor. (1985, February 26), *Wall Street Journal*, p. 4.

Clery, Daniels 1990 Organic transistor challenges amorphous silicon, *New Scientist*, **128** (1747), 24.

Clery, Daniels 1993 Memorable future for the lone electron, *New Scientist*, **137** (1862), 17.

Coats, Pamela K.1986 Artificial Intelligence: Replacing managerial judgement with computer, *Journal of Business Forecasting*, **5** (1), 22–23.

Cochran, Tracy (1992, Fall), *Samsara* squared: Buddhism and Virtual Reality, *Tricycle: The Buddhist Review*, **2** (5), 76–83.

Coghlan, Andy 1993 The cryptographer who took a crack at 'junk' DNA, *New Scientist*, **138** (1879), 15.

Coghlan, Andy 1993a. China's new cultural revolution and comment, *New Scientist*, **137** (1854), 4.

Coghlan, Andy 1993b Engineering the therapies of tomorrow, *New Scientist*, **138** (1870), 26–31.

Coghlan, Andy 1994b. Artificial antibodies cripple cancer protein, *New Scientist*, **144**, (1946) 23.

Cohen, Paul R. & Feigenbaum, Edward A. 1982 *The handbook of Artificial Intelligence* (Vol. III) London: Pitman.

Collins, H. M. 1975 The seven sexes: A study in the sociology of a phenomenon, or the replication of experiment in physics, *Sociology*, **9** (2), 78–83.

"Computer Array Interprets The Human Genome", *New Scientist* (6 May 1989): **122** (1663), 36.

Conrad, Michael 1996 Cross-scale information processing in evolution, development and intelligence, *Biosystems*, **38** (1), 97–109.

Conrad, Michael 1986 The lure of molecular computing, *IEEE Spectrum*, **23** (10), 56–60.

Corcoran, Elizabeth 1992 Robots for the Operating Room, *The New York Times*, July 19, 1992, Section 3, p. 9.

Cordes, Colleen 1986 Overseas trials of genetically altered vaccines raise questions about ethics for researchers, *Chronicle of Higher Education*, **33** (13), 6–8.

Coulborn, Rushton (Ed.). 1956 *Feudalism in history*, New Jersey: Princeton University Press.

Crow, Michael 1989 Technology development in Japan and the United States: Lessons from the high temperature superconductivity race, *Science and Public Policy*, **16** (6), 322–344.

Culbertson, William Y. (1990, February) Expert systems in finance, *Corporate Accounting*, **5** (3), 21–23.

Culotta, Elizabeth (1993, May 14). New startups move in as gene therapy goes commercial, *Science*, **260** (5110), 914–915.

Cyber wars: Logic bombs may soon replace more conventional munitions. (1996, January 13), *The Economist*, pp. 89–90.

Dambrot, Stuart 1988 Clever molecules for 'Thinking Computers', *New Scientist* **126** (1645), 29.

Davis, Howard & Scase, Richard 1985 *Western capitalism and State socialism*, Oxford: Basil Blackwell.

Dawkins, Richard 1976 *The selfish gene*, Oxford: Oxford University Press.

Day, Michael 1996 Repair kit for damaged nerves, *New Scientist*, **150** (2033), 22.

Dazzaniga, Michael S. 1992 *Nature's mind: The biological roots of thinking, emotions, sexuality, language and intelligence*, New York: Basic Books.

De Silva, Padmal 1984 "Buddhism and behavior modification", *Behavior Research and Therapy*, 1984, **22** (6), 661–678.

Denning, Peter J. 1990 Saving all the bits, *American Scientist*, **78** (5), 402–406.

Denser, faster, cheaper: The micro chip in the 21st century. (1991, December 29), *The New York Times*, p. 5.

Descartes, Rene, Discourse de la methode, quoted in *Dictionary of the history of ideas* (1973). Philip P. Wiener (Ed.), 1, 242.

Di Giammarino, Peter & Kuckuk, Matthew (1991, May/June). The move to advanced decision support and strategic systems, *Bankers Magazine*, p. 174.

Dibbell, Julian (1996, April 1). Two approaches represent an almost theological schism in computer science, *Time*, pp. 49–50.

Dickerson, Richard E. 1978 Chemical evolution and the origin of life, *Scientific American*, **239** (3), 16.

Dickson, David (1988, May 27). Europe grants first patent on plants, *Science*, **240** (4856), 1142.

Dizardt, Wilson, P. 1982, *The coming information age*, New York and London: Longman.

Dobrov, G.M. 1979 Technology as a form of organization, *International Social Science Journal*, **XXXI** (4), 66–72.

Doi, Noricha, Furukawa, Koichi & Fuchi, Kazuhiro (1987, July) The search for a thinking computer, *The Courier*, Paris: UNESCO.

Donaldson, Margaret 1992 *Human Minds An Exploration*, Penguin Books 1992 London p. 227.

Donnelley, Strachan (1989, July/August). Medicine, morality and culture: International bioethics, *Hastings Center Report*, 19 (4), pp. 1–2.

Doukidis, Georgios, I. & Dayo Forster 1990 The potential for computer-aided diagnosis of tropical diseases in developing countries: An expert system case study, *European Journal of Operational Research*, 49 (2), 23–29.

Downey, Gary Lee, Dumit, Joseph & Williams, Sarah 1995 Cyborg anthropology. In Chris Hables Gray (Ed.), *The Cyborg handbook*, pp. 341–347. New York & London: Routledge.

Drucker, Peter, F. 1969 *The Age of discontinuity: Guidelines to our changing society*, New York: Harper & Row.

Duda, R.O., Gasching, J. & Hart, P. 1981 Model design in the prospector consultant system for mineral exploration. In D. Michie (Ed.), *Expert systems in the micro electronic age*, Edinburgh University Press.

Durand, P., Reysenbach, A.L., Prieur, D. & Pace, N. 1993 Isolation and characterization of Thiobacillus-Hydrothermalis Sp-Nov, a Mesophilic Obligately Chemolithotrophic Bacterium isolated from a Deep-Sea Hydrothermal Vent in Fiji Basin, *Archives of Microbology*, 159 (1), 39–44.

Dyson, Esther 1993 Biology is destiny in computers too, *Computerworld* (COW), 27 (3), 33.

Eastmond, A & Robert, M.C. 1989 *Advanced plant biotechnology in Mexico: A hope for the neglected*, Geneva: ILO.

Ebel, Karl, H. 1989 Manning the unmanned factory, *International Labor Review*, 128 (5), 535–551.

Ebel, Karl, H. 1990 *Computer integrated manufacturing: The social dimension*, Geneva: ILO.

Edquist, C. 1978 *Social carriers of science and technology for development*, (Discussion Paper 123). Sweden: Lund University, Research Policy Program.

Edwards, Paul, N. 1990 The army and the microworld: Computers and the politics of gender identity, *Signs: Journal of Women in Culture and Society*, 16 (11), 124.

Eigen, Manfred, Gardiner, J. William, Schuster, Peter & Ruthild, Winkler-Oswatitisch 1982 The origin of genetic information. In John Maynard Smith (Ed.), *Evolution now: A century after Darwin*, London: Nature, MacMillan.

Eldredge, N. & Gould, S.J. 1972 Punctuated equilibria: An alternative to phyletic gradualism. In T.J.M. Schoff (Ed.), *Models of paleobiology*, San Francisco: W.H. Freeman.

Elmer-Dewitt, Philip (1992, October 5). Catching a bad gene in the tiniest of embryos, *Time*, pp. 81–82.

Elshtain, Jean Bethke (1991, March). Reproductive ethics, *Utne Recorder*, pp. 64–65.

Emmeche, C. "Life as an abstract phenomenon: is artificial life possible?" *Towards a Practice of Autonomous Systems: Proceedings of the First European Conference on Artificial Life* eds. F. J. Varela and P. Bourgine (MIT Press Cambridge, MA, 1992).

Emsley, John "Computer Chemistry – the shape of Things to Come" *New Scientist* 133 (1809) 19.

Etzkorn, Peter, K. 1985 Whither alienation?, *Sociologia Internationalis*, 23 (1), 43–48.

Factor, Lance, R. "What is the 'Logic' in Buddhist Logic?" *Philosophy East West*, 33, 183–188, AP 83.

Ezrahi, Yaron 1971 The Political Resources of American Science *Science Studies* 1, 1, 1971.

Farley, J. 1977 *The spontaneous generation controversy from Descartes to Oparin*, Baltimore: Johns Hopkins University Press.

Farrington, John (Ed.). 1989 *Agricultural biotechnology: Prospects for the Third World*, London: Overseas Development Institute.

Favello, A., Hillier, L. & Wilson, R. 1995 Genomic DNA sequencing, *Methods in Cell Biology*, 48, 571–582.

Feigenbaum, Edward & McCorduck, Pamela (1983, June). Land of the rising Fifth Generation, *High Technology*, pp. 25–28.

Fenema, E. & Sherman, J. 1977 Sex related differences in mathematics achievement, spatial visualization, and affective factors, *American Educational Research Journal*, 14.(1), 51–71.

Ferry, Georgina 1986 Parallel learning in brains and mac hines, *New Scientist*, 109 (1499), 37.

Feuer, L S. 1978 Telelogical principles in science, *Inquiry: An Interdisciplinary Journal of Philosophy and the Social Sciences*, 21 (4), 37–44 Oslo: Universitets Forlaget.

Finkelstein, Joanne, L. (1990, July/August). Biomedicine and technocratic power, *Hasting Center Report*, 20 (4), 13–16.

Fisher, Lawrence, M. 1992 "Pairing chips and Living Cells to Test Drugs" *The New York Times* (March 25, 1992), p. D 7.

Flamm, Kenneth 1987 *Targeting the Computer* Washington, DC, Brookings Institution.

Fisher, Lawrence, M. 1992 "Pairing Chips and Living Cells to Test Drugs" *The New York Times* (March 25, 1992), p. D 7.

Fleissner, Peter, & Hofkirchner, Wolfgang 1996 Emergent information: Towards a unified information theory, *Biosystem*, 38 (1), 243–248.

Flower, Joe 1996 A life in Silicon? *New Scientist*, 150 (2034), 33–35.

Flynn, Laurie (1996, March 4). Prototypes of Virtual Shoppers 'Avatars' : With your head on their shoulders, navigate cyberspace, *The New York Times*, p. D3.

Forman, Paul, 1971 Weimar culture, causality and Quantum Theory 1918–27: Adaptation by German physicists and mathematicians to a hostile intellectual environment, *Historical Studies in the Physical Sciences* (1971) 3: 1–116. Philadelphia: University of Pennsylvania Press.

Forsyth, Richard & Naylor, Chris 1986 *The hitch-hiker's guide to Artificial Intelligence*, New York: Chapman and Hall/Methuen.

Forsythe, Diana, E. 1993 The construction of work in Artificial Intelligence, *Science, Technology and Human Values*, 18 (4), 460–480.

Freeman, Chris 1987 Quoted in *Plant biotechnology including tissue culture and cell culture*, p.15. (1989). New York: UNDP.

Fulton, L. L., Hillier, L. & Wilson, R. K. 1995, Large-scale complementary-DNA Sequencing methods, *Methods in Cell Biology*, 48, 571–582.

Furst, Steven & Covert, Ranel (1988, March/April). National budgeting with micros — and without tears, *Computers in Africa*, pp. 20–24.

Gaasterland, T. & Sensen, C.W. 1996 Magpie-automated genome interpretation. *Trends in Genetics*, 12 (2), 76–78.

Garrett, John & Wright, Geoff 1978 Micro is beautiful, *Undercurrents*, 2(3), 27.

Garson, Barbara 1988 *The Electronic Sweatshop: How Computers are transferring the office of the Future into the Factory of the Past*, New York, Simon and Schuster.

Geister, Elieger (1986, July/Aug). Artificial management and the artificial manager, *Business Horizons*, 29 (4), 38–42.

Gene may be clue to nature of nurturing. (1996, January 26), *The New York Times*, p. A21.

Gene triumph. 1990 *New Scientist*, 127 (1733), 33.

Gene linked to diabetes found. (1993, January 12), *The New York Times*, p. C3.

Gene implanted in mice via pregnant mothers. (1995, February 28), *The New York Times*, p. 3.

Gene clues to changes that precede leukemia. (1993, February 23), *The New York Times*, p. 3.

Gianturco, Michael (1990, September 17). Bullish on biotech, *Forbes*, 146(6). p.208.

Gibson, William 1984 *Neuromancer*, New York: Ace Science Fiction Books.

Gilbert, G. N. 1976 The development of science and scientific knowledge: The case of radar meteor research. In O. Lemaino (Ed.), *Perspectives on the emergence of scientific discipline*, The Hague & Paris: Mouton.

Giuliano, Vincent, E. 1982 The mechanization of office work, *Scientific American* 252 (1), 23–31.

Goleman, Daniel 1981 "Buddhist and Western psychology: Some commonalities and differences" *Journal of Transpersonal Psychology* 1981 13(2), 125–136.

Goodman, Billy 1990 The genetic anatomy of US (and a few friends), *BioScience*, 40 (7), 484–9.

Goonatilake, Lalith 1989 Appropriate computer education for industrial growth in developing countries, *Computers in Industry*, 12 (1), 59–65.

Goonatilake, Suran (1991a, July 4). Working towards a molecular revolution, *Computing*, p. 26.

Goonatilake, Suran (1991b, July 18). Virtually certain of the meaning of life, *Computing*, p. 20.

Goonatilake, Suran & Khebbal, Sukhdev (Eds.). 1995 *Intelligent hybrid systems*, Chichester, New York: John Wiley & Sons.

Goonatilake, Suran & Treleaven, Philip (Eds.). 1995 *Intelligent systems for finance and business*, Chichester, New York: John Wiley & Sons.

Goonatilake, Susantha 1979 Technology as a social gene, *Journal of Scientific and Industrial Research*, 38 (2), 15–23.

Goonatilake, Susantha 1982 Colonies and scientific expansion (and contraction), *Review: Journal of the Fernand Braudel Center*, V (3), 78–85, New York: SUNY Press.

Goonatilake, Susantha 1984 *Aborted discovery: Science and creativity in the Third World*, London: Zed.

Goonatilake, Susantha, 1991 *The evolution of information: Lineages in gene, culture and artefact*, London: Pinter Publishers.

Gould, Stephen Jay 1983 The politics of evolution, *Psychohistory Review*, 11 (2–3), 15–35.

Gray, Chris Hables & Mentor, Steven 1995 In Chris Hables Gray (Ed.), The cyborg body politic: Version 1.2, *The Cyborg handbook*, New York & London: Routledge. pp 341–347.

Gray, Chris Hables, Mentor, Steven, & Figueroa-Sarriera, Heidi, J. 1995 "Cyborgology: Constructing the knowledge of cybernetic Organisms." In Chris Hables Gray (Ed.), *The Cyborg handbook*, New York & London: Routledge, pp 1–17.

Graziella, Mazzoli 1996 Advanced Technology in Hyper Complex Society: Between Creativity and Planning, *Tokyo International Workshop on Industrial Culture and Human Centred Systems*, Tokyo Kezai University.

Greene, Marjorie 1985, Perception, interpretation and the sciences: Toward a new philosophy of science. In David J. Depew & Bruce H. Weber (Eds.), *Evolution at cross roads: The new biology and new philosophy of science*, Cambridge Mass.: MIT Press.

Greenhouse, Steven (1992, Oct 14). Greenspan sees risks globally, *The New York Times*, p. D 1.

Gregorio, Domenico de (1987, July). The new world of Artificial Intelligence, *The Courier*, Paris: UNESCO.

"Groping at atoms" *Economist*, July 18th 1992, pp 87–88.

Gross, Neil (1990, June 15). 'Biochips': Life mimics electronics, *Business Week*, p. 94.

Gross, Neil (1996, August 5). Remembrance of things past on a chip, *Business Week*, p. 81.

Grossing, Gerhard 1988 How does a quantum system perceive its environment?. In A. Van der Merwe, F. Selleri, G. Tarozzi (Eds.), *Microphysical reality and Quantum Formalism*, pp. 225–238, Dordrecht: Kluwer Academic Publishers.

Gruson, Lindsey (1993, February 16). When 'mom' and 'grandma' are one and the same, *New York Times*, p. B 1.

Guilmet, George 1983 Impact of the computer revolution on human cognition, *Cultural Futures Research*, **8** (1), 45–56.

Gunaratne V.F. 1982 *Buddhist Reflections on Death*, Buddhist Publication Society, Kandy 1982, p. 12.

Gwynne, P. 1996 Gene sequencers seek to boost the speed of their technology, *R&D Magazine*, **38** (2), 41–42.

Hahlweg, Kai & Hooker, C.A. 1989 Evolutionary epistemology and philosophy of science. In Kai Hahlweg & C.A. Hooker (Eds.), *Issues in evolutionary epistemology* pp. 25–30, Albany: State University of New York Press.

Hallberg, Margareta 1990 Science and feminism, Vetenskop och feminism, *Sociologisk - Forskning*, **27** (3), 27–34.

Halpert, Julie Edelson (1993, Aug. 29). One car, worldwide, with strings pulled from Michigan, *The New York Times*, Section 3, p. 7.

Hamer, Dean & Copeland, Peter 1995 *The science of desire: The search for the gay gene and the biology of behavior*, New York: Simon & Schuster.

Hannah, Eric, C. & Soreff, Jeffrey 1983 Single chip computers, *Interdisciplinary Science Reviews*, **8** (1), 35–39.

Haraway, Donna 1988 Situated knowledges: The science question in feminism and the privilege of partial perspective, *Feminist Studies*, **14**, 575–599.

Haraway, Donna 1995 Cyborgs and Symbionts. Living together in the New World Order in Gray, Chris Hables (ed) *The Cyborg hand book*, Routledge New York p. xi–xx

Harding, Sandra 1986 *The science question in feminism*, Ithaca, New York: Cornell University Press.

Harding, Sandra 1991 *Whose science? Whose knowledge?*, Ithaca, New York: Cornell University Press.

Hessen, Boris 1930 The social and economic roots of Newton's Principia, *International Congress of the History of Science and Terminology*, London.

Hilts, Philip, J. 1996 Photos show mind recalling a word, *The New York Times*, Nov 11 1991.

Hindley, Martin 1996 Bionic brain cells teach the language of nerves, *New Scientist ISO* (2032), 22.

Hinton, Geoffrey, E. 1992 How neural networks learn from experience, *Scientific American*, **267** (3), 145–151.

Hitomi, K. 1990 Computer aided design, manufacturing and management, International conference on industrial culture and human centered systems, Tokyo: Keizai University.

Ho, Maw-Wan, Saunders, Peter & Fox, Sidney 1986 A new paradigm for evolution, *New Scientist*, **109** (1496), 23–24.

Hoffmeyer, Jesper (forthcoming) "The Unfolding semiosphere' in van de Vijver, Gertrudis; Salthe, Stanley S.; Delpos, Manuela; (Eds.) *Evolutionary Systems*, Kluwer Academic Publishers, Dordrecht (forthcoming)

Hoffman, Carol, A. 1990 Ecological risks of genetic engineering of crop plants, *Bioscience*, **40** (6), 24.

Holderness, Mike 1990 Neural Networks names niffs, *New Scientist*, **125** (1719), 34.

Holm, N.G. 1992 Marine hydrothermal systems and the origin of life — Preface, Special issue, *Origins of Life and Evolution of the Biosphere*, **22** (1–4), 1.

Holton, Gerald 1973 *Thematic origins of scientific thought: Kepler to Einstein*, Cambridge, Mass: Harvard University Press.

Holusha, John (1993, Oct. 31). Carving out real-life:Uses for Virtual Reality, *The New York Times*, Section 3, p. 11.

Holusha, John (1996, March 20). Making the shoe fit, perfectly, *The New York Times*, pp. D1, D7.

Holzmuller, Werner 1984 *Information in biological systems: The role of macromolecules*, Cambridge: University Press.

Horgan, John 1993 Trends in behavioral genetics: Eugenics revisited, *Scientific American*, **268** (6), 122–131.

Horowitz, Irving Louis 1987 Limits of standardization in scholarly journals, *Scholarly Publishing*, **18** (2), 125–130.

Horton, Allan quoted in 1983 Electronic access to information: Its impact on scholarship and research, *Interdisciplinary Science Reviews*, **8** (1), 67.

Huberman, Bernado, A. & Hogg, Tod 1988 The behaviors of computational ecologies. In B.A. Huberman (Ed.), *The Ecology of Computation*, Amsterdam: North-Holland Publishing.

Hudson, C.A. (1982, February 12), Computers in manufacturing, *Science*, **218** (3546), 149.

Hunt, Morton 1986 The total gene screen, *New York Times Magazine* Jan. 19; pp. 32–33

Hut, Piet & Sussman, Gerald Jay 1987 Advanced computing for science, *Scientific American*, 257 (4), 144–153.

Huws, Ursula 1986 The effects of AI on women's lives. In K.S.Gill (*Ed.*), *Artificial Intelligence for society*, Brighton: Wiley.

Inada, Kenneth, K. 1979 "Problematics of the Buddhist Nature of Self." *Philosophy East West*, 29, 141–158, Ap. 79.

Inada, Kenneth, K. & Jacobson, Nolan. P. (Eds.) 1984 *Buddhism and American Thinkers*, SUNY Press Albany 1984.

Jacobson, N. P. 1969 'The Philosophy of Oriental Influence in Hume's Philosophy', *Philosophy East and West*, **XIX** (1), University of Hawaii Press, Honolulu, Hawaii, January 1969.

Inside the gene machine, 1996 *New Scientist*, 150 (2027), 26–29.

James, Barry (1993, Dec 23). Sorting out the 'library' of genes, *International Herald Tribune*, p. 7.

Jansen, Sue Curry 1988 The ghost in the machine: Artificial Intelligence and gendered thought patterns, *Resources for Feminist Research/Documentation sur La Rocherche Feministe*, 17, 4–7.

Jansen, Sue Curry 1990 Is science a man? New feminist epistemologies and reconstruction of knowledge, *Theory and Society*, 19 (2), 235–246.

Jantsch, Eric 1976 Evolution: Self realization through self-transcendence. In Erich Jantsch & Conrad H. Waddington (Eds.), *Evolution and consciousness*, pp. 37–70, Reading, Mass: Addison-Wesley.

Jerison, Harry, J. 1985 Paleoneurology and the evolution of mind, *Scientific American*, 252 (9), 45–48.

Johnson, George, Same gene may shape face, heart and hands, *The New York Times*, February 13, 1996, pp. C1, C7.

Johnson-Laird, P.N. 1988 *The computer and the mind: An introduction to cognitive science*, London: Fontana.

Jones, Stacy V. 1987 "Designing Proteins" *The New York Times*, Nov. 14, 1987.

Joyce, G.F. 1993 Evolution of catalytic function, *Pure and Applied Chemistry*, 65 (6), 1205–1212.

Joyce, Christopher 1991 Prospectors for tropical medicines, *New Scientist*, 132 (1791), 36–40.

Juma, Celestous 1989 *The gene hunters: Biotechnology and the scramble for seeds*, Princeton, NJ: Princeton University Press.

Junne, Gerd, Komen, John and Tomei, Frank 1989 Dematerialisation of production: Impact on raw material exports of developing countries, *Third World Quarterly*, 11 (2), 128–142.

Kabat-Zinn, Jon.; Massion, Ann O.; Kristeller, Jean; Petersen, Linda Gay; Fletcher, Kenneth, E.; Pert, Lori; Lenderking, William, R.; Santorelli, Saki, F. (1992) "Effectiveness of a Meditation-Based Stress Reduction Program in the Treatment of Anxiety Disorders" *American Journal of Psychiatry*, July 1992, 149 (7), 936–943.

Kahn, J.S. & Llobera, Joseph R. 1981 *The anthropology of precapitalist societies*, London: Macmillan.

Kahn, Patricia 1993 Genome on the production line, *New Scientist*, 138 (1870), 32–36.

Kairamo, Kari 1987 Longer-term impacts of information and communication technologies, *Interdependence and co-operation in tomorrow's world* (p. 41). Paris: OECD.

Kajikawa, Kin-ichiro (1989, July/August) Japan: A new field emerges, *Hastings Center Report*, 19 (4), 29–30.

Kaminuma, Tsuduchika & Matsumoto, Gen. 1991 *Biocomputers: The next generation from Japan*, London: Chapman and Hall.

Kampis, George (forthcoming) "Evolution as its own cause and effect" in van de Vijver, Gertrudis; Salthe, Stanley S.; Delpos, Manuela; (eds) *Evolutionary Systems*, Kluwer Academic Publishers, Dordrecht.

Kaplan, S.J. & Ferris, D. (1982, August). Natural language in the DP world, *Datamation*, pp.114–20.

Keen, G., Burton, J., Crowley, D., Dickinson, E., Espinosalujan, A., Franks, E., Hargar, C., Manning, M., Maech, S., Mclecd, H., Oneill, J., Power, A., Pumilia, M., Reinert, R., Rider, D., Rohrlich, J., Schwertteger, J., Smyth, L., Thayer, N., Troup, C. & Fields, C. (1996). The Genome-Sequence-Database (Gsdb) — Meeting the challenge of Genomic Sequencing, *Nucleic Acids Research*, 24 (I), 13–16.

Kimura, M. 1985 The neutral theory of molecular evolution, *New Scientist*, 111 (1516), 24.

Kingman, Sharon 1989 Antibody takes poison darts to lymph cancers, *New Scientist*, 122 (1658), 26.

Klappenburg, Jack & Kenney, Martin 1984 Biotechnology, seeds and the restructuring of agriculture, *The Insurgent Sociologist*, 12 (3), 3–17.

Kluckhohn, Clyde 1959 *Mirror for man*, New York: Fawcett World Library.

Knee, C. 1985 The hidden curriculum of the computer. In T. Solomonides & L. Levidos (Eds.), *Computer technology: Computer as culture*, pp. 72–85. London: Free Association Books.

Knight, Jerry (1987, December 16). Were calculating computers the culprits behind the crash?, *Washington Post*, National Weekly Edition, pp. 7.

Knorr-Certinca K. 1981 *The manufacture of knowledge*, Oxford: Pergamon.

Kobayashi, Koji 1983 Integration of computers and communications, C + C: The influence of space technology, *Interdisciplinary Science Reviews*, 8 (1), 22–26.

Kohyama, Kenichi, (1968 Winter). Introduction to information society theory, *Chuo Koron*.

Kolata, Gina (1992, July 28). Biologist's speedy gene method scares peers. But gains backer, *New York Times*, p. C1.

Kolata, Gina (1993, Oct 26). Cloning human embryos: Furious debate erupts over ethics, *The New York Times*, p. A1.

Kolata, Gina (1994, Jan 6). Fetal ovary transplant is envisioned, *The New York Times*, p. A 16.

Kolata, Gina (1995a, February 28). Man s world, woman s world? Brain studies point to differences in approaches to understanding male-female brain differences, *The New York Times*, pp. C1, C7.

Kolata, Gina (1995b, December 26). Will alcoholic mice teach scientists about human behavior?, *The New York Times*, p. C 12.

Kolata, Gina (1996, April 25). Map of yeast genes promises clues to diseases of humans, *The New York Times*, p. B11.

Kolata, Gina (1996a, May 30). Study finds way to produce an animal s sperm cells in another species, years later, *The New York Times*, p. A 24.

Kolata, Gina (1996b, December 10). With major math proof, brute computers show flash of reasoning power, *The New York Times*, p. C1.

Kolm, Serge-Christopher 1986 "The Buddhist theory of 'no-self'" in Elster, Jon (ed) *The Multiple Self* Cambridge University Press Cambridge, 1986, 233–265.

Kosko, Bart & Isaka, Satoru (1993, July). Fuzzy logic, *Scientific American*, 269 (1), 62–67.

Kramer, Pamela S. & Lehman, Sheila 1990 Mismeasuring women: A critique of research on computer ability and avoidance, Signs: *Journal of Women in Culture and Society*, 16 (1), 171.

Kramer, Peter, D.1993 *Listening to Prozac*, Harmondsworth: Penguin.

Kuhn, T. S. 1962 *The structure of scientific revolutions*, Chicago: University of Chicago Press.

Kuppers, Bernd-Olaf 1990 *Information and the origin of life*, Cambridge, Mass: The MIT Press.

Kurtzman, Joel 1993 *The death of money: How the electronic economy has destabilized the world's markets and created financial chaos*, New York: Simon & Schuster.

Lancaster, F.W., Lee, Sun-Yoon, Kim & Diluvio, Catalina 1990 Does place of publication influence citation behavior, *Scientometrics*, 19 (3–4), 239–244.

Langley, P. W. 1977 Rediscovering physics with BACON 3, *Proceedings of International Joint Conference on Artificial Intelligence*, 6, 505–7.

Lansdown, John & Earnshaw, Rae A. (Eds.). 1989 *Computers in art, design and animation*, New York: Springer-Verlag.

Lappe, Marc (1990, November/December). Genetics, neuroscience and biotechnology, *Hastings Center Report*, 19 (6), 21–22.

Large, Peter 1984 *The micro revolution*, New Jersey: Rowman & Allanheld. Quoted in Wurman, Saul Richard (1989), *Information anxiety*, p. 35, New York: Doubleday.

Larson, Eric D., Molt, Ross & Williams, R. H. 1986 Beyond the era of materials, *Scientific American*, 254 (6), 24–31.

Latour, B. & Woolgar, S. 1979 *Laboratory life: The social construction of scientific facts*, London: Sage.

Lauhon, C. & Szostak, J. 1993 Invitro selection of RNA molecules that specifically bind riboflavin, *Faseb Journal*, 7 (7), A1087–A1087.

Laurel, Brenda 1995 Virtual Reality *Scientific American* 273 ISS: 3 September 1995, p. 90.

Laurence, Jeremy (1995, April 3). Test-tube babies blessed with more loving parents, *The Times* (London), p. 3.

Lawren, William 1988 *The General and the Bomb*, New York: Dodd Mead & Co.

Lawrence, Lucy & Rogers, Lois (1996, 16 June). Women sell their eggs through agent for 750 pounds, *The Sunday Times* (London), p. 8.

Leakey, Richard & Lewin R. 1977 *Origins*, London: Macdonalds & Janes.

Leary, Warren E. (1996, March 22). Gene study finds link to type of epilepsy in surprising place, *The New York Times*, p. A19.

Lederman, Leonard L. 1987 Science and technology policies and priorities: A comparative analysis, *Science*, 237 (4819), 1125–1133.

Leigh, David 1995 Neural networks for credit scoring. In Suran Goonatilake, & Philip Trelevaven (Eds.), *Intelligent systems for finance and business*, pp. 78–89 Chiseter and New York: John Wiley & Sons.

Lemonick, Michael D. (1996, June 10). The sperm that never dies, *Time*, p. 49.

Lenat, Douglas 1983 Eurisko: A program that learns new heuristics and domain concepts, *Artificial Intelligence*, 21 (3), 3–14.

Lenat, Douglas B. 1995 Artificial Intelligence, *Scientific American*, 273 (3), 62–65.

Lesser, William H. (ed) 1989 *Animal Patents — the legal, Economic and Social issues* Macmillan Press, Basingtoke

Levy, Steven 1993 *Artificial life*, New York: Vintage Books.

Lewin, Roger 1990 In the beginning was the genome, *New Scientist*, 127 (1726), 34–38.

Lewontin, R.C. 1978 Adaptation, *Scientific American*, 239 (3),156–169.

Lind, Per 1991 *Computerization in developing countries: Model and reality*, London: Routledge.

Lorenz, Konrad quoted in Hahlweg, Kai and Hooker, C.A. 1989. Evolutionary epistemology and philosophy of science. In Kai Hahlweg & C.A. Hooker (Eds.), *Issues in evolutionary epistemology*, Albany: SUNY Press.

Lorenzo's oil malady: Biologists find gene. (1993, March 2), *The New York Times*, p. PS

Lovelock, J.E. 1987 *Gaia: A New look at Life on Earth* New York Oxford University Press.

Loy, David 1992 "Avoiding the Void: The lack of Self in Psychotherapy and Buddhism" *The Journal of Transpersonal Psychology*, 1992, 24 (2), 151–179.

Lukacs, George 1923 *Geschichte und Klassen Bewusstein* (History and class consciousness). Berlin: Malik.

Luke, Timothy W. (1996, March). On being digital in the electronic village and info-city, *Futures Bulletin*, p. 12.

Luukkonen, Terttu 1990 Publication structures and accumulative advantages, *Scientometrics*, 19 (3–4), 167–184.

Mac Cormac, Earl R. 1984 Men and machines: The computational metaphor, *Technology in Society*, 6 (3), 207, 216.

Mackenzie, D. & Barnes, S.B. 1978 Scientific judgement: The biometry - Mendalism controversy. In S.B.Barnes, & B. Shapin (Eds.), *Natural order*, pp. 62–75, Beverly Hills, California: Sage Publications, (Sage Focus Editions).

Mackenzie, D. 1978 Statistical theory and social interests: A case study. *Social Studies of Science*, **8**, (1) 35–83.

Mackenzie, Debora 1992 Europe debates the ownership of life, *New Scientist*, 133 (1802), 9–10.

Maes, Pattie 1995 Intelligent software, *Scientific American*, 273 (3) , 66–68.

Mahowald, Mary B., Silver, Jerry & Rakheson, Robert A. (1987 January/February). The ethical options in transplanting fetal tissue, *The Hastings Center Report*, 17 (1), 9–15.

Malaska, P. 1985 Outline of a policy for the future. In S. Aida (Ed.), *The science and praxis of complexity* pp. 104–111, Tokyo: United Nations University Press.

Manning, Elizabeth (1996, July 27). DNA strands learn to add, *United Press International reports.*

Marbach, William (1993, March 15). The new jam-packed chips are coming: Just don't ask how. *Business Week*, p. 93.

Marien, Michael (1983, September/October). Some questions for the information society, *World Future Society Bulletin.*

Marijuan, Pedro C. 1996 First conference on foundations of information science: From computers and quantum physics to cells, nervous systems, and societies, *Biosystems*, 38, 87–96.

Markle, Gerald E. & Robin, Stanley S. 1985 Biotechnology and the social construction of molecular biology, Science, Technology and Human Values, 10, (1) 70–79.

Markoff, John (1993, February 23). A novel microscope probes the ultra small, *The New York Times*, p. C 1.

Markoff, John (1992a, March 31). Pioneering the computer frontier, *The New York Times*, p. D 1.

Markoff, John (1992b, August 6). New ways to store more data, *The New York Times*, p. D 1.

Markoff, John (1995 May 15) "Information technology and now, computerized sensibility" *The New York Times*, p. D 6.

Markoff, John (1991, November 5). So who's talking: Human or machine, *The New York Times*, p. D 1.

Marks, Paul 1996 Bio-diode could lead to superchip, *New Scientist*, 149 (2014), 23.

Marti, John & Zeillenger, Anthony 1982 *Micros and money: New technology in banking and shopping.* London: Policy Studies Institute.

Martin, James 1981 *Telematic society: A challenge for tomorrow*, Englewood Cliffs NJ: Prentice Hall.

Maruyama, M. 1976 Toward human futuristics. In W. Maruyama, & A. Harkin (Eds.), *Cultures of the future*, pp. 33–60. The Hague: Mouton.

Masuda, Yoneji 1981 *The information society as post-industrial society*, Bethesda: World Future Society.

Matsuno, Koichiro 1996 Internalist stance and the physics of information, *Biosystems* 38, 111–118.

Maturana, Humberto R. & Varela, Francisco J. 1986 *The tree of knowledge: The biological roots of human understanding*, Boston & London: New Science Library, Shambhala.

Mayr, Ernst 1985 How biology differs from the physical sciences. In David J. Depew, & Bruce H. Weber (Eds.), *Evolution at the cross roads: The new biology and the new philosophy of science*, pp. 200–201 Cambridge: MIT Press.

McLuhan, Marshall 1964 *Understanding media: The extensions of man*, New York: McGraw Hill.

McNeill, Daniel, & Freiberger, Paul 1993 *Fuzzy logic*, New York: Simon & Schuster.

Michael Balick, Director, New York Botanical Garden's Institute of Economic Botany, quoted in (1991, September 23), *Time*, p. 52.

Michie, D. & Johnston, R. 1985 *The creative computer*, London: Pelican.

Michie, D. 1974 *On machine intelligence*, Edinburgh: Edinburgh University Press.

Miles, Ian, Muskens R. & Grupelaan W. 1988 *Global telecommunications networks/ Strategic considerations*, Doordech: Kluwer Academic Publications.

Miller, Susan Katz 1993 To catch a killer gene, *New Scientist*, 138 (1870), 37–40.

Miller, Henry J. & Ackerman, Stephen J. (1990, March). Perspective on food biotechnology, *FDA Consumer Research*, p. 32.

Miller, Stuart & O'Neill, Bill 1996 From Cradle to grave on memory chip *The Guardian*, July 18th 1996, p. 1.

Milner, Peter A. The mind and Donald O. Hebb *Scientific American*, (January, 1993), 268 (1), 124–129.

Milstead, Jeff & Milhon, Jude. (Interview with Mike Saenz). 1991. The carpal tunnel of love: Virtual sex, *Mondo 2000*, 4.

Minch, Eric (forthcoming) "The beginning of the end: What is the origin of final cause?" in van de Vijver, Gertrudis; Salthe, Stanley S.; Delpos, Manuela; (eds) (forthcoming) *Evolutionary Systems*, Kluwer Academic Publishers, Dordrecht.

Mitsubishi's biochip. (1989, May 4), *Japan Chemicals*, p. 23.

Molecular evolution on a fast track. (1993, July 12), *The New York Times*, p. D 2.

Morin, E. 1985 Blind intelligence. In Shlomo Giora Shoham, & Francis Rosensteil (Eds.), *And he loved big brother*, pp. 165–170. Lourdes: Macmillan, Council of Europe.

Morin, E. 1981 Self and autos. In M. Zeleny (Ed.), *Autopoiesis: A theory of living organization*, pp. 230–242. New York: North Holland.

Mostow, D.J. & Hayes, Roth, F. 1979). Machine-aided heuristic programming: A paradigm for knowledge engineering, *Rep. No. Rand N-1007-NSF*, Santa Monica, Calif: Rand Corp.

Mostow, D.J. 1981 Mechanical transformation of task heuristics into operational procedures, *Rep. No. CS-81-113*, Computer Science Dept., Carnegie-Mellon Univ. (Doctoral Dissertation).

Murdock, Graham, Hartmann, Paul, & Gray, Peggy 1993 Contextualising home computing. Resources and Practices Department of Human Sciences, Brunel University.

Nagel, Thomas (1974, October). What is it like to be a bat? *The Philosophical Review*, p. 27–30.

Nagel, Roger (1993, June). Virtual winners, *International Management*, p. 64.

Narin, F. & Noma, E. 1985 Is technology becoming science? *Scientometrics*, 7 (3–6), 369–381.

Needham, Joseph 1956 Mathematics and science in China and the West, *Science and Society*, 20.

Needham, Joseph 1972 The emergence and institutionalization of modern science. In Barry Barnes (Ed.), *Sociology of science: Selected readings*, pp. 10–21. Harmondsworth: Penguin.

Nelsen, Rolf Haugaard 1992 Gene test may assess chance of conceiving a handicapped child. *New Scientist*, 135 (1830), 19.

Neurological gain seen. (1993, February 16), *The New York Times*, p. C 2.

Neville, Robert C. 1984 "Buddhism and Process Philosophy" in Inada, Kenneth K.; and Jacobson, Nolan B. (Eds.) *Buddhism and American Thinkers* State University of New York Press, Albany 1984.

Nishioka, M, Tanizoi I., Fujita A., Katsura S. & Mizuno, A. 1995. Fix, cut and succesive recovery of fragments of single DNA molecule for high speed sequencing, *Institute of Physics Conference Series*, 143, 335–338.

No looking back. (1990, Jan 9), *Indian Express*, p. 11.

Noble, T. 1981 *Structure and change in modern Britain*, London: Batsford.

Noble, David 1986 *Forces of production: A social history of industrial automation*, New York: Oxford University Press.

OECD 1989 *Information computer communications policy: Major R and D programmes for information technology*, Paris: OECD.

OECD 1989 *Biotechnology: Economic and wider impacts*, Paris: OECD.

OECD 1981 *Information activities, electronics and communication technologies*, Series No. 6. Paris: ICCP.

Office of Technology Assessment 1989 *Patenting life*, Washington D.C.

Ojulu, Epajjar (1988, Sept/Oct.). A backlog of computer illiteracy, *Computers in Africa*, pp. 3–7.

Olson, Arthur J. & Goodsell, David S. 1992. Visualizing biological molecules, *Scientific American*, 267 (5), 44–51.

Open University 1971 *Science and society*, Science Foundation Course, Units 33 and 34, Buckinghamshire: The Open University Press.

Ormerod, Paul (1990, December). Future issues: Chaotic systems and neural networks in the planning process, *Long Range Planning*, 23 (6), 78–82.

Osborn, L. (1979, November) Managing the data from respiratory measurements, *Medical Instrumentation*, 13 (6), 83–87.

Osborne, John 1979 *Running wild: The next industrial revolution*, New York: McGraw Hill.

Page, Richard C. & Berkow, Daniel N. 1991 "Concepts of the Self: Western and Eastern Perspectives" *Journal of Multi cultural Counseling and Development*, April 1991, 19, 83–93.

Pagel, Walter 1973 The spectre of Von Helmont. In Teich & Young (Eds), *Perspectives in the history of science*, pp. 87–94. Boston: Reidel.

Paul, R.P. 1981 *Robot Manipulators: Mathematics, Programming and Control*, MIT Press, Cambridge MA.

Parfit, Derek 1984 *Reasons and persons*, Oxford: Oxford University Press.

Parker, Barnett R. 1990 In quest of useful health care decision models for developing countries, *European Journal of Operational Research*, 49 (2), 32–38.

Pask, Gordon, & Curran, Susan 1982 *Microman: Living and growing with computers*, London: Century Publishing Co.

Passarelli, Ben 1989 Neural networks: Profiles in learning, *UNIX Review*, 7 (5), 50–57.

Patel, Vibhuti (n.d.). *Misuse of prenatal diagnostic techniques in India: A case-study of sex determination tests leading to female foeticide*, Bombay: SNDT Women's University.

Peerenboom, R.P. 1989 "Buddhist Process Ethics: Dissolving the Dilemmas of Substantialist Metaphysics." *Indian Philosophical Quarterly*, 16, 247–268, J1 89.

Pelet, Abraham 1987 The next computer revolution, *Scientific American*, 257 (4), 34–43.

Patterson, David A. Microprocessors in 2020 *Scientific American*, September 1995, 273 (3), 62–67.

Pelton, Joseph N. (1989, September/October). Telepower: The emerging global brain, *The Futurist*, p. 10.

Pelton, Joseph N. 1982 Global talk and the world of telecomputer energetics. In Howard F. Didsbury (Ed.), *Communication and the future: Prospects, promises & problems*, pp. 78–87. Bethesda: World Future Society.

Perry, Ruth, & Greber, Lisa 1990 Women and computers: An introduction, *Signs: Journal of Women in Culture and Society*, 16 (1), 93–95.

Pfeiffer, J. L. 1969 *The Emergence of man*, London: Nelson.

Pickering, Andrew 1989 Editing and epistemology: Three accounts of the discovery of the weak neutral current, *Knowledge and Society: Studies in the Sociology of Culture Past and Present*, 8, 217–232.

Pickering, A. 1984 Against putting the phenomena first: The discovery of the weak neutral current, *Studies in History and Philosophy of Science*, 15, 85–117.

Pinch, T. J. 1976 What does a proof do if it does not prove. In E. Mendelsohn, P. Weingar, & R. Whitley (Eds.), *The social production of scientific knowledge*, pp. 171–218. Doordrecht: Reidel.

Pinsky, Robert (1995, May 14). The muse in the machine: Or, the poetics of Zork, *The New York Times Book Review*, pp. 3, 26.

Pollack, Andrew (1992, August 19). Computer dictionary: Back to basics, *The New York Times*, p. D 5.

Pollack, Andrew (1993, January 29). Computer translator phones try to compensate for Babel, *The New York Times*, p. A 1.

Pool, Ithiel de Sola 1984 *Communication flows: A census in the United States and Japan*, New York: North Holland.

Pool, Robert 1996 Bright future for brainy chips, *New Scientist*, 149 (2023), 20.

Porat, M.U. 1978 Emergence of an information economy, *Economic Impact*, 24, United States of America International Communication Agency.

Port, Otis (1991, July 29). Creating chips an atom at a time, *Business Week*, pp. 54–55.

Premack, D. 1971 Language in chimpanzee, *Science*, 172, 808–822.

Price, D. J. de Solla 1963 *Little science, big science*, London: Macmillan.

Prigogine, Ilya 1980 *From being to becoming*, New York: W.M. Freeman.

Rada, Juan F. 1986 Information Technology and Services ILO 1986

Rahula, Walpola 1978 *What the Buddha Taught* Gordon Fraser 1978 London

Rajapakse, Vijitha 1985 "Buddhism in Huxley's Evolution and Ethics." *Philosophy East and West*, 35, 295–304, J1 85

Renn, Ortwin, & Peters, Hans Peter 1986 Micro and macro sociological consequences of new information technologies, Paper presented at Xth World Congress of Sociology, New Delhi.

Rennels, Glenn D. & Shortcliffe, Edward 1987 Advanced computing for medicine, *Scientific American*, 257 (4), 146–153.

Rennie, John 1993 DNA's new twists, *Scientific American*, 266 (3), 88–96.

Rheingold, Howard 1993 *The virtual community: Homesteading on the electronic frontier*, New York: Addison Wesley.

Ridley, Mark 1985 *The problems of evolution. New York:* Oxford University Press.

Rifkin, Jeremy 1987 Genetic engineering may threaten humanity. In Julie S. Bach (Ed.), *Biomedical ethics: Opposing view points*, pp. 23–30 Minnesota: Greenhaven Press.

Rogers, Lois, & Craig, Olga (1996, June 16). The hardest choice, *The Sunday Times*, p. 16.

Rose, Hilary, & Rose, Steven 1976 *The radicalization of science*, London: Macmillan.

Rosner, Judah L. (1992, May 10). Reflections of science as a product, *Nature*, pp. 108.

Ross, Philip E. 1993 Endangered genes, *Scientific American*, 268 (1), 17.

Rossler, O.E. 1987 Endophysics. In J.L. Casti, & A. Karlqvist (Eds.), *Real brains: Artificial minds* pp. 25–46. New York: North-Holland.

Rossler, O.E. 1996 Ultraperspective and endophysics, *Biosystems*, 38 (1) 211–219.

Rothbart, Daniel 1984 The semantics of metaphor and the structure of science, *Philosophy of Science*, 51, 595–615.

Rothfeder, Jeffrey 1986 *Minds over matter*, Sussex: Harvester Press.

Rothstein, Edward (1996, May 27). Connections dscribing intelligence through a virtual symphony, *The New York Times*, p. 31.

Rule, James B. 1988 Biotechnology: Big money comes to the university, *Dissent*, 354 (153), 430, 436.

Rumelhart, D.E. & McLelland, J.C. "PDP Models in Cognitive Science" in "Rumelhart, D.E., & MCLelland, J.C." (Eds.). 1986 *Parallel distributed processing: Explorations in the microstructure of cognition*, pp. 110–146. Cambridge, Mass: MIT Press.

Ruscio, Kenneth P. 1984 The changing context of academic science: University-industry relations in biotechnology and the public policy implications, *Policy Studies Review*, 4 (2), 259–275.

Ruskin, F.R. (Ed.). 1986 *Micro computers and their application for developing countries*, Boulder, Colorado: Westview Press.

Salisbury, J.K. 1984 Interpretation of contact geometries from force measurements, *Proceedings of the international symposium on robotics*, Vol.1. Cambridge Mass.: MIT Press.

Salthe, S. 1985 *Evolving hierarchical systems*, New York: Columbia University Press.

Salthe, S.N. 1989 Self organization of/in hierarchically structured systems, *Systems Research*, 6, 201.

Salthe, Stanely (forthcoming) "The Role of Natural Selection Theory in Understanding Evolutionary Systems" in *van de Vijver, Gertrudis*; Salthe, Stanley S.; Delpos, Manuela; (Eds.)

Samuel, A.L. 1959 Some studies in machine learning using the game of checkers, *IBM J. Research and Development*, 3, 210– 229.

Sasson, Albert 1988 *Biotechnologies and development*, Paris: UNESCO.

Scheffler, Samuel (1984, May 4). Ergo: Less ego, *The Times Literary Supplement*, p. 4231.

Schiller, Herbert I. 1987 Old foundations for a new (information) age. In Jorge Reina Schement, & Leah A. Lievrouw (Eds.), *Competing visions, complex realities: Social aspects of the information society*, pp. 76–83. Norwood, New Jersey: Ablex Publishing.

Schiller, H.I. 1981 *Who knows: Information in the age of the Fortune 500*, Norwood, New Jersey: Ablex Publishing.

Schrodinger, E. 1945 *What is life?*, London: Cambridge University Press.

Schroedinger, E. C. 1957 *Science and theory and man*, New York: Dover Publications.

Schwartz, Evan I. (1994, Jan. 9). Software valets that will do your bidding in cyberspace, *The New York Times*, Section 3, p. 11.

Scientists try to disarm cancer gene. (1993, April 4), *The New York Times*, p. C 6.

Scientists finish first phase in mapping of human genes. (1996, March 19), *The New York Times*, p. C7.

Scraggs, G.W. 1975 Answering questions about processes. In D.A. Norman, & D.E. Rumelhart (Eds.), *Explorations in cognition*, pp. 77–83. San Francisco: W. H. Freeman.

Sculley, John (1989, October). Technology is reshaping both work and workers, *Personal Computing*, p. 218.

Searls, David B. (1992, November/December). The linguistics of DNA, *American Scientist*, 80, 579–592.

Seidel, George E. (1989, October). Biotech on the farm geneticists in the pasture, *Current*, pp. 21–27.

Sejnowski, T. & Rosenberg, C. 1986 NET talk: A parallel network that learns to read aloud, *Electrical Engineering and Computer Science Technical Report, JHU/ EEC-86/01*, John Hopkins University.

Sen, Amar K. & Lee, Tyronne 1988 *Receptors and ligands in psychiatry*, Cambridge: Cambridge University Press.

Shannon. C.E. & Weaver, W. 1949 *The mathematical theory of communication*, Urbana, Ill: University of Illinois Press.

Sherman, Barrie 1985 *The new revolution*, Chichester, New York: John Wiley and Sons.

Shinn, Terry (1989, December 4). Progress and paradoxes in French science and technology 1900–1930, *Social Science Information*, 28, 659–683.

Shiva, Vandana (1991, Nov. 30). Biotechnology development and conservation of bio-diversity, *Economic and Political Weekly*, pp. 78–92.

Shri Purohit Swami (Trans.) 1977 *The Bhagavat Gita*, New York: Vintage Books.

Siebert, Charles (1996, January 5). At the mercy of our genes, *The New York Times*, p. 15.

Silverstone, Roger 1991 Beneath the bottom line: Household and information and communication technologies in an age of the consumer. The Third Charles

Read Memorial Lecture. Centre for Research into Innovation, Culture and Technology, Brunel University.

Sklair Leslie 1972 The political sociology of science: A critique of current orthodoxies, *The Sociological Review Monograph*, 18. Staffordshire: J.H. Brooks Ltd.

Sloan, Douglas 1992 *The computer in education*, New York: Teachers College.

Slutsker, Gary (1991, January 7). Patenting mother nature, *Forbes*, 147 (1), 290.

Smith, J. Clarke (1991, May/June). A neural network: Could it work for you?, *Financial Executive*, pp. 26–30.

Sylwester, Robert, 1990 Expanding the range, dividing the task: educating the human brain in an electronic society *Educational Leadership*, October 1990, 48 (2), 71–78.

Sutton, C. 1987 The race for a high temperature superconductor hots up, *New Scientist*, 113 (1545), 33.

Smith, Emily T. (1986, June 2). Computers that come awfully close to thinking, *Business Week*, pp. 98–100.

Smith, G. W. & Debenham, J. D. (1983, February). Mass producing intelligence for a rational world, *Futures*, pp. 18–23.

Sterling J. 1991 Plane truth, *Scientific American*, 264 (5), 6.

Stone, Richard (1993, May 14). Biotech sails into heavy financial seas, *Science*, 260, 908–910.

Stonier, Tom 1996 Information as a basic property of the universe, *Biosystems*, 38, 135–140.

Sussman, G.J. 1975 *A computer model of skill acquisition*, New York: American Elsevier.

Sweet, Michael J.; Johnson, Craig G. 1990 "Enhancing empathy: The interpersonal implications of a Buddhist meditation technique. Special Issue: Psychotherapy and religion," *Psychotherapy*; 1990 Spr., 27 (1), 19–29.

The ghost in the machine. (1993, May 8), *The Economist*, p. 92.

Trawling the heavens. (1995, September 9), *The Economist*, pp. 107–108.

The world on a screen. (1990, Oct. 21), *Time*. p. 80.

Tank, David W. & Hopfield, John J. 1987 Collective Computation in Neuron like Circuits *Scientific American*, Dec. 1987, 257 (4), 104.

Thimbleby, Harold (1991, April). Can viruses ever be useful?, *Computers & Security*, 10 (2), 111–114.

Thought Control *New Scientist* 149 (2020), pp. 38–42.

Torrero, E.A. (Ed.). 1985 *Next generation computers*, New York: IEEE Press.

Toufexis, Anastasia (1996, January 15). What makes them do it, *Time*, p. 42.

Travis, John (1993, Aug. 27). Putting antibodies to work inside cells, *Science*, 261 (5125), 1114.

Turkle, Sherry 1995 *Life on the screen: Identity in the age of the internet*. New York: Simon & Schuster.

Turkle, Sherry, & Papert, Seymour 1990 Epistemological pluralism: Styles and voices within the computer culture, *Signs: Journal of Women in Culture and Society*, 16 (1), 144.

Turkle, Sherry 1984 *The second self: Computers and the human spirit*, New York: Simon and Scuster.

Turner, Ronny E. 1987 Language and knowledge: Metaphor as the mother of knowledge, California Sociologist, 10 (1), 44–61.

Uenohara, Michiyuki & Linuma,Kazumoto 1989 Machine translation activities in Japan, Paper presented at IXth General Conference of the International Federation of Social Science Organisations (IFSSO).

UNLTC UN Centre on Transnational Corporations 1990 *Transnational corporations and the transfer of new and emerging technologies to developing countries*, New York: United Nations.

UNCTAD 1991 *Trade and development aspects and implications of new and emerging technologies: The case of biotechnology*, Geneva: UNCTAD.

UNCTC 1983 *Transborder data flows: Access to the international on-line data base market*, New York: UNCTC.

UNDP 1989 *Plant biotechnology including tissue culture and cell culture*, New York: UNDP.

UNIDO 1986 *The impact of expert systems*, Vienna: Regional and Country Studies Branch, Studies and Research Division.

Varela, F.J., Maturana, H.R. & Uribe, R. 1974 Autopeosis: The organization of living systems, its characterization and a model, *Bio-Systems*, 5 (4), 187–96.

Varela, Francisco F.; Thompson, Evan; Rosch, Eleanor 1993 *The Embodied Mind: Cognitive Science and Human Experience* The MIT Press Cambridge, Massachussets 1993, p. xiv.

Wachtershauser, Gunter 1987 Light and life: On the nutritional origins of sensory perception. In Gerard Radnitzky, & W.W. Bartley (Eds.), *Evolutionary epistemology, rationality and the sociology of knowledge*, pp.121–137. Illinois: Open Court, La Salle.

Waddington, Conrad H. 1976 Evolution in the sub-human world. In Erich Jantsch, & Conrad H. Waddington (Eds.), *Evolution and consciousness:Human systems in transition*, Massachusetts: Addison-Wesley.

Wade, Nicholas (1996, December 31). Alteration of genes in brain cells shows how mice remember maps, *The New York Times*, p. C3.

Walbridge, Charles T. (1989, January). Genetic algorithms: What computers can learn from Darwin, *Technology Review*, pp. 47–53.

Waldrop, M. Mitchell 1990 Learning to drink from a fire hose *Science* 248: 674–675 (11 May).

Walser, Randal quoted in Welter, Therese R. (1990. October 1). The artificial tourist: Virtual reality promises new worlds for industry, *Industry Week*, p. 66.

Walsh, Roger 1988 "Two Asian Psychologies and their Implications for Western Psychotherapists," *American Journal of Psychotherapy*, XLII (4), October 1988.

Wang, Hao 1984 Computer theorem proving and artificial intelligence, *Contemporary Mathematics*, 29 (5), 44–50.

Ward, Salomon (1989, February/March). The biotechnological revolution, *The OECD Observer*, p. 156.

Washburn, Sherwood 1960 Tools and human evolution, *Avenues to antiquity: Readings from Scientific American*, p.11. California: W.H. Freeman & Co.

Watson, James D. (1990, April). The Human Genome Project: Past, present and future, *Science*, 248, 44–49.

Watson, J.D., Tooze, J. & Kurtz, D.J. (Eds.). 1983 *Recombinant DNA: A short course*, New York: Scientific American Books.

Watts, Susan 1990 Drugs industry turns animals into bioreactors', *New Scientist*, 126 (1712), 26.

Weinberg, Nathan 1990 *Computers in the information society*, Boulder: Westview Press.

Weiss, R. (1987, Aug 5). Animal patent debate heats up, *Science News*, 132 (8), 112.

Weiss, Rick (1989, March 4). Test screens live 'test tube' embryos, *Science News*, 135 (9), 132.

Weiss, Rick (1992, Sept. 8). Techy new products hum DNA's tune, *Science Times*, *The New York Times*, p. C 3.

Wessells, Michael 1990 *Computer, self and society*, Englewood Cliffs, NJ: Prentice Hall.

Wheeler, David L. (1991, February 27). Ethicist urges public debate on medical therapies that could cause genetic changes in offspring, *Chronicle of Higher Education*, 37 (24), p. A 5.

Wickelgren, Ingrid (1989, August 19) Please pass the genes, *Science News*, 136 (8), 120–124.

Wickelgren, Ingrid (1996, December 3). Very smart fruit flies yield clues to the molecular basis of memory, *The New York Times*, p. C 3.

Wiener, Philip P. (Ed.). 1973 *Dictionary of the history of ideas*, New York: Charles Scribner's Sons.

Wiggen, Regina (1990, October). Mapping the plant genome, *Agricultural Research*, 38 (10), 2.

Wind, James P. (1990, July/August). What can religion offer bioethics, *Hastings Center Report, A Special Supplement*, 20 (4), 18–20.

Witt, Patricia L., Barnerle, Cynthia, Derouen, Diane, Kamel, Freja, Kelleher, Patricia, McCarthy, Monica, Namenworth, Marion, Sabatini, Linda, & Voytovich, Marta 1989. The October 29th Group: Defining a feminist science, *Women's Studies International Forum*, 12 (3), 253–259.

Wobbe, Werner 1990 Anthropocentric production systems in the context of European integration, *Tokyo International Workshop on Industrial Culture and Human Centered Systems*, Tokyo: Kezai University.

Wuketits, Franz M. 1990 *Evolutionary epistemology and its implications for human kind*, Albany: SUNY Press.

Wurman, Saul Richard 1989 *Information anxiety*, New York: Doubleday.

Wynne, B.1976 C. G. Barkla and the J. Phenomenon: A case study of the treatment of deviance in physics, *Social Studies of Science*, 6 (2), 72–98.

Yam, Phillip 1991 Atomic turn-on, *Scientific American*, 266 (5), 20.

Yam, Phillip 1993 A gene for hypertension, *Scientific American*, 268 (1), 24.

Yang, Dori Jones (1992, Nov. 16), *Business Week*, pp. 73–76.

Yasdani, Masoud (Ed.). 1986 *Artificial Intelligence: Principles and applications*. London: Chapman and Hall.

Yearly, Steven (1987, March). The social construction of national scientific profiles: A case study of the Irish republic, *Social Science Information*, 26 (1), 191–210.

Young, R. M. 1973 The historiographic & ideological contexts of the nineteenth century debate on man's place in nature. In M. Teich and R. M. Young (Eds.), *Changing perspectives in the history of science*, pp. 47–51, London: Heinemann.

Yu, V. L. 1979 Antimicrobial selection for meningitis by a computerized consultant: A blinded evaluation by infectious disease experts, *Journal of the American Medical Association*, 242 (3), 1279–1282.

Yuanliang, M. 1989 *Modern plant biotechnology and rural society: Today and tomorrow*, Shanghai: Shanghai Institute of Scientific and Technical Information.

Zuboff, Shoshana 1988 *In the age of the smart machine: The future of work and power*, New York: Basic Books.

Zuckerman, Laurence (1995, November 6). I.B.M.'s robotic army of computers Chip soldiers, *The New York Times*, p. D 5.

INDEX

Abu-Mostafa, Yaser 54, 59, 221
Ackerman, Stephen, J. 73, 74, 242
Adaptation 3, 17, 19, 22, 161, 225, 240
Adenine 17, 80
Aesthetic criteria 178, 179
Agents, electronic 200, 204
Ahamed, Ifthikhar 133, 221
Albery, John 69, 221
Alexander, Tom 56, 221
Allen, Peter, M. 93, 182, 221
Altman, Lawrence, K. 77, 221
Amato, Ivan 161, 162, 221
Ames, Van Meter 211, 221
Amniocentesis 127
Analytical Engine 36
Anderson, Ian 78, 155, 221
Anderson, Christopher 64, 79, 221
Anderson, French, W. 77, 78, 79, 221
Anderson, Arthur 65, 70, 221
Andima, Haron, S. 100, 221
Angier, Natalie 125, 127, 142, 143, 222
Annas, George, J. 126, 132, 222
Anthropomorphism 103
Aristotle 209
Arndt, Stephen 103, 222
Arriaga, Patricia 100, 222
Arrow of time 21
Artefactual information 35, 36, 47, 50, 109, 186, 205, 206
Artefactual (Information) lineages 4, 50, 87, 88, 184, 191
Artificial life 161, 175
Artificial organisms 82, 200

Artificial Intelligence (AI) 5, 40, 55, 57, 59, 61, 62, 82, 93, 105, 108, 111, 158, 165, 171, 175, 190, 213
Artificial evolution 200
Artigiani, Robert 26, 190, 222
ATAS Bulletin 99, 100, 222
Auotopoiesis 22, 184, 185
Automated sequencing 156
Automation 82
Avatars 204, 219
Ayala, Francisco, J. 19, 21, 222
Ayres, Robert & Miller, Steve 42, 51, 74, 223

Baark, Jamison 130, 131, 132, 223
Babbage, Charles 36
Baby farms 138
Bacon, Francis 30, 57
BACON program 57
Bagchi, Amiya, K. 99, 223
Bahutar 219
Bains, Sunny 54, 223
Bajaj, Y.P. 72, 74, 223
Balsamo, Anne 111, 114, 223
Bankowski, Zbigniew 128, 223
Baringa, Marcia 126, 223
Barnes, Barry 27, 29, 30, 223
Base pairs 20
Beardsley, Tim 79, 82, 137, 223
Becoming 19, 67, 191
Being 19
Bendix, Reinhard 23
Berer, Marge 127, 223
Berman, B.J. 92, 223
Bi- chips 117, 150

Bibliographical control 172
Bifurcation 32, 181
Bio-computers 149, 150, 152
Bio-diversity 123, 169
Bio-epistemology 188
Bio-ethics 128, 138
Bio-morphs 162
Bio-sensors 69, 152, 153, 154
Biological determinism 135
Biological motherhood 135
Biological evolution 3, 6, 60
Biology as information science 77, 156
Biomolecules 151
Biotechnological knowledge 83, 120
Biotechnology information 119
Biotechnology revolution 83
Birnbaum, N. 23, 64, 223
Birnbaum, Joel, S. 23, 223
Bishop, Jerry, E. 77, 223
Bishop, Donald, H. 77, 223
Blackmore, John, T. 77, 211, 224
Blakeslee, Sandra 142, 224
Blank, Robert, H. 127, 224
Bledsoe, W.W. & Loveland, D.W. 56, 224
Bloch, Marc 23, 224
Bloom, Barry, R. 77, 224
Boden, Margaret 5, 57, 60, 63, 224
Bograt, Greg 212, 224
Bonte, P. 23, 224
Borman, Stu 156, 224
Boulding, Kenneth, E. 6, 182, 224
Bourdieu, Pierre 30, 225
Bower, B. 103, 225
Bowers, C.A. 92, 225
Boyer, R.S. & Moore, J.S. 42, 56, 225
Boyer-Moore Theorem Prover 56

Brain Opera 203
Brain cells 141
Brain structures 143
Brain death 129
Brain-as-scan 154
Brandon, Robert, N. 16, 17, 198, 225
Braverman, Avishay 100, 225
Bricoleur programmers 94
Brodner, Peter 91, 225
Brody, Herb 60, 225
Bromley, Allan 36, 225
Brooks, Daniel, R. 5, 21, 182, 225
Brown, F. 27, 160, 225
Broyles, William Jr. 90, 225
Brzezinski, Zbigniew 37, 225
Buchanan, B.G. 57, 225
Buddhaghosa 216
Buddhism 210, 211, 212, 215, 216, 217, 218
Buddhist Encyclopedia 216, 226
Bugliarello, George 149, 226
Burgess, John 89, 204, 226
Bylinsky, Gene 74, 107, 226
Bylinsky, Gene & Moore, A.H. 42, 226

Calem, Robert, E. 66, 226
Callahan, Daniel 128, 129, 132, 226
Carpenter, Betsy 158, 226
CD-ROM 51, 52
Cell fusion 72
Cerebral anatomy 29
Chan, Vincent, W.S. 45, 226
Chaos theory 40
Chithelen, Ignatius 40, 226
Chomsky, A.N. 174
Christopher, Joyce 169, 226

Chromosomes   19, 82, 156
Churchland, Paul, M.   60, 226
Clark, Andy   58, 59, 226
Clay, Carr   40, 226
Clery, Daniels   150, 227
Clevenger, James   103, 227
Cloning   136
Coats, Pamela, K.   41, 227
Cochran, Tracy   75, 212, 227
Coevolution   18, 172, 208
Coghlan, Andy   19, 75, 76, 78, 119,
    124, 143, 158, 159, 227
Cognitive windows   191
Collins, H. M.   27, 29, 227
Commonsensical knowledge   63
Communication technologies   101
Communication network   66
Communities, transformed   218
Computational ecologies   67
Computational molecular
    biology   158
Computer Aided Design (CAD)   41,
    99, 104, 108, 160, 177
Computer Aided Production and
    Management (CAPM)   99
Computer Aided Manufacture
    (CAM)   99, 104, 177
Computer architecture   148
Computer culture   88
Computer graphics   41
Computer/human interphase   114
Computer Integrated Manufac-
  ·   ture   43, 91, 99, 176
Computer densities   52
Computer interfacing   112
Computer mediated communica-
    tion   98
Computer Numerical Control
    (CNC)   41
Computer vision   60

Computers from biological
    models   147
Computers, thought control of   176
Conrad, Michael   17, 21, 149, 227
Conservation of past memory   19
Construction of biotechnology   120,
    130
Construction of scientific fact 29
Copeland, Peter   142, 158, 227
Cordes, Colleen   123, 227
Corcoran, Elizabeth   154, 227
Coulborn, Rushton   23, 227
Coulomb Blockade devices   54
Covert, Ranel   100
Crow, Michael   28, 228
Culbertson, William, Y.   40, 41, 228
Culotta, Elizabeth   78, 228
Cultural bias of programs   93
Cultural diversity   123
Cultural flow lines   24, 25, 87, 88
Cultural information   3, 94, 110,
    131, 144, 170, 174, 184, 185,
    186
Cultural stream   31, 32
Cultural structures 113
Cultural tree   26
Cultural windows   190
Culture embedded genes   132
Culture-to-artefact merger   111
Cybernetics   5, 147
Cyberspace   61, 107, 155, 206, 207
Cyborgs metaphor   147
Cyborgs   147, 207, 212, 214, 215,
    219
Cystic fibrosis   78, 79
Cytosine   17, 80

Dambrot, Stuart   150, 151, 228
Darwin, Charles   13, 16, 17, 60,
    177, 209

Data gloves   108, 212
Day, Michael   141, 228
Davis, Howard,   23, 212, 228
Dawkins, Richard   162, 184, 228
Dazzaniga, Michael, S.   142, 228
De Silva, Padmal   212, 228
DENDRAL program   58
Denning, Peter, J.   49, 228
Descartes, Rene   216, 228
Developing countries   28
Di Giammarino, Peter   41, 228
Diachronic transmission   8
Dibbell, Julian   200, 228
Dickerson, Richard, E.   13, 228
Dickinson, E.   13
Dickson, David   124, 228
Diderot   172, 179
Difference Engine   36
Digital biodiversity reserve   200
Digital ecologies   200
Digital jungles   200
Direct mergers   109, 113, 164
Direct interactions   87
Disjunctures   25, 34, 67, 181
Dissipative structures   181
Dizardt, Wilson, P.   172, 228
DNA computers   151
DNA sequencers   81, 156
DNA, junk   157
DNA   6, 14, 18, 19, 21, 73, 79, 80,
   82, 151, 156, 172, 174, 177,
   178, 197, 198
Dobrov, G.M.   38, 229
Doi, Noricha,   55, 229
Donaldson, Margaret   212, 229
Donnelley, Strachan   129, 229
Doukidis, Georgios, I.   100, 229
Downey, Gary Lee   207, 229
DRAM   50, 51, 88
Drucker, Peter, F.   37, 229

Duda, R.O.   58, 229
Dumit, Joseph   207
Durand, P.   14, 229
DVD ROMs   52
DVD-Digital Video Disc   52
Dyson, Esther   115, 149, 229

Eastmond, A.   133, 229
Ebel, Karl, H.   91, 229
Ecologies   203
Ecosystems   21
Edquist, C.   118, 140, 229
Edwards, Paul, N.   90, 229
Egocentricity   185, 191
Eigen, Manfred   19, 230
Einstein, Albert   31
Eldredge, N.   21, 230
Electronic links   45
Electronic immigrant   89, 204
Electronic age   37, 89
Electronic communities   45
Electronic processing   48
Electronic roof   201
Electronic commons   48, 200
Electronic sub ecosystems   200
Elmer-Dewitt, Philip   80, 230
Elshtain, Jean Bethke   128, 135,
   136
Embedded products   100, 230
Embedded micro controllers   66
Embedded cultural
   information   132
Employment effects   132
EMYCIN   58
Encyclopeadists   172
Encyclopedia of Buddhism   213
End of history   194
End-effectors   69
Endophysics   6, 217
ENIAC   36, 37, 65

Entropy   21, 168, 181
Environment   18, 25, 26, 32, 122
Environmental politics   122, 123
Epistemological pluralism   94
Ethical issues   138
Ethicists   139
Etzkorn, Peter, K.   98, 230
Eugenics   136
EURISKO program   62, 63
Evocative objects   102, 103
Evolutionary perspective   208
Evolutionary processes   16, 60, 67, 184
Evolutionary epistemology   187, 191
Evolutionary lineages   35
Evolutionary system   192
Evolutionary theory   31
Evolutionary tree   191, 192
Evolving epistemologies   187, 189
Evolving realities   218
Evolving whole   195
Excision of a gene   128
Exosomatic lineage   182
Expert systems   40, 41, 43, 57, 58, 62, 63, 68, 100, 106, 107
Extended sociology   197

Farley, J.   27, 29, 230
Farrington, John   72, 73, 230
Favello, A.   157, 175, 230
Feigenbaum, Edward   55, 57, 66, 230
Feminist research   30
Feminists   30
Fenema, E. & Sherman, J.   93, 230
Ferris, D.   56
Fetal neural transplants   181
Fetal transplants   137
Feuer, L.S.   31, 231

Fifth Generation Computer   55
Figueroa-Sarriera, Heidi, J.   209
Finkelstein, Joanne, L.   126, 132, 231
Fisher, Lawrence, M.   153, 158, 159, 231
Flamm, Kenneth   90, 231
Fleissner, Peter   6, 231
Flexible production   43, 96
Flow of human history   23, 24
Flow line of culture   23, 132
Flower, Joe   100, 200
Flynn, Laurie   204, 231
Forces of production   24
Forman, Paul   27, 231
Forsyth, Richard   58, 61, 62, 63, 92, 231
Forsythe, Diana, E.   92, 231
Fox, Sidney   19
Franks, E.   214
Freeman, Chris   87, 231
Freud, Sigmund   209
Fulton, L.L.   158, 188, 231
Fuzzy logic   40, 57, 61
Fuzzy systems   107

Gaasterland, T.   156, 176
Gaia   198
Garrett, John   97, 231
Geister, Elieger   40, 232
Gender bias   93
Gender construction   93
Gender roles   176
Gene therapy   78, 143
Gene probes   118
Gene screen   127, 138
Gene screened babies   138
Generic technologies   95
Genes and behavior   142
Genetic screening   79, 138

Genetic defects 127, 142
Genetic information 20, 120, 128, 174, 175, 184, 186
Genetic interventions 77
Genetic system 7, 140
Genetic lineage 26, 70
Genetic tree 26
Genetic mechanisms 127
Genetic pool 18
Genetic markers 82
Genetic tests 127
Genetic autonomy 132
Genetic diversity 122, 123
Genetic map 81, 82
Genetic factors 142
Genetic determinism 142
Genetic disorders 77, 138
Genetic counseling 128, 137
Genetic diseases 78
Genetic stream 132, 144
Genetic bombs 76
Genetic algorithms 8, 40, 57, 60, 61, 63, 67, 105, 107, 111, 151, 152, 174
Genetic engineering 72, 74, 120, 122
Genetics, homosexuality 142
Genome sequence 127
Genome maps 82, 120
Ghosts 40, 185
Gianturco, Michael 119, 232
Gibson, William 107, 232
Gilbert, G. N. 29, 232
Gina 62, 125, 136, 137, 140, 141, 142, 150
Giuliano, Vincent, E. 41, 232
GLAUBER program 57
Global trade patterns 134
Global informatization 89
Global semiosphere 198

Globalization 43, 170, 201, 204
"Glove-puppet" in information 184, 187
Goleman, Daniel 212, 232
Goodman, Billy 80, 232
Goonatilake, Lalith 99, 232
Goonatilake, Suran 53, 108, 149, 150, 151, 152, 155, 162, 163, 165, 181, 182, 232
Goonatilake, Suran & Khebbal, Sukhdev 40, 61, 232
Goonatilake, Suran & Treleaven, Philip 40, 232
Goonatilake, Susantha 24, 26, 29, 32, 139, 182, 184, 185, 232, 233
Gould, Stephen Jay 21, 31, 233
Gray, Chris Hables 207, 209, 233
Green Politics 123
Green Revolution 120
Greene, Marjorie 20, 188, 233
Greenhouse, Steven 48, 233
Gregorio, Domenico de 55, 233
Gross, Neil 117, 179, 233
Grossing, Gerhard 5, 233
Gruson, Lindsey 135, 138, 233
Guanine, G. 17, 18
Gunaratne, V.F. 215, 234
Gwynne, P. 156, 234

Hackers 57, 103
Hahlweg, Kai 188, 234
Hallberg, Margareta 30, 234
Halpert, Julie Edelson 201, 234
Hamer, Dean 142, 234
Hannah, Eric, C. & Soreff, Jeffrey 50, 51, 53, 234
Haraway, Donna 30, 207, 234
Harding, Sandra 30, 234
Hartshorne, Charles 211

Hayes Roth, F.   57
Hebbs, Donald   148,   174
Heisenberg, N.   31
Hessen, Boris   27, 234
Hierarchies in computer systems   110
Hills, Dany   154, 162
Hilts, Philip   54, 234
Hindley, Martin   150, 234
Hinton, Geoffrey, E.   174, 234
Historical process   118
Historical struggle   132
Historical evolution   1
Hitomi, K.   176, 235
Hiving-off   69
Ho, Maw-Wan   19, 22, 235
Hoffman, Carol, A.   122, 235
Hoffmeyer, Jesper   198, 208, 210, 217, 235
Hofkirchner, Wolfgang   6
Hogg, Tod   67
Holderness, Mike   152, 235
Holland, John   60
Hollerith, Herman   36
Holm, N.G.   14, 235
Holograms, holography   54
Holton, Gerald   31, 235
Holusha, John   43, 155, 202, 235
Holzmuller, Werner   20, 187, 235
Homeostasis   147
Horgan, John   142, 143, 235
Horowitz, Irving Louis   29, 235
Horton, Allan   172, 235
Huberman, Bernado, A.   67, 235
Hudson, C.A.   42, 235
Human centered technologies   85, 95
Human/computer interactions   111
Human Genome Initiative   49, 77, 79, 80, 81, 82, 120, 125, 138, 156, 159, 171, 175

Hume, David   208, 210
Huntington's   disease   77
Hut, Piet   62, 236
Huws, Ursula   105, 236
Huxley   208, 210, 211
Hybrid communities   203
Hybrid space   206
Hybrid systems   61
Hybrid-net-travelers   204
Hybrid-nets   201, 218, 219
Hybrids   40, 107, 210

IBM   36
Idealized rationality   92
Identity, politics, questions   206, 214
Ideology of the computer   94
Imaging   154, 158
Implanted chips   179
Implications of merging   167
Inada, Kenneth   211, 236
Indirect mergers, mergings   113, 177
Indirect interactions   87
Indirect processes   110
Industrial Revolution   1, 3, 7, 26, 87, 97
Industrial production   3
Information technology   1, 37, 39, 40, 87, 88, 89
Information shifts   169
Information hybrids   219
Information society   1, 37, 39, 46, 88
Information hierarchies   69
Information stores   26, 69
Information transfers   173
Information artefacts   6
Information sectors   38, 39
Informatization   47, 96

Inheritance mechanism   16
Inherited characteristic   17
Innate hypotheses   189
Input-output devices   107, 109
Intelligent behavior   148
Interaction with computers   109
Interconnectedness   211
Intermingling of information
   streams   117
Internet   50, 101, 199, 200

Jacobson, N.P   210, 211, 236
James, Barry   82, 236
Jamison, Andrew   130, 131, 132
Jansen, Sue Curry   30, 93, 236
Jerison, Harry, J.   20, 189, 236
Johnson-Laird, P.N.   127, 190, 212,
   236
Jones, Stacy, V.   158, 236
Joyce, G.F.   14, 121, 236
Juma, Celestous   121, 171, 236
Junne, Gerd   167, 237

Kabat-Zinn, Jon   212, 237
Kahn, J.S.   23, 77, 143, 237
Kahn, Patricia   77, 82, 83, 143, 237
Kairamo, Kari   64, 237
Kajikawa, Kin-ichiro   129, 237
Kaminuma, Tsuduchika   148, 154,
   237
Kampis, George   198, 208, 210, 217,
   237
Kaplan, S.J.   56, 237
Keen, G.   157, 237
Kenney, Martin   211
Kimura, M.   17, 237
Kingman, Sharon   76, 237
Klappenburg, Jack   119, 237
Kluckhohn, Clyde   23, 237
Knee, C.   92, 238

Knight, Jerry   39, 238
Knorr-Certinca, K.   27, 238
Know bots   111
Knowledge society   37
Kobayashi, Koji   44, 238
Kohyama, Kenichi   37, 238
Kolata, Gina   62, 79, 80, 125, 136,
   137, 140, 141, 151, 156, 238
Kolm, Serge-Christopher   215, 238
Kosko, Bart & Isaka, Satoru   61, 238
Kramer, Pamela, S. & Lehman,
   Sheila   93, 238
Kramer, Peter, D.   143, 238
Kuhn, T.S.   34, 239
Kuppers, Bernd-Olaf   13, 18, 239
Kurtzman, Joel   49, 239

Lancaster, F.W.   28, 239
Langley, P.W.   57, 239
Lansdown, John & Earnshaw,
   Rae, A.   177, 239
Lappe, Marc   30, 138, 239
Large, Peter   47, 239
Large Scale Integration LSI   37, 137
Latour, B. & Woolgar, S.   29, 239
Lauhon, C. & Szostak, J.   15, 239
Laurence, Jeremy   36, 136, 239
Lawren, William   180, 239
Lawrence, Lucy & Rogers, Lois   79,
   137, 239
Leakey, Richard & Lewin,
   Roger   23, 82, 239
Learning systems   111
Leary, Warren, E.   77, 239
Lederman, Leonard, L.   27, 239
Leibniz, G.W.   36
Leigh, David   60, 240
Lemonick, Michael, D.   78, 79, 240
Lenat, Douglas, B.   54, 57, 62, 63,
   240

Levy, Steven   162, 163, 240
Lewontin, R.C.   17, 240
Limits on culture   184
Lind, Per   94, 240
Linguistic metaphors   174
Living process   75
Logic Theorist   56
Lorenz, Konrad   188, 189, 240
Lou Gehrig's disease   143, 145
Lovelock, J.E.   198, 240
Loy, David   215, 240
LUIGI program   56
Lukacs, George   100, 190, 240
Luke, Timothy, W.   203, 240
Luukkonen, Terttu   28, 240

Mac Cormac, Earl, R.   147, 240
Mach, Ernst   208, 210, 211
Machine Creativity   55
Mackenzie, Debora   125, 240
Mackenzie, D. & Barnes, S.B.   27, 30, 240
Macro lineage   193
Maes, Pattie   200, 201, 205, 241
Mahowald, Mary, B., Silver, J. & Rakheson, A.   138, 241
Malaska, P.   182, 241
Manning, Elizabeth   151, 241
Marbach, William   51, 241
Marien, Michael   37, 241
Marijuan, Pedro, C.   5, 6, 197, 241
Market niches   176
Markle, Gerald, E. & Robin, Stanley, S.   130, 241
Markoff, John   51, 52, 63, 64, 65, 241
Marks, Paul   150, 241
Marti, John & Zeillenger, Anthony   41, 104, 241
Martin, James,   37, 242

Maruyama, M.   5, 242
Masuda, Yoneji   37, 242
Material and energy use   167
Mathematical theorem proving   56
Matsumoto, Gen   148, 154
Matsuno, Koichiro   5, 21, 242
Maturana, Humberto, R. & Varela, Francisco, J.   22, 190, 191, 212, 213, 242
Mayr, Ernst   21, 242
McLuhan, Marshall   37, 242
McNeill, Daniel 61 & Freiberger, Paul   61, 242
Medical intervention   126
Meiskey, Lori   29
Memory retention   22
Memory   34
Mendel, Gregor   16
Mental control of computers   153
Merged evolution Dynamics   181
Merged evolution   167, 177
Merged hybrid communities   218
Merger of computing and biology   149
Merging process   174, 177, 194
Merging of culture and genes   117, 144, 145
Merging interactions   113, 115
Merging of culture into biology   130
Merging of information   173
Meta communicating system   197
Meta DENDRAL program   57
Michael, Balick   121, 242
Michie, D.   57, 242
Michie, D. & Johnston, R.   58, 68, 242
Micro communities   203
Micro propagation   72
Microbes   14

Microprocessors 64
Miles, Ian, Muskens, R. &
    Grupelaan, W. 44, 242
Military culture 90
Miller, Susan Katz 77, 242
Miller, Henry, J. 73, 74, 242
Milner, Peter, A. 148, 242
Milstead, Jeff & Milhon, Jude 155,
    242
Minch, Eric 217, 242
Mind-body 216
Minsky, Marvin 92
Mitchell, T.M. 57
Models of reality 189
Models of biology 147, 189
Modern Synthesis 17
Molding of biotechnology 134
Molecular biology 77
Molecular computer graphics 160
Molecular switches 8, 52
Molecular genetics 16
Molecular computers 53, 77
MOLGEN program 58
Monoclonal antibodies 75, 119
Moore's Law 51
Moore's spleen 51, 126
Morin, E. 20, 188, 191, 243
Mostow, D.J. 57, 243
Music and dance of genes 179
MYCIN program 43, 58, 114

Nagarjuna 114
Nagel, Roger 140, 202, 208, 243
Nagel, Thomas 20, 140, 189, 202,
    208, 243
Nano technology 52, 53, 171
Nano electronics 8
Napier, John 35
Napier's Rods 8
Narin, F. & Noma, E. 118, 243

National approaches to science 28
Natural selection 16, 198
Naylor, Chris 58, 61, 62, 63
Needham, Joseph 27, 243
Nelsen, Rolf Haugaard 143, 243
Nested lineages 184, 185
Nestedness of the different
    lineage 185
Neural networks 40, 41, 57, 58,
    60, 61, 67, 105, 107, 111,
    148, 152
Neural computers 54, 117
Neurological diseases 141
Neuromancer 107
Neville, Robert, C. 211, 243
New organisms 123
New Communities 197
New Synthesis 16
Newell, Allen 56, 93, 211
Newton, Isaac 27, 31, 57
Nishioka, M., Tanizoi, I., Fujita, A.,
    Katsura, S. & Mizuno, A.
    157, 243
Nitrogen fixing 73
No-self 215
Noble, David 38, 244
Noble, T. 23, 38, 244
Novelty seeking 142
Novelty creation 19, 22, 185
Nuclear Magnetic Resonance
    NMR 154, 159
Nucleotides 19

Occean of communities 219
Occupational structures 39, 43
OECD 38, 73, 76, 77, 117, 133,
    134, 167
Office of Technology Assessment
    124

Ojulu, Epajjar 100, 159, 160, 244
Olson, Arthur, J. & Goodsell, David, S. 159, 160, 244
Open University 7, 49
Optical techniques 150
Optical computing 54, 150
Optical neural computers 54
Opto electronics 8, 52
Orgware 38
Ormerod, Paul 40, 244
Osborn, L. 58, 244
Osborne, John 64, 65, 244
Outer lineage 182
Ownership of body 126

Pagel, Walter 30, 244
Paradigmatic changes, breaks 30, 34
Parentage 138
Parfit, Derek 209, 210, 244
Parker, Barnett, R. 48, 100, 244
Parkinson's disease 141
Pascal, Blaise 35, 36
Pask, Gordon & Curran, Susan 36, 37, 244
Passarelli, Ben 148, 245
Patel, Vibhuti 127, 245
Patriarchal control 135
Patriarchal science 30
Peerenboom, R.P. 215, 245
Pelet, Abraham 44, 66, 245
Pelton, Joseph, N. 45, 48, 49, 50, 89, 204, 245
Perceptron 48, 174
Perfect offspring 127, 210
Perry, Ruth & Greber, Lisa 105, 245
Person 210
Pfeiffer, J.L. 7, 26, 245

Photosynthesis 15
Phylogenesis 22, 189
Phylogenetic ascendancy 193
Phylogenetic necessity 182
Phylogenetic tendency 7, 20, 187
Piaget 98
Pickering, Andrew 27, 29, 245
Pinch, T. J. 27, 29, 245
Pinsky, Robert 178, 245
Plato 30
Pollack, Andrew 56, 107, 153, 154, 245
Pool, Robert 150, 245
Porat, M.U. 38, 39, 246
Port, Otis 54, 246
Post industrial society 37
Premack, D. 35, 246
Prethas 219
Price, de Solla, D. J. 7, 49, 246
Prigogine, Ilya 21, 181, 246
Process philosophy 211
Programming style 93
Propositional Logic 56
Psaltis, Demetri 59
Publications behavior 28
Punctuated equilibrium 21, 67, 162

Rahula, Walpola 215, 246
Rajapakse, Vijitha 211, 246
Rate of evolution 187, 194
Ray, Thomas 200
Recombinant DNA 72
Recursive loops 113, 187
Regulatory genes 131
Renn, Ortwin & Peters, Hans Peter 96, 246
Rennels, Glenn, D. & Shortcliffe, Edward 58, 246
Rennie, John 19, 246

Reproductive technology   136

Rheingold, Howard   203, 207, 212, 246

Ridley, Mark   16, 17, 246

Rifkin, Jeremy   214, 246

RNA   14, 18, 174

Robcop   147

Robotic scalpels   43

Rogers, Lois & Craig, Olga   79, 137, 246

Rose, Hilary & Rose, Steven   29, 246

Rosner, Judah, L.   130, 246

Ross, Philip, E.   120, 246

Rossler, Otto, E.   6, 21, 217, 246

Rothbart, Daniel   247

Rothfeder, Jeffrey   63, 68, 247

Rothstein, Edward   203, 247

Rule, James, B.   130, 247

Rumelhart, D.E. & McLelland, J.C.   59, 247

Ruscio, Kenneth, P.   130, 247

Ruskin, F.R.   100, 247

Salisbury, J.K.   69, 247

Salthe, S.N.   21, 208, 247

Samuel, A.L.   57, 247

Sasson, Albert   119, 120, 247

Scheffler, Samuel   209, 247

Schickard, Wilhelm   35, 36

Schiller, Herbert, I.   44, 95, 247

Schroedinger, E.C.   31, 248

Schwartz, Evan, I.   61, 248

Scientific information   131

Scientific knowledge   7, 27

Scientific Management   91

Scientific Revolution   7, 26, 27, 216

Scraggs, G.W.   56, 248

Sculley, John   48, 56, 248

Searls, David, B.   174, 248

Second Law of Thermodynamics   21

Secondary storage   51

Seidel, George, E.   73, 74, 75, 248

Sejnowski, T. & Rosenberg, C.   60, 248

Self repair   151

Self organization   13, 22, 151, 182, 163, 181, 184, 185

Self construction   34

Self blurred in cyberspace   207

Self organizing systems   6, 58

Self   34, 213, 215, 216

Semiotics of evolution   210

Semiotics   217

Sen, Amar, K. & Lee, Tyronne   143, 248

Service society   37

Shannon, C.E. & Weaver, W.   5, 248

Shaw, J.C.   93

Sherman, Barrie   36, 248

Shinn, Terry   28, 248

SHRDLU program   56

Shri Purohit Swami   179, 248

Siebert, Charles   142, 248

Silverstone, Roger   102, 248

Simon, Herbert   56, 57, 92, 93, 113

Sklair, Leslie   27, 249

Sloan, Douglas   92, 249

Slutsker, Gary   124, 249

Smith, G.W. 68 & Debenham, J.D.   68, 249

Smith, Emily, T.   60, 249

Smith, Clarke, J.   60, 68, 249

Social construction of computers   88

Social construction of science   27, 31

Social epistemology   131, 190

Social genes   101

Social imprint on computer   93

Social isolation   104
Social   parenting   135
Social subjectivity   33
Social transformations   24
Socially constructed knowledge   90
Societal evolution   24
Societies of machines   199
Socio-physical environment   24
Socio-technological shifts   25
Socio-technological systems   24
Speciation   22, 34, 181, 184, 185, 194
Speech recognition   59
Sperm cell therapy   78
Sperm cells   79
Stem cell therapy   78
Sterling, J.   42, 249
Stone, Richard   249
Stonier, Tom   5, 249
Stress on environment   167
Structural genes   131
Sub cultures   25
Subcultures in the Internet   203
Subject-object   216
Subjective limits   140
Subjectivities   6, 20, 34, 67, 140, 191, 212
Sudden changes   34
Supply of information   48
Surrogacy   136
Sussman, Gerald Jay   54, 57, 62, 249
Sweet Michael, J. & Johnson, Craig, G.   212, 249
Symbolic manipulation   104
Synchronic information   5

Tank, David, W. & Hopfield, John, J.   59, 249
Telecommuting   97

Telemarketing   204
Telematic   society   37
Telepresence   154
Thermodynamics of open systems   23, 181
Thimbleby, Harold   163, 249
Third Wave technologies   1
Thought streams   213
Thymine   17, 80
Tissue culture   71, 72
Torrero, E.A.   55, 250
Toufexis, Anastasia   142
Trajectory for science   33
Transfers of information   171
Transgenesis   74
Transgenic information   185
Transgenic technologies   78
Transgenic animals   74
Transparency   106
Travis, John   76, 250
Tree of knowledge   26, 33
Tree of information   32
Tree of evolution   33
Tube worms   14
Turing Test   63
Turkle, Sherry   94, 102, 103, 109, 111

Ubiquitousness of computing   68
Uenohara, Michiyuki   107, 250
Ultra Large Scale Integration
   ULSI   37
UNCTC   44
Undesirable genes   128
UNDP   71
Uni-Nets   197
UNIDO   55

Varela, F. J., Maturana, H. R.
   & Uribe, R.   21, 22, 190, 191, 212, 213, 250

Very Large Scale Integration
    VLSI 37
Virtual genetic products 176
Virtual Reality VR 107
Virtual selves 205
Virtual micro cultures 203
Virtual communities 201
Virtual corporation 202
Virtual offices 202
Visuddhi Magga 215
Voice recognition 56

Wachtershauser, Gunter 188, 250
Waddington, Conrad, H. 5, 6, 251
Wade, Nicholas 141, 251
Walbridge, Charles, T. 60, 251
Waldrop, Mitchell, M. 49, 251
Walser, Randal 108, 251
Walsh, Roger 212, 251
Wang, Hao 56, 251
Washburn, Sherwood 19, 251
Watson, J.D. 73, 78, 80, 81, 82,
    251
Watts, Susan 75, 82, 251
Webs of meanings 219
Weinberg, Nathan 93, 251
Weiss, Rick 127, 178, 251
Wessells, Michael 41, 48, 90, 97,
    102, 252

Wet ware 176
Wheeler, David, L. 139, 252
Whitehead, Northrop 208, 210,
    211, 218
Wickelgren, Ingrid 73, 141,
    252
Wiener, Norbert 147
Wiener, Philip, P. 31, 252
Wiggen, Regina 83, 252
Wind, James, P. 129, 252
Winograd, T. 56
Witt, Patricia, L. 30, 252
Wobbe, Werner 98, 252
World views 20, 22, 188, 189,
    190, 191, 194, 207
Worm's eye view 33
Wuketits, Franz, M. 188, 252
Wurman, Saul Richard 47, 252
Wynne, B. 29, 252

Yam, Phillip 53, 77, 252
Yang, Dori Jones 252
Yasdani, Masoud 69, 252
Yearly, Steven 28, 252
Yu, V.L. 43, 253
Yuanliang, M. 133, 253

Zuboff, Shoshana 104, 108, 253
Zuckerman, Laurence 66, 253

Other titles in World Futures General Evolution Studies

VOLUME 13
THE QUEST FOR A UNIFIED THEORY OF INFORMATION
Edited by Wolfgang Hofkirchner

VOLUME 14
MERGED EVOLUTION: LONG-TERM IMPLICATIONS OF BIOTECHNOLOGY AND INFORMATION TECHNOLOGY
Susantha Goonatilake